Literacy in the Lives of Working-Class Adults in Australia

Adult Learning, Literacy and Social Change

SERIES EDITORS:

Anna Robinson-Pant (University of East Anglia, UK)
Alan Rogers (University of East Anglia, UK and University of Nottingham, UK)

This series explores the complex relationship between adult learning and social change. Instead of the common focus on adult literacy as kick-starting development, the series considers how adult learning and literacy can also emerge from processes of social change. Each volume introduces new theoretical and methodological lenses to investigate insights into adult learning and literacy based on original empirical research by the authors. Recognizing that Governments from the Global North as well as the Global South have recently signed up to the Sustainable Development Goals, this series brings together research conducted in a wide range of countries, including Malawi, Nepal, China, the Philippines and the UK.

ADVISORY BOARD:

Dennis Banda (University of Zambia, Zambia)
Lesley Bartlett (University of Wisconsin, USA)
Maria Lucia Castanheira (Federal University of Minas Gerais, Brazil)
Mostafa Hasrati (Seneca College, Canada)
Li Jiacheng (East China Normal University, China)
Judy Kalman (CINVESTAV, Mexico)
Simon McGrath (University of Nottingham, UK)
Tonic Maruatona (University of Botswana, Botswana)
Tony Mays (Commonwealth of Learning)
Hendrik Nordvall (Mimer, The Swedish Network for Research on Popular Education, Sweden)
Mastin Prinsloo (University of Cape Town, South Africa)
Anita Rampal (University of Delhi, India)
Bonnie Slade (University of Glasgow, UK)

Also available in the series:

Adult Learning and Social Change in the UK: National and Local Perspectives,
edited by Jules Robbins and Alan Rogers
Migrant Workers' Education in China: Changing Discourses and Practices,
by Fusheng Jia
Literacies, Power and Identities in Figured Worlds in Malawi,
by Ahmmardouh Mjaya

Literacy in the Lives of Working-Class Adults in Australia

Dominant versus Local Voices

Stephen Black

BLOOMSBURY ACADEMIC
LONDON · NEW YORK · OXFORD · NEW DELHI · SYDNEY

BLOOMSBURY ACADEMIC
Bloomsbury Publishing Plc, 50 Bedford Square, London, WC1B 3DP, UK
Bloomsbury Publishing Inc, 1385 Broadway, New York, NY 10018, USA
Bloomsbury Publishing Ireland, 29 Earlsfort Terrace, Dublin 2, D02 AY28, Ireland

BLOOMSBURY, BLOOMSBURY ACADEMIC and the Diana logo
are trademarks of Bloomsbury Publishing Plc

First published in Great Britain 2024
This paperback edition published in 2025

Copyright © Stephen Black, 2024

Stephen Black has asserted his right under the Copyright,
Designs and Patents Act, 1988, to be identified as Author of this work.

All rights reserved. No part of this publication may be: i) reproduced or transmitted in any form, electronic or mechanical, including photocopying, recording or by means of any information storage or retrieval system without prior permission in writing from the publishers; or ii) used or reproduced in any way for the training, development or operation of artificial intelligence (AI) technologies, including generative AI technologies. The rights holders expressly reserve this publication from the text and data mining exception as per Article 4(3) of the Digital Single Market Directive (EU) 2019/790.

Bloomsbury Publishing Plc does not have any control over, or responsibility for, any third-party websites referred to or in this book. All internet addresses given in this book were correct at the time of going to press. The author and publisher regret any inconvenience caused if addresses have changed or sites have ceased to exist, but can accept no responsibility for any such changes.

A catalogue record for this book is available from the British Library.

A catalog record for this book is available from the Library of Congress.

ISBN: HB: 978-1-3503-7810-0
PB: 978-1-3503-7811-7
ePDF: 978-1-3503-7812-4
eBook: 978-1-3503-7813-1

Series: Adult Learning, Literacy and Social Change

Typeset by Integra Software Services Pvt. Ltd.

For product safety related questions contact productsafety@bloomsbury.com.

To find out more about our authors and books visit www.bloomsbury.com
and sign up for our newsletters.

Contents

Series' Foreword vi
Adult Learning, Literacy and Social Change ix
List of Abbreviations xi

1 Literacy, Politics and Working-Class Adults 1
2 Prisoners and Literacy 21
3 Long-Term Unemployed People and Literacy 39
4 Local Council Workers and Literacy 55
5 Production Workers and Literacy 73
6 Adult Literacy Students and Literacy 99
7 Marginalized Young People and Literacy 119
8 Vocational Education and Training Students and Literacy 135
9 Diabetes Patients and Literacy 157
10 Countering Deficit 173

References 191
Index 223

Series' Foreword

This series explores the complex relationship between adult learning, literacy and social change through empirical research conducted within and beyond educational programmes in a wide range of countries in the Global North and South. Since the launch of the 2030 Sustainable Development Goals, there has been growing interest in how adult literacy – sometimes referred to as 'the invisible glue' (LWG, 2007) – connects the seventeen goals. Much research has focused on how to measure literacy progress quantitatively (through literacy rates) against such development indicators and assumed that most literacy learning takes place formally within institutions or educational programmes. Rather than taking this instrumental approach, this series investigates the 'why' and 'how' of the assumed relationship between adult learning, literacy and social change.

The UNESCO Chair in Adult Literacy and Learning for Social Transformation (based at University of East Anglia, UK) has strongly shaped the approach and stance of this series. Aiming to develop understanding about how adult literacy and learning – particularly for women and young adults – can help address inequalities in the poorest communities of the world, the UNESCO Chair brings together university departments specializing in adult literacy and community learning in the UK, Ethiopia, Nepal, Malawi, Egypt and the Philippines. Several of the books in this series emerged from in-depth qualitative research studies conducted by researchers within this international partnership.

Providing a much-needed critical perspective on adult literacy and development, the series challenges the usual starting point of international and national policy discourse and research in this field. First, the shift to consider social change rather than development offers a broader, holistic lens, since 'development' implies a limited perspective on social change as predetermined, planned, staged, and often with an envisaged endpoint (Castles, 2001). Conceptual debate on 'social transformation' (defined as 'big' social change by Haas et al., 2020) informs this analysis – particularly the notion that 'social transformations are deeply political in nature, an insight which dominant, "technocratic" development theories and ideologies ignore and actively try to conceal' (ibid: 7). This alternative lens provides a way to step outside development frameworks that focus only on literacy and development outcomes in order to re-centre attention onto people's lived experiences of social change.

Secondly, this series is grounded on an 'ideological' rather than an 'autonomous' model of literacy (Street, 1984). In contrast to much international development policy and research which has drawn on an understanding of literacy as decontextualized skills learned in a classroom, the series takes a 'situated' approach (Barton, Hamilton and Ivanič, 2000) to investigate literacy and adult learning in everyday life. Researching informal and non-formal learning – both within and beyond educational institutions and development programmes – the authors offer original insights into how adults are engaging with an ever-increasing diversity of literacies, languages, cultural values and technologies. Resisting the common tendency to conflate literacy, learning and education, they explore the complex relationships around power, knowledge and identities that are shaping people's lives and social change.

Thirdly, this series accepts the now widely held view of adult learning as comprising formal, non-formal and informal elements (UNESCO, 2009: 27), not necessarily as discrete activities but often inextricably mixed in a lifelong and life-wide process of interaction between social members. Learning can no longer be seen as the sole prerogative of educational institutions in time-limited activities; it takes multiple forms and occurs in multiple locations throughout life. The volumes in this series will explore how such adult learning is inspired by and at the same time contributes to social change.

As the world now grapples with the devastating effects of the global Covid-19 pandemic, climate change, conflict, migration and widening inequalities, the focus of this series is particularly relevant. More than ever before, social change is seen as unpredictable, and new educational challenges are emerging. The authors in this series do not set out to advocate solutions for policymakers or educational providers. However, these in-depth research accounts share rich first-hand experiences, observations, analysis and voices that are often unheard, thereby introducing new ways to understand adult learning, literacy and social change.

Anna Robinson-Pant
Alan Rogers

References

Barton, D., Hamilton, M. and R. Ivanič (2000). *Situated Literacies: Reading and Writing in Context*. London: Routledge.

Castles, S. (2001). 'Studying Social Transformation'. *International Political Science Review*, 22 (1): 13–32

Haas, H., Fransen, S., Natter, K., Schewel, K. and Vezzoli, S. (2020). *Social Transformation*. International Migration Institute Working Papers, Paper 166, July 2020, Oxford: IMI.

Street, B.V. (1984). *Literacy in Theory and Practice*. Cambridge: Cambridge University Press.

University of East Anglia UNESCO Chair. Available online: https://www.uea.ac.uk/groups-and-centres/unesco-chair-programme

UK Literacy Working Group (2007). 'Literacy and international development: The next steps', LWG Position Paper. Available online: http://balid.org.uk/pdfs/LWG%20Position%20Paper%20Final%20June07%20CD%20final.doc

UNESCO. (2009). *Global Report on Adult Learning and Education*. Hamburg: UIL

Adult Learning, Literacy and Social Change

'I'm not much in the reading and writing, but I know how to start a shovel.' (Phil)

This fourth book in our series on Adult Learning, Literacy and Social Change presents a powerful challenge to the prevailing discourses around adult literacy and learning for social change. Drawing on rich ethnographic data from many years of research in Australia, Stephen Black speaks back to the pervading images of low-literate adults that dominate popular narratives and show them as lacking self-esteem, knowledge and skills. Through the experiences of Phil, a construction worker with the local council; Athena, who acts as the 'memory' for her husband during hospital consultations, and many others, we see a contrasting picture of how people in very different situations navigate and engage with complex literacy and numeracy learning in everyday life. We also begin to understand the reasons why adults may feel reluctant to sit in classrooms for formal training or literacy programmes. The author's concluding hope is that the book highlights 'how groups of working-class adults manage their everyday lives while subject to a dominant discourse on literacy that oppresses them and subjects them to symbolic violence' (p. 190). These insights into the ways in which literacy is connected with power and identity through people's everyday lives are both moving and thought-provoking.

The other ethnographic volumes in this series – from the very different country contexts of Malawi and China – also demonstrated all too clearly, the word 'literacy' is problematic and often contested. Stephen Black recognizes the tensions in being a literacy researcher, yet simultaneously trying to avoid putting 'literacy' centre-stage, as he explains: 'Literacy has always been my main focus, and in the chapters of this book I try to direct my discussions specifically to literacy, but it is not always possible or desirable' (p. 13). This is because taking a 'situated' approach to researching literacy contrasts with the 'autonomous' model held by policymakers and their tendency to put 'literacy first'. The author uses *Lost for Words*, a popular TV series about 'eight brave Australians' who embark on an intensive adult literacy programme, to illustrate such wide-spread assumptions about literacy and illiteracy. In the TV series, the reported stereotypes and feelings of shame are framed within a narrative about the 'literacy crisis' in Australia, which resonates with similar accounts from countries in the Global South.

Stephen Black moves beyond simply analysing how low-literate adults are represented in policy discourses and the media to address the reasons why such images are perpetuated. Of particular relevance to this Bloomsbury series on literacy and social change is his analysis of the political agenda behind what he terms the 'literacy=jobs axiom' (p. 41). This is the assumption that literacy will automatically lead to better jobs, serving to obscure, as he comments, 'there was a less a skills gap, more a jobs gap' (p. 46). In the Global South, we might see this as the message that literacy leads to development, which is perpetuated through similar deficit discourses on 'illiterate' individuals and poorer communities. As the author reflects: 'In this era of neoliberal capitalism, it is in the interests of governments and dominant groups to focus on victim-blaming individuals with literacy problems because it effectively shifts responsibility away from the need to address the broader structural issues of social class inequalities in society' (p. 16).

Rooted in the debates around literacy as a social practice and using 'ethnographic-style' research, the book explores a variety of programmes and sectors – health, TVET, youth programmes, adult literacy courses, workplaces, 'jobseeker' programmes, local councils and prisons. The rich vignettes of individuals take the reader straight into these diverse contexts and the analysis of how literacies are embedded in identities, values and social networks. The book illustrates vividly how the assumed 'stigma' of illiteracy is important for some, but by no means for all of these people. Above all, in all these contexts, Stephen Black challenges any causal notions of literacy and social change. For instance, in the chapter on prison literacy, he observes that 'prisoner illiteracy rates were linked to organizational power; they were political' (p. 23). These reflections bring out some of the complex links between literacy and social change that this series is aiming to interrogate and have important implications for the field of literacy and development in the Global South.

Anna Robinson-Pant
March 2023

Abbreviations

ABE	Adult Basic Education
ABS	Australian Bureau of Statistics
ACAL	Australian Council for Adult Literacy
ACEA	Australasian Corrections Education Association
ACSF	Australian Core Skills Framework
AFE	Adult Foundation Education
AIG	Australian Industry Group
AIN	Assistant in Nursing
ALL	Adult Literacy and Life Skills
ALN	Adult Literacy and Numeracy
ALLP	Australian Language and Literacy Policy
CALD	Culturally and Linguistically Diverse
CES	Commonwealth Employment Service
CGVE	Certificate in General and Vocational Education
COAG	Council of Australian Governments
DCS	Department of Corrective Services
DEET	Department of Employment, Education and Training
DEST	Department of Education, Science and Training
EAL	English as an Additional Language
EN	Enrolled Nurse
ESOL	English for Speakers of Other Languages
ESL	English as a Second Language

FE	Further Education
HSC	Higher School Certificate
IALS	International Adult Literacy Survey
ISC	Industry Skills Council
ITAB	Industry Training Advisory Board
L&N	Literacy and Numeracy
LLN	Language, Literacy and Numeracy
NESB	Non-English-Speaking Background
NLS	New Literacy Studies
LANT	Literacy and Numeracy Training
LLND	Language, Literacy, Numeracy and Digital
LLNP	Language, Literacy and Numeracy Programme
NCVER	National Centre for Vocational Education Research
OECD	Organization for Economic Co-operation and Development
PIAAC	Programme for the International Assessment of Adult Competencies
SAS	Survey of Adult Skills
SBS	Special Broadcasting Service
SCOTESE	Standing Council for Tertiary Education Skills and Employment
SEE	Skills for Education and Employment
SIP	Special Intervention Programme
TAFE	Technical and Further Education
TVET	Technical and Vocational Education and Training
UNESCO	United Nations Educational, Scientific and Cultural Organization
UTS	University of Technology Sydney
VET	Vocational Education and Training
WELL	Workplace English Language and Literacy

1

Literacy, Politics and Working-Class Adults

Introduction

This book features first-hand accounts – the voices – of groups of adults who are usually labelled by others as lacking literacy skills, the reading and writing deemed necessary for individuals to participate in society. At the time of writing this book (during the Covid-19 pandemic 2020–2), there has been heightened awareness in Australia of adults lacking literacy skills with the release of a national TV series called *Lost for Words* (SBS, 2021a). This series follows the 'emotional and confronting journey' of eight adult students as they progress through a nine-week intensive literacy programme. In the promotion and content of the series, viewers are informed at various times that 7 million adults, or more than 43 per cent of the Australian adult population, do not have 'the necessary literacy skills needed for everyday life' (SBS, 2021b). Contemporaneous with the TV series, a federal parliamentary committee has sought public submissions and reported on an inquiry into 'Adult literacy and its importance' (House of Representatives, 2022). These two organizational events, particularly the TV series, have served to highlight, shape and reinforce public perceptions in Australia of literacy deficiencies in the adult population, the latest iteration of the long-held 'literacy crisis' narrative (Hodgens, 1994; Kamler, 1999).

The focus of this book is on the perspectives of different groups of adults, those labelled low literate or deficient in literacy skills, on the role of literacy in their lives. How do they manage their lives? What role does literacy play in their participation in society, in their work and non-working lives? These groups of adults are quite diverse, and they include prisoners, unemployed people, outdoor workers in a local council, manufacturing workers, students engaged in a range of different courses in vocational education and training (VET), and people experiencing a chronic health condition, type 2 diabetes. Beyond their low literacy status, what links these groups is that they all feature in research studies I have undertaken over more than forty years in a professional career in the field of adult literacy education. They also share a common status as working-class adults in Australian society.

In this book, I draw on my previous publications and unpublished research data to revise and account for the perspectives of these adult groups. In the Australian adult literacy field, there are extensive and wide-ranging accounts of what others think of low-literate adults in the community, including the perspectives of teachers and allied professionals (Campbell, 2010; Osmond, 2021; White, 1983) and various industry groups (Australian Industry Group, 2010, 2012, 2016; Industry Skills Councils, 2011). Much less commonly sought or documented, however, are the first-hand accounts of adults in the community who are labelled low literate, in what can be termed 'the view from below' (Hart, 1992) or 'hearing other voices' (Hull, 1993). Notwithstanding my own publications expounded in the following chapters, there are some exceptions to this trend (e.g. Bee, 1993; Grant, 1987; Kell, 2005), but there has been little replication in Australia of ethnographic accounts of the role of literacy in the lives of working-class adults as found in many overseas studies (e.g. Barton and Hamilton, 2012; Barton et al., 2007; Duckworth, 2013; Gowen, 1992; Heath, 1983; Hull, 1993). One book reviewer has commented that 'Australia does not have a history of ethnographers recording studies focused on literacy and rooted deeply in community' (O'Maley, 2014). In this introductory chapter, I explain how I began my work with the adult groups, and the socio-political orientations that have underpinned this work. This will be followed by the perspectives of other people and organizations – dominant society, those with greater status and power – on the adults they define in a normative sense as low literate. The key theme that runs through this book is the stark contrast or contradiction between the perspectives of dominant society on those they define as low literate and the perspectives of the working-class adults so defined. Dominant groups in society perceive literacy primarily in terms of a set of autonomous skills that people either have or do not have, and that the acquisition of these skills is essential for participation in everyday life, particularly for economic advancement in work contexts. This is the taken-for-granted, dominant discourse on literacy that I outline in the pages of this introductory chapter. But as the following chapters of this book demonstrate, when the everyday lives and literacy practices of these so-defined low-literate, working-class adults are examined from their own 'situated' perspectives, alternative, complex and often contradictory understandings of literacy are provided. Each chapter in this book features firstly the 'skills' perspectives on literacy promoted by dominant groups, followed by 'situated' or 'social practice' perspectives on literacy obtained through close, ethnographic-style accounts of how people manage their everyday lives. For the most part in this book, when I refer to literacy 'skills' I am referring to dominant perspectives on literacy, and it follows that when I refer to people as 'low-literate' or deficient in literacy skills, I am referring to normative, dominant constructions of literacy as a set of autonomous skills. When I refer to literacy 'practices', it is usually in reference to ethnographic-style studies of how people engage with literacy in their everyday lives.

My engagement and subsequent research with diverse groups of working-class adults began in early 1980 when, as a disillusioned high school history teacher, I commenced a postgraduate degree in education at the University of New South Wales in Sydney. Having taken unpaid leave from my full-time teaching position in Melbourne, I needed a source of income to support my postgraduate studies. I then applied for a part-time 'remedial English' teaching position at the local Long Bay Prison Complex in Sydney, and despite having no experience teaching either adults (let alone adult prisoners) or English literacy, I was successful in obtaining a job that it appeared few others applied for. It was a job that markedly changed the trajectory of my professional working life, and teaching and researching literacy in the lives of adults has played a significant role in my life ever since. In the years following that initial foray into prison literacy teaching, I began a lengthy career teaching, managing and researching literacy programmes in TAFE (Technical and Further Education, Australia's public VET provider) in Sydney (1988–2009). Following my retirement from TAFE, for more than a decade I have worked at the University of Technology Sydney (UTS) on a range of adult literacy–related research projects.

To add context to my research studies, for the most part they have been undertaken as an 'add-on' to my paid professional role as an educator working with the same adult groups. In the case of prisoners, for example, my academic study of the role of literacy in their lives was motivated by and was complementary to my professional role at the time as a prison educator. The research was undertaken part-time for a master's honours thesis (Black, 1989a). In 1992, I commenced a PhD part-time, and for almost a decade I managed the dual roles of working in TAFE as a teacher and frontline manager of literacy programmes, and doctoral researcher into the role of literacy in the lives of a range of adult groups (Black, 2001). These adult groups included, for example, long-term unemployed people referred to TAFE literacy programmes in a federal government initiative aimed ostensibly at improving their work prospects. Another group were maintenance and construction workers in a local council. As part of a 'return-to-industry' project designed to assist TAFE teachers to better understand the contemporary world of work, I worked with and researched the role of these outdoor council workers who were in the process of having their work restructured into 'competitive teams' as part of the 'new work order' (Gee, Hull and Lankshear, 1996). Necessarily, my priority with each adult group was my substantive paid role as an educator, but my research role was always complementary, providing a two-way relationship in which my paid role provided access to adult groups and legitimacy and trust as an educational service provider, and my research role provided some deep insights into the perspectives and needs of the adult groups.

Federal government research funding from the National Centre for Vocational Education Research (NCVER) also played a role in my later years at TAFE and at UTS. At TAFE, this included two projects that examined student and teacher perspectives on the role of social capital in TAFE and community literacy programmes (Balatti, Black and Falk, 2006, 2009), and one project that examined the role of VET in government welfare to work initiatives (Black, 2008a). At UTS, NCVER funding enabled a study of worker and employer perspectives on literacy and numeracy in several manufacturing companies (Black, Yasukawa and Brown, 2013).

Working-class adults

I refer to the main subjects of this book as working class because low levels of literacy in the adult population can be viewed predominantly as a matter affecting working-class people (Black and Bee, 2018a; Quigley, 2021; Zacharakis, Becker Patterson and Quigley, 2021), and the adult groups featured in this book reflect this. Their working-class status was based on their location in the economic hierarchical structure, poor material circumstances reflected in socio-economic indicators such as income and occupation, and their relation to the means of production as producers of surplus labour (Wood, 1995). These were wage labourers with low levels of formal schooling/education. Collectively, they lacked power and status in society, and this was readily apparent in the operator-level work contexts of outdoor workers in a local council (Chapter 4) and workers in manufacturing companies (Chapter 5) where top-down management structures allowed little worker autonomy. In the case of prisoners (Chapter 2), low socio-economic status and lack of power were self-evident, with long-established correlations with poverty and lack of education (Vinson, 1999; Australian Institute of Health and Welfare, 2019). Most TAFE college students

(Chapters 6, 7 and 8) were also likely to fit within a working-class classification given that the TAFE system of VET was formed in the early 1970s with an educational and social brief to redress the disadvantaging effects of class and poverty (Clemans and Seddon, 2000). In the comparable further education (FE) sector in the UK, VET (also commonly referred to as TVET – Technical and Vocational Education and Training) has been seen to be for the waged-labour class, for 'other people's children' (Avis, 2021; Orr, 2018; Thompson, 2009).

While I refer to the various adult groups in terms of their working-class status in society, in contemporary times, social distinctions based on social class are not popularly invoked. Teachers of adult literacy, for example, view their students through the prism of their own more privileged middle-class backgrounds, and they usually describe their students with less politically contentious terminology such as disadvantaged or marginalized (Black and Bee, 2018a). Commonly, they claim through their pedagogy to be 'empowering' students, but they rarely challenge capitalist power relations based on social class (Black and Bee, 2018b). In relation to FE teachers in the UK, this form of pedagogy has been termed 'comfort radicalism' (Avis, 2017; Brown, 2019). In the higher education academy, mainstream research paradigms in the social sciences have largely moved beyond conflict theories and social class analyses. In the field of applied linguistics, for example, social class is considered to have been 'erased' as a research construct (Block, 2014) as the politics of recognition have displaced the politics of redistribution (Fraser and Honneth, 2003). Social class still features in some research paradigms, but rarely prominently, and with the qualification that it is viewed 'in all its complex relations to language, people, discourse, practices, place and change' (Pennycook, 2015: 276).

My perspective reflected in this book is that highlighting social class in educational research is central in a neoliberal era of global capitalism where social, economic and educational inequalities in society are exacerbated, and wealth, power and privilege are concentrated increasingly in the hands of elites (Connell, 2013; Hill and Kumar, 2009; Leathwood and Archer, 2004; Reay, 2006, 2017; Simmons and Smyth, 2018). Class inequalities and exploitation are necessary in-built features of neoliberal capitalism, as winners in the perpetual pursuit of profit and society's goods invariably require there to be losers (Connell, 2013). Educational systems, as essential elements of the capitalist state apparatus, serve to both reflect and support social and economic inequalities. They ensure that people are educated to the level 'deemed suitable by capital for work' (Hill, Greaves and Maisuria, 2009: 120). I experienced this first-hand through my own schooling in working-class East London in the 1950s and 1960s. The low-status secondary modern schools were designed to ensure that the great majority of working-class children were prepared for lower skilled jobs required in Britain's post-war reconstruction (McCulloch, 1998, 2011; Sanderson, 2007). This was achieved through their entry criterion of failure at the eleven-plus exam, a curriculum based largely on 'practical' subjects such as metalwork and woodwork, and harsh cultures of discipline and punishment. Grammar schools on the other hand, with their selective entry and academic curriculum, were designed for the expanded middle class, and students were prepared for higher education and establishment careers in management and the civil service (Jones, 2016; Power et al., 2003). I experienced the 'different worlds' (Brine, 2006a: 6) of both types of schools, and the impact on me has been long-lasting.

Social class in education remains personal for me (Black, 2020), and in a broad sense, it has been reflected in my research orientations in which I have chosen to take the side of working-class people. At the time of my earliest research in prisons in the 1980s, Brennan and Brennan (1984: 237) wrote in their prison research about the need to choose sides: 'The issue of whose side you are on dominates all daily interactions. It is doubtful that any person or group can remain neutral for long.' They were referring to the need for educators in prison to provide a 'human alternative' to the custodial regulations that dominated prisoners' lives. While I agreed with this sentiment as hopefully chapter two of this book will demonstrate, taking sides went further than working with prisoners. In all of my research studies featured in this book, I have presented the perspectives of working-class adults which invariably ran counter to official or dominant group perspectives, and it has meant taking sides. The working-class adults I worked with experienced inequalities and sometimes punitive treatment in part because, related to their low literate status, they were perceived by dominant groups to be less worthy and less productive as individuals in society, particularly in employment contexts. This has been referred to symbolically as the 'violence of literacy'; in the hands of dominant groups, literacy 'oppresses' (Stuckey, 1991). This applied especially to unemployed people often coerced by government agencies to undertake literacy programmes (Chapter 3) and to local council workers and manufacturing workers (Chapters 4 and 5) who were blamed for low productivity in their workplaces and were being required to work smarter and leaner (and harder). They were on the wrong side of the wealth/power/class divide in a neoliberal world consumed with efficiencies in the name of increased profits.

A focus on the Global North

From the academic citations mentioned so far in this chapter, it should be apparent that my examination of the role of literacy in the lives of Australian adults set within a social-class construct is framed primarily from the viewpoint of wealthier industrial societies of the Global North. Many references in this chapter and in later chapters are to studies undertaken in the UK, the United States and Canada. It needs to be acknowledged, however, that the central theme of this book – literacy 'skills' versus 'practices', dominant autonomous understandings of literacy versus ethnographic understandings of local practices – goes well beyond the largely English-speaking contexts of the countries of the North that I focus on. Street's (e.g. 1984, 1993, 1995, 2001; Kalman and Street, 2013; Rogers and Street, 2012) many publications of ethnographic studies undertaken in a wide range of global contexts demonstrate the enduring contribution of studies of local literacy practices to academic debates on the role of literacy in different communities of the North and South (numeracy also, see Yasukawa et al., 2018). While my focus is on the Global North, due mainly to policy, systems and sociocultural commonalities between Australian adult literacy contexts and the UK and North America, there have been many significant ethnographic studies of the role of literacy in local communities in the Global South, including in Africa (e.g. Gebre et al., 2009; Prinsloo and Breier, 1996; Trudell, 2019), South America (e.g. Kalman and Reyes, 2016; Kalman and Street, 2013; Stromquist, 1997; Zavala, 2018) and a wide range of development studies (e.g. Basu, Maddox and Robinson-Pant, 2009; Mjaya, 2022; Robinson-Pant, 2004, 2015). There are similarities in ethnographic research approaches adopted in the literacy studies of the Global North and South. Similarities also extend to understandings of literacy, promoted by governments, dominant groups and major international organizations, as a set of generic (autonomous) skills required for individuals, communities and indeed countries to develop and prosper. Except that in the Global North, these dominant skills approaches to literacy are influenced and represented largely by the OECD (Organization for Economic Co-operation and Development), which, through its international large-scale literacy surveys, has defined and constructed literacy as a set of skills essential for participation in economic activities and everyday life. In the Global South, UNESCO (United Nations Educational, Scientific and Cultural Organization), largely through its Global (Education) Monitoring Reports (e.g. UNESCO, 2006, 2012), plays a key role as the organization with 'the power to name and define' literacy skills

(Street, 2011). But there are also some differences in the adult literacy studies of the North and South. International development studies, for example, focus largely on women (as mothers, caregivers and those with the lowest literacy rates) as the key target group for literacy programmes (Eldred et al., 2014; Robinson-Pant, 2015, 2016). The professionalization of the field of adult literacy education also differs. Since the early efforts of volunteer tutors in the 1970s (e.g. British Association of Settlements, 1974; Jones and Charnley, 1978; Mace, 1979), adult literacy education in the countries of the North has become increasingly professionalized (i.e. training, qualifications, salaries) as an established career, whereas in international development contexts of the South, there is still an assumption that teachers will work as volunteers or on a very small stipend and with minimal training (Rogers and Gizaw, 2022). A further difference is that the concept of social class as adopted in this book is problematic when used in relation to caste-based societies of the Indian subcontinent.

The politics of adult literacy education and the crisis discourse

In the context of adult literacy programmes in the TAFE system of VET that have dominated much of my working life and research, my perspective is that in this neoliberal era, the almost exclusive curriculum focus on literacy as foundation skills for employability serves primarily to control and regulate working-class students in the interests of capital (Black, 2018). These employability-focused programmes, as accounts from similar UK programmes indicate, effectively disempower working-class adults by preparing them only for marginal, low-paid jobs (Atkins, 2013; Brine, 2006b). Adult literacy programmes in TAFE and VET generally have not always been about job skills and social control; moreover, in an earlier era it was about the antithesis, as teachers promoted the empowerment of students. Around the time when I first began teaching literacy in prisons in the early 1980s, when adult literacy provision in TAFE was growing fast, teachers and researchers drew inspiration from the emancipatory pedagogy of Freire (1972), which aimed to empower oppressed groups by developing critical consciousness to transform relations of power and exploitation in society. The term 'empowerment' was very popular with adult literacy teachers in TAFE; indeed, it 'belongs' to the field in the 1980s (Campbell, 2010: 141), but rarely in the Freirean transformative sense that focused on the emancipation of oppressed groups. Rather, it focused primarily on the personal development of individual students in a pedagogy some have termed 'liberal progressive' (Black and Bee, 2018b; Lee and Wickert, 1995), which reflected the social democratic educational ideals of the era. It was the Whitlam Labor government that promoted these ideals when it established TAFE colleges in the early 1970s (Australian Committee on Technical and Further Education, 1974). The prevailing principles of adult literacy education were based on empowering individual students through a student-centred pedagogy. According to this pedagogy, in a student/teacher partnership, both partners were 'sometimes learner, sometimes teacher' (White, 1986: 36) as pedagogy was expected to be negotiated in a dialogic and mutually respectful way (Black and Bee, 2018b; Campbell, 2010; Grant, 1987; Osmond, 2021; White, 1983).

Central to personal empowerment in adult literacy programmes was the self-confidence that students developed from the student-centred pedagogy (Charnley and Jones, 1980; Jones and Charnley, 1978). Later research indicated that adult literacy students developed new and qualitatively different social networks (social capital) and that these networks could be linked to the socio-economic well-being of students (Balatti, Black and Falk, 2006, 2009). More recently, some UK researchers have highlighted the transformation of working-class students' identities in adult literacy programmes, but only if curriculum and pedagogy are based on 'contextualised and emancipatory learning' founded on those Freirean-inspired principles of respect for students' needs and dialogic engagement to create a meaningful learning (Duckworth, 2013; Duckworth and Tett, 2019). These pedagogical principles are highly unlikely to be promoted in the contemporary state of adult literacy education (now foundation skills) in TAFE, where the curriculum is nationally accredited and prescribed based on competencies defined by industry groups, and an uncompromising audit culture ensures conformity in the way every aspect of the curriculum is taught. There are examples of 'everyday resistance' to this industry agenda from some adult literacy teachers (Black, 2010; Osmond, 2021; Yasukawa and Osmond, 2019), but broadly speaking, the mantra of student empowerment has been replaced in the neoliberal era by compliance with government and industry norms (Black, 2018).

As the chapters in this book highlight, literacy levels in society are inherently political, and the view that these levels are so low that they represent a crisis is a recurrent theme in Australian society (Green, Hodgens and Luke, 1994). Traditionally, the main focus has been on literacy levels at school, and the political response to literacy crises is usually to target aspects of schooling systems or pedagogical practices, especially ones deemed progressive, that governments and other dominant groups wish to change (Sawyer, 2006). Literacy crises in the adult population are also sometimes highlighted as a way of reflecting critically on aspects of schooling, and a clear example was provided early in my TAFE career. In March 1988, a new conservative government had come to power in the state of New South Wales (NSW), and later in the year, a daily newspaper reported on 'Fury over illiterate students' (*Daily Telegraph* 21 November) as a survey had indicated that a high percentage of TAFE students experienced literacy difficulties that seriously impaired their TAFE training ('they cannot read their own textbooks'). The same newspaper article reported that the Minister for Education was angered by these findings, and he linked them to children leaving school without adequate literacy and numeracy skills. In turn, this justified his decision to introduce state-wide basic skills tests in schools for children as young as eight. Literacy professionals in TAFE sought unsuccessfully to learn more about this survey of TAFE student literacy abilities, and then, a few weeks after the first news story, a different daily newspaper reported that it appeared there was no survey and that the claim about illiteracy rates was 'totally spurious' (*Sydney Morning Herald* 5 December). TAFE adult literacy professionals thus concluded that the original 'illiterate students' survey was a fabrication, an opportunistic attempt by a new Minister for Education to justify the need for state-wide basic skills testing in schools (Black and Sim, 1989). This was an early lesson for me about the politics of literacy.

Over my forty-plus years of working in the adult literacy field there have been several literacy 'crises' in Australia linked to various surveys on the low literacy rates of adults. These surveys and subsequent crises are important to discuss in some detail because they provide important background to the perspectives of most people, dominant interest groups in particular, on low-literate adults. Invariably it is a picture of deficit and debilitation, and the news media often plays a significant role by providing alarmist and reductionist headlines. For example, the very first large-scale survey of adult literacy skills in Australia in the late 1970s, based on the Sydney metropolitan area (Goyen, 1977), brought forth newspaper headlines such as 'A nation of illiterates: 225,000 adults cannot read this headline' (cited in Sawyer, 2006: 249). Since that first survey there have been four major national surveys of adult literacy. The first argued that literacy standards were relative ('to social and cultural norms, to time and place, to purpose and intent'), and thus there was 'no single measure' or level of literacy required for participating in society (Wickert, 1989: 4).

The next three surveys were designed by the OECD, initially in conjunction with Statistics Canada, and conducted in Australia under the auspices of the Australian Bureau of Statistics (ABS, 1997, 2008a, 2013). These three surveys measured skills across the domains of literacy (prose and document), numeracy and problem-solving. One of these surveys, the Adult Literacy and Life Skills (ALL; see ABS, 2008a), had a particularly significant impact in Australia, with news media headlines that included 'Half of Australians are illiterate' (cited in Yasukawa and Black, 2016: 27). The authors of the survey, the ABS, encouraged this type of reporting by applying a level of competence in the ALL, Level Three, used previously by the OECD to indicate the 'minimum required for individuals to meet the complex demands of everyday life in the emerging knowledge-based economy' (ABS, 2008a). While the application of Level Three has been critiqued as statistically 'unjustified' (Black and Yasukawa, 2014a; St. Clair, 2012), and according to a senior analyst at the OECD, 'manifestly false' (Thorn, 2013 cited in Smythe, 2015: 10), it nevertheless enabled the ABS, news media and many other stakeholders in literacy debates, including industry, to claim and highlight that a very high percentage and number of adults were unable to properly participate in society. The ALL data based on the Level Three criterion became a powerful tool for use by dominant groups in Australian society. In effect, this criterion level created a dichotomy little different to earlier simplistic notions of people being either literate or illiterate (Addey, 2018); it determined those who were 'fit' or 'unfit' to participate in society (Atkinson, 2012).

Deficit ideology

The ALL survey (referred to in many Australian publications as ALLS) and the subsequent reporting of it provided a textbook example of 'deficit thinking' (Valencia, 2010), or as I prefer, 'deficit ideology' (Gorski, 2018). Large swathes of the adult population were found to be deficient, and the survey served to 'blame the victims' insofar as responsibility for literacy inequalities was located largely within the individuals and communities found to be deficient, that is, working-class adults (Black and Bee, 2018a). These adults have long been described as disadvantaged or forming 'at risk' groups, and consistently over the decades they have been portrayed to experience shame and guilt at their low literacy (White, 1983; Adult Learning Australia, 2021; House of Representatives, 2022). This was exemplified in the recent national television series on adult literacy,

Lost for Words (SBS, 2021a), mentioned briefly at the beginning of this chapter. The series featured individual students experiencing emotions of shame and embarrassment, set within the country's 'staggeringly low adult literacy rate'. In the popular media, contrasted with 'upright and worthy' literate citizens, 'illiterates' are often viewed as 'seedy and hopeless, even irresponsible' (Wickert, 1993: 31), reflecting the assumed moral virtue of possessing literacy skills (Cook-Gumperz, 2006). There is a history in literacy studies of blaming the victims for low literacy levels while ignoring structural issues of poverty and social-class inequalities (Lankshear and Lawler, 1987). Blaming the victims appears especially prevalent in bad economic times. In the recessionary period of the early 1990s in Australia, for example, there was a focus in the news media on 'Australia's underclass' with families described as 'part of a debilitating cycle of illiteracy and unemployment'. Such is the hegemony of this literacy narrative that members of this underclass (working class) believed themselves to be unworthy. In one newspaper article, for example, a family member referred to another non-literate family member as 'a bum', with 'no hope' of getting a job (cited in Black, 1995b: 24).

The deficit ideology encouraged by the ALL survey was particularly pronounced in workplaces and relates to many of the adult groups featured in this book. Progressively since the early 1990s, the dominant discourse on adult literacy policy and practice has been the human capital argument that increasing literacy (and numeracy) levels will have an economic pay-off in increased workplace productivity (Australian Industry Group, 2015; Department of Employment, Education and Training [DEET], 1991; House of Representatives, 1991). In line with this shift to economic benefits, literacy has been incorporated within the broader discourse of foundation skills that also include English language, numeracy, digital literacy and employability (Standing Council for Tertiary Education Skills and Employment [SCOTESE], 2012). Australian policy and practice in the field of adult literacy for the past decade have been driven by the federal government's National Foundation Skills Strategy for Adults (SCOTESE, 2012). This National Strategy is premised almost entirely on what Australian adults lack in literacy and numeracy skills as measured by the ALL survey (Black and Yasukawa, 2016). On the very first page of the strategy document, the federal government minister responsible for vocational education claimed, based on ALL statistics, that '[m]ore than 7.5 million Australian adults do not have the literacy and numeracy skills needed to participate fully in today's workforce' (SCOTESE, 2012: i).

Nomenclature

At this point in this introductory chapter, it may be appropriate to discuss nomenclature. Already it may be unclear that while this book is about literacy, discussion has also touched on numeracy and the term 'foundation skills'. As later chapters indicate, there is also overlap at times between literacy and spoken English language proficiency. Literacy has always been my main focus, and in the chapters of this book I try to direct my discussions specifically to literacy, but it is not always possible or desirable. Conceptually, as indicated already in this chapter, literacy is presented by governments and international organizations such as the OECD and UNESCO in a quite narrow 'autonomous' sense as the ability to read and write (in English) which in turn will lead to economic and social rewards in society. But the 'situated' or 'social practice' perspectives of the many adult groups featured in this book involve more than literacy skills (Papen, 2005). From these perspectives, literacy is a more complex, socially constructed concept (Cook-Gumperz, 2006) that intersects with the many sociocultural factors that influence how adults engage with literacy practices in their everyday lives. It requires broader discussion than simply whether people have the ability to read and write. As later chapters will elaborate, these 'situated' perspectives are represented in academic research with terms such as the 'new literacy studies' (e.g. Barton, Hamilton and Ivanič, 2000; Street, 2003, 2012a; Gee, 2000, 2015) or 'literacy studies' (e.g. Baynham and Prinsloo, 2009; Hamilton, 2016).

As a professional field of pedagogy, adult literacy education fits within or overlaps with a number of different disciplinary fields and namings. In my career in TAFE, I was employed as a teacher, and later head teacher, of Adult Basic Education (ABE). The term 'ABE' essentially incorporates literacy and numeracy, though literacy has always dominated. ABE has been the preferred term used by some Australian researchers (Osmond, 2021; Yasukawa and Osmond, 2019), but use of the term is not universal in Australia. While it is common in the state of NSW, in Victoria, the term 'ALBE' (Adult Literacy and Basic Education) has long predominated. Literacy and numeracy have often been viewed together as complementary skills (i.e. L&N teachers), and many research studies, including some of my own that have been government funded, have focused on both. Language also plays a key role. In 1987 Australia had its first National Policy on Languages (Lo Bianco, 1987), which focused mainly on languages and, to a lesser extent, adult literacy. A few years later came the Australian Language and Literacy Policy (ALLP; see DEET, 1991), which highlighted the role of both language and literacy. In the decades that followed it has been quite common for some teachers to be referred to as language, literacy and numeracy (LLN) teachers, especially in workplace and vocational learning contexts. As is apparent in several chapters of this book, many of the participants interviewed were born overseas in countries where English was not their first language. While my focus is on (English) literacy, necessarily there is overlap at times with the disciplinary fields of English as a second or additional language (ESL/EAL) or English for speakers of other languages (ESOL).

Since 2012, as the previous section of this chapter indicated, the term 'foundation skills' has gained dominance for governments and industry and skills groups following the National Foundation Skills Strategy for Adults (SCOTESE, 2012). As indicated, foundation skills have been defined to include not only literacy but also English language, numeracy, digital literacy and employability. Internationally, the term 'foundation skills' has been adopted by organizations such as UNESCO to describe basic skills (UNESCO, 2012). In Australia, the term 'foundation skills' developed following scoping studies by private consultants funded by the federal government (Perkins, 2009; Roberts and Wignall, 2010), and the term represents primarily the interests of governments and industry/skills stakeholders who promote the human capital rationale for improving literacy skills (Black, 2018; Black and Yasukawa, 2016). A similar trend has been apparent in some other countries with the promotion of 'essential skills' in Canada (Hayes, 2013; Jackson, 2005a) or 'functional skills' in the UK (Burgess and Hamilton, 2011). In recent years, the interest of government and industry stakeholders has focused increasingly on digital technologies and automation, and it is now common to refer to language, literacy, numeracy and digital (LLND) skills (Joyce, 2019). But through these various iterations of skills, literacy retains its prominence as a generic label, as demonstrated by the recent federal parliamentary inquiry into adult literacy in which the term 'literacy' is seen to encompass LLND (House of Representatives, 2022: 4).

Human capital, victim-blaming and the neoliberal individual

The National Strategy symbolized the culmination of the shift in the professional field of adult literacy from its social democratic origins in the 1970s to human capital dominance in the contemporary era. It was produced with considerable support from national industry and skills organizations whose own reports drew extensively on the ALL survey data (Australian Industry Group, 2010,

2012; Industry Skills Councils, 2011; Productivity Commission, 2010; Skills Australia, 2010). The Australian Industry Group (AIG), which nationally represents employers, has been a major player in promoting the human capital implications of low literacy in workplaces. The CEO of the AIG, drawing on the ALL data, once highlighted in a national radio interview that 'there are seven million people in the Australian workforce that just can't do it. They can't read standard operating procedures, for example ... ' (cited in Black, Yasukawa and Brown, 2015: 610). Such was (and remains) the unanimity of support from government, industry and skills organizations for this deficit ideology reflected in the National Strategy that these stakeholders have been referred to as 'singing off the same hymn sheet' (cited in Black, Yasukawa and Brown, 2015: 610; Black and Yasukawa, 2016: 173).

While the economic agenda has dominated adult literacy policy and practice in recent decades, another field to have embraced literacy deficit ideology based on the ALL survey data has been health, following a separate ABS (2008b) report on health literacy (see Chapter 9 of this book). It thus became standard in a range of academic studies to state that 60 per cent of the Australian adult population lacked the health literacy skills to cope with everyday life (e.g. Barber et al., 2009; Nutbeam, 2009; Peerson and Saunders, 2009). The ALL survey data became instrumental in highlighting health literacy deficits in the Australian adult population and, as with workplace literacy, elevating them to the level of a 'crisis' requiring a national policy response (Australian Commission on Safety and Quality in Health Care, 2014).

The deficit ideology expressed in the National Strategy represents a contemporary blame-the-victim discourse. The strategy expresses consensus among dominant groups that low literacy and numeracy represent a crisis affecting the nation's economic prosperity and health. The proposed remedy is to improve the literacy and numeracy levels of adult Australians, and to do this, the strategy aims 'to encourage, inspire and empower individuals to develop the courage and confidence to improve their foundation skills' (SCOTESE, 2012: 11). Responsibility for the literacy crisis and the potential remedy therefore is seen to rest primarily with individuals choosing or not choosing to improve their literacy skills through various programmes or interventions. They are held responsible for their own level of literacy, their own level of human capital. This blame-the-victim strategy is congruent with the neoliberal ideal of individuals being responsible consumers who have choices, in this case, to improve their literacy levels to 'secure a less parlous participation in the increasingly precarious labour markets of a globalising, neoliberal capitalism' (Argent, Brown and Kelly,

2022: 49). The National Strategy has been referred to recently as a 'neoliberal apparatus' (Argent, Brown and Kelly, 2022), and the tenets of 'individualization' and 'responsibilization' have become key to neoliberal governance in education and society more broadly (Keddie, 2016; Peters, 2017).

The role of the OECD

The OECD has played a key role in adult literacy policy in Australia due to its international surveys, and particularly the ALL survey (ABS, 2008a). The OECD is a promoter of neoliberal education reforms, including those involving competition mechanisms, standardization, core curriculums, corporatization and accountability regimes (Teodora, 2020). Its international adult literacy surveys have been described as 'technologies of neoliberal governance' (Atkinson, 2012: 81), which aim to promote neoliberal versions of what it is to be a worthy citizen – individual consumers who are knowledgeable and autonomous (Atkinson, 2019; Sellar and Lingard, 2013; Walker, 2009). So influential are the surveys that their constructions and measures of literacy have become the taken-for-granted 'common sense' discourses on literacy in the Global North (Rubenson, 2015). A similar argument has been made in relation to the dominant role of UNESCO's definitions of literacy in the Global South (Street, 2011). The Literacy Assessment and Monitoring Programme (LAMP; see UNESCO Institute for Statistics, 2009), not unlike earlier OECD international surveys (Guadalupe, 2015), defines literacy as a continuum of skills across five proficiency levels (for recent perspectives on the interplay and comparative aspects of the large-scale literacy (and numeracy) surveys of the OECD and UNESCO, see Addey, 2021; Grotlüschen, Desjardins and Liu, 2020). In Australia, there has been unanimity within governments and dominant groups regarding the extent of literacy and numeracy deficiencies in the adult population as measured by the ALL survey, and the level of skills that the nation should be aiming for (Black and Yasukawa, 2016). The National Strategy states that the Australian governments (State and Territory) have agreed: 'By 2022, two thirds of working age Australians will have literacy and numeracy skills at Level 3 or above' (SCOTESE, 2012: 10).

In this era of neoliberal capitalism, it is in the interests of governments and dominant groups to focus on victim-blaming individuals with literacy problems because it effectively shifts responsibility away from the need to address the broader structural issues of social-class inequalities in society. Neoliberal notions of people acting as self-managing individuals assuming personal responsibility for their lives apply not only to workplaces covered by the National Strategy but to other areas including health and well-being (Brown and Baker, 2012), with similar potential for victim-blaming (Jamrozik, 2010).

Much of the discussion in this chapter has focused on deficit ideology resulting from the ALL survey (ABS, 2008a) and the National Strategy that followed a few years later (SCOTESE, 2012). This was the era in which much of my research with adult groups was undertaken. Writing this chapter now in 2022, however, it appears little has changed in the intervening years. It should be noted that the OECD survey that followed the ALL, the Survey of Adult Skills (SAS), an initiative of the Programme for the International Assessment of Adult Competencies (PIAAC), produced statistics very similar to the ALL, but without explicitly recognizing a minimum level of skills to meet the complex demands of everyday life (ABS, 2013). This was consistent with the OECD's major report on PIAAC, which stated that their proficiency levels have no normative element and should not be understood as 'standards' or 'benchmarks' (OECD, 2013: 61). Unlike the ALL survey, the SAS/PIAAC results have received very little media attention in Australia (Yasukawa, 2019). This has not, however, prevented peak Australian industry organizations such as the Australian Industry Group (2016: 10) from inserting their own benchmark references to Level Three as 'the minimum requirement to operate effectively in workplaces and society' when discussing PIAAC results. In this way the deficit momentum created by the ALL has been maintained.

It was not only the reporting of national adult literacy and numeracy levels that has been revised in recent years. A new national health literacy survey has been conducted by the ABS (2019) using a multidimensional health literacy tool 'grounded in the daily lives of citizens, practitioners and policymakers' (Osborne et al., 2013). The survey was not comparable with the ALL data and did not feature an overall criterion level of health literacy required to meet the demands of everyday life. Thus, it is no longer tenable to state that 60 per cent of adult Australians have inadequate health literacy.

Contemporary perspectives on adult literacy

In the contemporary era in Australia, as indicated at the beginning of this chapter, adult literacy is again on the national agenda. With the National Strategy due to expire in 2022, the federal government commissioned a scoping study into foundation skills to inform future policy (Department of Education, Skills and

Employment, 2020) and produced a draft framework (Australian Government, 2022). A federal parliamentary committee has also recently completed its inquiry into 'Adult literacy and its importance' (House of Representatives, 2022). The many public submissions made to this inquiry provide important organizational and community insights into contemporary perspectives on adult literacy in Australia, and they are particularly pertinent for this book's focus on the role of literacy in the lives of working-class adults. One group of people, tutors from a volunteer literacy tutoring programme, provided a considerable number of submissions to the enquiry (available at https://www.aph.gov.au/Parliamentary_Business/Committees/House/Employment_Education_and_Training/Adultliteracy/Submissions). These tutors, writing about their experiences working with low-literate adults, provided exclusively deficit-oriented perspectives. For example, low literacy was described as causing 'social isolation, feelings of hopelessness, poor or no job prospects, and a withdrawal from society' (Submission 9). It was also seen to run through families: 'a cycle of unemployment, under-employment and poverty that repeats itself through generations' (Submission 7). The personal lives of low-literate individuals were described as 'empty' (Submission 22) and 'prevented ... from enjoying the most basic things in life' (Submission 16). Students were presented essentially as deficient, non-functioning adults and dependent almost entirely on others for assistance. One spouse wrote of her partner: 'From finances to health, every facet of my husband's life, and that of our children, would be precarious if he did not have the ready assistance of a willing reader and scribe – me' (Submission 27). These comments about the apparent helplessness of low-literate adults appeared indicative of models of cultural deprivation critiqued in the academy almost half a century ago in the 1970s (e.g. Hoyles, 1977; Keddie, 1973). While academics in the adult literacy field are often dismissive of these social pathology models, referring to them as myths (Grant, 1987; Hamilton and Hillier, 2006), they are nevertheless a salient reminder of the prevalence of deficit models in the general community.

In this introductory chapter, I have deliberately highlighted deficit ideology in adult literacy, focusing on significant economic and health discourses, and also general community perspectives. The chapter provides dominant perspectives on adults in society who are deemed to be low literate, and it serves as the background context to the chapters that follow which examine the perspectives of these adults on the role of literacy in their lives. The dominant perspectives can be summarized briefly as follows: low-literate adults are disadvantaged members of society (I refer to them as working class); they experience shame and guilt about their low literacy and are unable to function properly in their everyday lives; they are more likely to be unemployed, and in their working lives, their low literacy limits their individual productivity and economic worth; in relation to health literacy, they have difficulty maintaining individual health and well-being. Finally, and particularly significant in this neoliberal era, responsibility for their low literacy skills lies with them and their motivation and choice over whether to seek to improve their skills. These characteristics indicate a depressing picture of how dominant society – those with more power and status – view adults who are deemed to lack literacy skills. In the next chapter, I begin to provide an alternative picture. After outlining dominant perspectives on prisoner literacy levels, I explain the 'social practice' approach to literacy research and explore the perspectives of prisoners on how literacy affects their lives, documenting their voices on their lived experiences.

2
Prisoners and Literacy

All the time I can turn around and ask my cellmate how to spell words.
(Jackie, NSW prisoner)

Reading's not going to help you fuckin stop your face getting kicked in.
(Jeffrey, NSW prisoner)

If you're going to break the law, you'll break the law, and you're gonna come back to jail again. It's not going to stand on the reading and writing basis.
(Harry, NSW prisoner)

Introduction: Illiterate prisoners and crime

The above quotes from prisoners are drawn from interview data collected as part of a research thesis I completed in the late 1980s for a higher education degree (Black, 1989a). This chapter draws extensively on this research to provide first-hand accounts of prisoners on the role of literacy in their lives. Their voices and the perspectives they provide are rarely heard or documented in the public domain. Instead, dominant perspectives on prisoners and literacy are usually provided by organizations and individuals related to the field of criminology or with an interest in it. I begin with this dominant perspective.

As part of the recent Australian parliamentary inquiry into 'Adult literacy and its importance' (House of Representatives, 2022), a submission (No. 35) by the Australasian Corrections Education Association (ACEA) commenced with two quotes, both from overseas sources: 'Crime is significantly linked to illiteracy'; and 'Up to 85 per cent of juvenile delinquents are functionally illiterate'. These quotes were followed by reference to another overseas study (Morken, Jones and Helland, 2021) that indicated prisoner literacy (and language) 'disorders' potentially contributed to maladjustment and recidivism. The ACEA is a network of academics, practitioners and policymakers committed to 'best practice education and training programs' in prisons (https://www.acea.org.au/). Other submissions to the parliamentary inquiry indicated that approximately 62 per cent of Australian prisoners had less than functional literacy and up to 80 per cent in one prison in Tasmania (House of Representative, 2022: 133). These submissions demonstrate that in the forty years since my first involvement in prison education, little has changed in dominant perspectives on literacy in prisons. In the 1980s, the implied link between crime and illiteracy was apparent in a range of NSW government publications. An annual report of the NSW Department of Corrective Services (NSW DCS, 1984) claimed that nearly 30 per cent of prisoners were functionally illiterate. This followed the 30 per cent illiteracy statistic cited in the 1978 Royal Commission into NSW Prisons (NSW Government, 1978), based on prisoners' levels of formal schooling. It also followed an internal NSW DCS report by a prison psychologist (Dodd, 1980), in which the 30 per cent functional illiteracy rate was based on low scores on a verbal reasoning test and a school-based reading comprehension test. Leading NSW prison education bureaucrats in the mid-1980s claimed that functional illiteracy 'runs at least three times higher in the prisoner population than in the general community' (Noad and Hancock, 1984: 20). Thus, the dominant perspective on prisoners was then, and remains, at least among leading contemporary prison educators and allied stakeholders, predominantly deficit-oriented with the focus on high 'illiteracy' rates. It suggests that a large swathe of prisoners, an 'anonymous docile mass' (Wilson, 2004: 68), is unable to function properly in society because they lack literacy skills. This perception of illiterate prisoners, as I explain in the following paragraphs, serves a number of stakeholder interests.

The idea that crime is linked to illiteracy is highly problematic for me, in part because the corollary, that crime will be reduced if literacy levels improve, is a fanciful suggestion based on my own prison education experiences. It also runs contrary to my academic studies of literacy, even in the 1980s, as I became aware of the ideological role of literacy in different social contexts (Graff, 1979; Levine, 1982, 1986; Street, 1984). It needs to be recognized nevertheless that these crime/illiteracy links correspond with the idea that prisoners can be rehabilitated through programme interventions, including education, which is implicit in the term 'corrective' services. I grappled with these ideas from the time I was first employed by the NSW DCS and entered prisons as a part-time 'remedial English' teacher in 1980. As a qualified secondary school teacher, I always saw my role foremost as an educator and quite removed from any rehabilitative role. I perceived and articulated the view that education in prison was a human right and an end in itself (Black, 1989b). Decades later, the human rights versus rehabilitation arguments about the role of prison education continue (Czerniawski, 2015; Galloway, 2019, 2021; Muñoz, 2009; Vorhaus, 2014). An additional contemporary element is the focus within the field of criminology on the concept of desistance, examining how and why people refrain from offending (Farrall and Maruna, 2004; Graham and McNeill, 2017). This includes a recent study undertaken in NSW prisons which has examined how learning in a basic skills programme may support desistance from crime (McGregor, 2020).

My first-hand experiences and observations of prison education in the 1980s indicated that prisoner illiteracy rates were linked to organizational power; they were political (Lankshear and Lawler, 1987). They were used, for example, by prison education bureaucrats as leverage to argue their case for resources in competition with other areas of need within the prison system. Prison education was always viewed as a minority element in a corrective services department that garnered few votes in the wider electorate. With tight budgets, custodial matters were prioritized, and education, badged as 'Programmes Division', was forced to compete for scarce financial resources with a range of other non-custodial areas, including prison industries, psychological services, and welfare. This fight for resources appears to be a generic problem in prison jurisdictions, as critics have argued that education in prisons should not become 'simply an add-on should resources "allow" it' (Muñoz, 2009: 165). To appeal to departmental overlords for a share of financial resources, and indeed to justify and promote their own jobs, it was hardly surprising that prison education bureaucrats would promote high illiteracy rates among prisoners and encourage the link with recidivism and rehabilitation generally. This same dominant illiteracy/crime discourse can be seen to underpin the recent ACEA submission outlined at the beginning of this chapter. As has been long contended in literacy studies, illiteracy rates are often used as 'counters in a political game over resources: if campaigners can inflate the figures, then the public will be shocked and funds will be forthcoming from embarrassed governments' (Street, 1990: 5).

Promoting education as a 'human right' was then in the 1980s, and is now, unlikely to count for much in competition over limited prison resources. An additional factor hindering the case for education in prisons has always been the high cost of qualified educators relative to other prison personnel. This even led to a suggestion (though thankfully not enacted) by the Minister for Corrective Services in the late 1980s that custodial staff should assume the role of educators in prisons (Black, 1989b). Fast-forward several decades to the contemporary era, and the Minister for Corrective Services NSW in 2016 attempted to resolve the high cost of prison education services by outsourcing most of it to a private contractor. This was in accord with neoliberal ideology that has increasingly been applied to criminal justice systems in Australia (Mills, 2017). So powerful is the rehabilitation argument in prison education discourse that critics of this privatization of prison education argued as part of their case that privatization represented 'an abandonment of the state's obligations to rehabilitate and reform prisoners' and that reducing recidivism required highly qualified educators (Community Justice Coalition, 2016, 2018).

The popular perception of large numbers of illiterate prisoners was always problematic for me to reconcile with my own experiences of working with prisoners. For a start, despite being employed as a 'remedial English' teacher, I only rarely met or worked with prisoners who could be considered illiterate, however defined, to the extent that I wondered if such prisoners existed to any great extent in the prison system. Many of the prisoners I worked with wanted primarily to improve their spoken English, in fact at one time the classroom was referred to by some prisoners as 'little Beirut'. Many prisoners also wanted assistance with study units from an array of correspondence courses, including at university level. But there was a general absence of prisoners seeking my assistance to improve their basic literacy skills, and this became the genesis for my master's research thesis – examining the needs of low-literate prisoners and the factors that affected their participation in prison literacy programmes (Black, 1989a).

Research on prisoners and literacy practices

In this chapter, I draw on research data from my thesis, and in line with the central theme of this book, I focus primarily on how low-literate prisoners managed literacy practices in their everyday lives in prison and outside in the general community. In exploring the attitudes and motivations of these prisoners towards literacy education in prison, it was important to know how or to what extent literacy impacted their everyday living. As a teacher and later as an educational manager of prison education programmes, I was ideally positioned in my 'add-on' role as a researcher, to interview prisoners in a relatively informal way that explored their subjective perspectives on literacy. I began my prison education research in late 1984, and over the next few years I was influenced in my research approach by a number of contemporary sociological studies of literacy.

These included studies of the role of social networks in assisting low-literate adults (Fingeret, 1983), and a focus generally on the social contexts of literacy, indicating its functions and uses within local communities (Cook-Gumperz, 2006; Heath, 1980, 1983; Levine, 1982, 1986). I was unaware at the time that my research approach was largely in accord with what has since been termed the new literacy studies (NLS), an influential alternative approach to understanding and researching literacy that developed rapidly in this era (Barton, 2007; Barton and Hamilton, 2012; Baynham, 1995; Gee, 2015; Heath, 1983; Street, 1984). The main focus of the NLS is how people use literacy (or more accurately, literacies) in their everyday lives on the basis that

> [l]iteracy cannot be separated from what people are doing, how they are doing it, when, where, and under what conditions and with whom they are doing it; metaphorically, there is no separation of the dancer from the dance.
> (Bloome and Green, 2015: 20)

Street's (1984) work was particularly significant in indicating the ideological role, the politics of literacy practices in people's everyday lives that contrasted with dominant society's focus on an 'autonomous' model of literacy based on standardized norms. It was this latter model that was responsible for the shocking prisoner 'illiteracy' statistics.

In the field of prison literacy research in Australia in the early 1980s, coincidentally, a study had been undertaken with Victorian state prisoners using semi-structured interviews that mirrored my research method (Brennan and Brennan, 1984). This qualitative Victorian study explored the attitudes of prisoners to literacy education and was similar in research approach to other Australian studies at the time which explored subjective experiences on the role of literacy in community literacy programmes (Grant, 1985, 1987).

My research focused on a selection of low-literate prisoners in a male, maximum security prison in Sydney's Long Bay Prison Complex. Initially, to help identify the prisoners to be interviewed, I used departmental test scores from a standardized verbal reasoning test that was part of the regular classification process when prisoners first entered the prison system. These psychological test scores had value for me only in the broadest, normative sense in potentially identifying prisoners who could be termed 'low literate'. My substantive criterion for low literacy was self-reporting from the prisoners. In brief and initial one-to-one interviews with prisoners, I enquired about their literacy abilities, and only if they acknowledged that they experienced difficulties with literacy in their lives did I explain the nature of my research and seek their participation in later, more in-depth interviews. This self-reporting criterion was promoted in several UK studies at the time on the basis that in adult life, it is the individual's assessment of their own basic skills relative to the demands placed on them by their own life that is most relevant (Hamilton and Stasinopoulos, 1987; Jones and Charnley, 1978; Levine, 1986).

A total of eighteen prisoners were interviewed for the research. Two prisoners identified as transsexual. The average age of prisoners was thirty (ages ranged from seventeen to forty-six), and all were from English-speaking backgrounds. Based on their educational and work backgrounds, all the prisoners could be classified as working class. Most had left school at thirteen or fourteen years (one had no schooling), and only one had reached Year 10 level of schooling. All previous employment backgrounds were in manual or low-skilled jobs, with occupation/usual job described as labourer (3), unemployed (3), on a pension (3), farm work (2), prostitute (2, both transsexual), spray painter, truck driver, laundry, caretaker, off-sider (in a brewery). Twelve of the eighteen prisoners (66 per cent) had been to prison previously. All interviews with the prisoners were tape-recorded and later transcribed in full. Pseudonyms were provided for each of the interviewees.

Literacy and everyday life in prison

The range of self-reported literacy abilities described by the prisoners varied across the interviews. With some prisoners, it was clear in a normative sense that they struggled with reading and writing. One prisoner, Greg, an invalid pensioner on the outside, said he could read 'next to nothing'. Don, a farm worker, said he was 'not much of a reader at the best of times'. And Warren, unemployed on the outside, said he could read 'a little bit, not much'. Several prisoners focused primarily on their difficulties with spelling. Harry, for example, a building labourer, stated that 'writing becomes a little bit difficult, just remembering the words, how to spell them out'. In fact, several prisoners spoke about their difficulties in 'spelling it out'. These comments from prisoners in response to questions about their literacy abilities were to some extent predictable, as Wilson (2007) indicated based on her work with prisoners in the UK. They most likely reflected their experiences with literacy as an autonomous skill in the formal schooling sense, which in most cases had been negative. One prisoner, Jeffrey, related his experiences to a particular social practice, writing to his family. He said his writing was 'sloppy', and he confined his letters to 'small words they will understand, that the spelling'll be right'.

In this study, the literacy practices of prison life were distinguished from those that the prisoners engaged with in the general community beyond prison, and for some of the prisoners, the former were likely to be different and more complex to navigate. So much of daily life in prisons involved literacy practices. They included the forms to be completed for 'buy ups', those extra purchases such as tobacco, snacks, toiletries that made prison life slightly more bearable. Written requests on a blue application form (known as a 'bluey') were required for myriad reasons, from obtaining personal items from prison property to even seeking permission to grow a beard. And with restricted visits by and phone calls to loved ones and friends on the outside, letters took on heightened significance. Brennan and Brennan (1984: 228) wrote that letters 'contain everything that is precious to a prisoner's humanity and must be seen as the essence of the literate enterprise. Letters are the basic literature of prisons'. Prison jobs were another domain of literacy practices. While many were routine and manual and required few literacy abilities, such as the many 'sweeper' or kitchenhand jobs, there were some that were more varied and complex, such as the various administrative or 'clerk' jobs. Finally, there were the literacy practices that could be termed 'personal fulfilment' (Perry and Homan, 2015), including personal expression through poetry (Clemente, Higgins and Sughrua, 2011), and reading books and magazines for pleasure. These were important as a means of coping with prison life and may have provided 'a metaphorical escape from the confines of prison' (Perry and Homan, 2015: 438). Wilson (2000, 2004, 2007), in her studies of UK prisons, conceptualized some of these literacy practices as a 'third space', an in-between cultural space between the official, regulative prison world and the more informal social practices of prisoners. They helped prisoners retain a sense of personhood and enabled them to 'keep their minds' (Wilson, 2000: 68).

Independently managing this range of literacy practices was problematic for many of the prisoners interviewed. In their lives beyond prison (explained later in this chapter), invariably there was ready assistance with literacy practices from family, friends and a number of trusted 'mediators' (Baynham, 1993; Fingeret, 1983; Papen, 2010), but prison life necessarily disrupted this avenue of social support. For many of the prisoners, new social networks needed to be established, and the most obvious ones included fellow prisoners. One prisoner, Don, for example, indicated in a quite matter-of-fact way the help he received: 'I get someone else to do it for me, a couple of me mates, they all come from Queensland.' Another prisoner, George, indicated that he also received assistance from fellow prisoners, but from 'just the one' prisoner with whom he had developed a trust:

Neville, he's helped me a lot. He doesn't tell anybody else. He keeps to himself. He's not a bloke to mouth off. If I want a letter written, he'll make it, just like that. See, there was another bloke down there wanted to read a letter to me. I said, 'nope'.

Most commonly, and conveniently, given the time prisoners were locked together in their cells, it was cellmates who provided much assistance. Jackie, a transexual, who shared a cell with another transexual, indicated that for her, asking for help with a literacy task was a non-issue: 'All the time I can turn around and ask my cellmate how to spell words.'

For some prisoners, however, asking cellmates for assistance was found to be problematic. William, for example, was aware that his cellmate had other priorities and asking for help could be unwelcome: 'He's got his own problems at the moment, trying to sort his wife and that out. So that's why I don't interfere.' Michael also indicated some of the problems inherent in sharing a cell that would mitigate against asking for assistance:

> He said there one night, oh, if you don't stop snoring, I'll get up and smack you round the cell, you know. But I'd been with him for a week or more and, you know, he's a sort of real friendly attitude. Well, this showed me how quick people can change.

Wing sweepers, and in particular head sweepers, were an additional source of informal inmate support. These prisoners tended to be long termers who commanded high status and a degree of trust within the prison system. Part of their informal role was to assist other prisoners when required:

> Well, I had to fill out an application form, to get some money out of my bank, and I got Barry (head sweeper) to do it for me. Well, I was told by the wing officer, he told me to see Barry.

How prisoners managed everyday literacy practices depended to a large extent on the nature of the literacy task (event) and their own literacy abilities. The buy-up forms, for example, could be undertaken independently by most prisoners. One prisoner, Stephen, stated: 'I don't know everything that's on the form, but what I can see is what I want kinda thing.' For other prisoners, the buy-up forms could present some problems, but it was a routine task that they could usually master to some degree, even by those who considered they had very poor literacy skills. William, for example, stated: 'I know how to fill me name. I only buy up once a fortnight. I just put down two ounces of tobacco. I copy off the packets.'

In seeking assistance from fellow prisoners, it was clear that prisoners tried to retain some independence, particularly when it came to letter writing to family and loved ones. William, for example, though he struggled with his writing and had to seek the assistance of other prisoners, nevertheless tried to retain some individual agency, some personal power, in letters to his wife:

> I get other inmates to write it out for me, then I might change the letters. I'm starting to learn. I only use the top part of the letter, then I write how much I love her and all this.

But even this strategy was problematic. William later stated that his wife had told him to 'cut down on the writing. She was getting the same kind of letter every week'.

Other prisoners demonstrated not only better writing abilities but greater individual agency. Jeffrey, for example, said that with application forms, he would 'struggle through' on his own and would seek assistance only if really necessary, and then it was on his terms:

> If there's something that I want real bad, and I'm not sure how to go about it, I'll just get a mate to help with the spelling. I'll tell him what I want to write, and he'll just help me with the spelling.

While it was clear that fellow prisoners provided much help with literacy practices, relying on that support was problematic given the transitory nature of the prison system. That trusted fellow prisoner would at some stage be transferred to another prison or be released, and this would require the process of establishing new social networks of support with other prisoners. There was also the issue of trusting others to know your weaknesses, in this case, poor literacy, and the risk that this could be used against them. Harry alluded to this based on his previous experiences in a Queensland prison: 'It's a big drama in jail, you know, once they find out what you want. Don't let anything go. I found out by mistake from up Queensland.' Another prisoner, Tony, commented: 'Crims get to know these things, and people talk, and crims can be very nasty.'

Beyond assistance from fellow inmates, there were not too many options for prisoners. It was rare for prisoners to seek assistance from prison officers. As one prisoner, Harry, said: 'They stick together, we stick together.' Some other comments from prisoners were highly disparaging of prison officers, and one prisoner, Jeffrey, felt constrained in what he could say: 'All on tape! No way in the world. No way in the world. I wouldn't ask them for the time of day.'

Non-custodial staff also played a role, and as a teacher, I found my role was often more that of a literacy mediator than a teacher, helping prisoners with official forms and occasionally letters. One prisoner, Michael, commented on the degree of trust with educators and some other staff: 'the only time anyone uses your own name, or you can talk to anybody, is in here (education) or the psychologist.' During my time as a prison educator in the early 1980s, one tertiary educated prisoner actually established a role for himself as a literacy mediator for prisoners, a drop-in centre function within the education section of the prison where assistance could be provided for any prisoner who needed it. Interestingly, literacy research at the time had indicated the need for just this type of provision in the general community (Levine, 1986).

Some prison jobs required prisoners to work directly under the supervision of custodial officers, as in the various 'clerk' or 'store' jobs, and they invariably involved literacy practices. While it was rare for the low-literate prisoners I interviewed to seek these jobs, one prisoner, Tony, described how he managed to bluff his way along during a previous prison sentence:

> I was put into the store, and I managed to work in the store, at a desk, keeping files, doing bookwork, even though I couldn't really do it. I copied a lot of stuff. They never knew, they never picked to it.

Prisoners were asked in the interviews about their literacy interests, which related to the 'personal fulfilment' aspect of literacy practices, including poetry and reading books and magazines. While these prisoners all acknowledged that they experienced literacy difficulties in their lives, several of them indicated that they enjoyed reading for pleasure. Victor, for example, said he enjoyed 'westerns' and 'war stories' but not comics ('they're no good, they're not educational'). Leslie said he enjoyed 'poems and things like that', and Jim said he read 'comic books, bike books, Easy Rider stories'. One prisoner said he read the Bible, and several prisoners mentioned enjoying magazines. Jeffrey commented on the reading practices he enjoyed:

> I reckon some of the poetry I've seen in books are beautiful, you know, good to send sheilas. But I'm a comic man, I like the funnies. If I go through the Penthouses, I look at the jokes instead of the nude sheilas.

Poetry and expressive writing generally is viewed in the research literature as having a 'liberating function' in prisons that can momentarily locate prisoners beyond the walls of their confinement (Clemente, Higgins and Sughrua, 2011; Perry and Homan, 2015). In my research, one prisoner, Michael, experienced this quite differently. He had begun to participate in literacy classes and was encouraged by his teacher to express his feelings in writing. However, he found little joy in doing so as his feelings were too strong given his current life circumstances. He rather poignantly related his attempt at expressive writing to the story of a prisoner he knew who occupied the cell next to him:

> The bloke next door to me, you know, after I writ that. He'd been sorta going like that on the wall, sorta banging for about two weeks. And then the other night he got a razor blade and cut his wrists up, you know. So, he must've been feeling hard too, and that was after I writ that.

It was following this experience of his prisoner neighbour that Michael decided against exploring his own feelings in writing.

Literacy and everyday life on the outside

A key factor in determining how well these prisoners functioned on the outside world was their work history. As indicated earlier, previous employment for this group of prisoners was mainly low skilled. In most of their jobs, literacy practices played a relatively small role, and lacking literacy skills was not considered a problem. This was especially the case with work in sawmills, driving tractors and farm labouring work generally. It was certainly the case in Sandy's previous work: 'as a worker, a prostitute, you just need to know what the money looks like'. There were some examples of prisoners having to confront more complex literacy practices. Harry, for example, took on a new role in the construction industry and became a union delegate, a safety officer, and he was put on the spot occasionally due to spelling problems: 'that happened quite a few times actually. I just asked the next bloke how do you spell it? And they'd say, "you dumb bastard", you know'. This negative labelling, however, was not something that bothered him. He viewed it 'more like a joke, 'cos there's a whole heap of Europeans and Italians and that, and they can't even speak English'.

Quite a few of the prisoners did perceive that their lack of literacy held them back in their work. Greg, for example, was offered a staff job at BHP but claimed he had to refuse it due to his reading and writing difficulties. For the same reason another prisoner, Michael, felt unable to take on the fairly straightforward book work involved in logging truck weights on the wheat silos, making the excuse that 'oh no, I haven't got the time, too busy to do that sort of thing'. Again though, for some, the role of social networks came into play.

Victor, for example, established himself as a spray painter, but the business side of things he left to his wife: 'any paperwork comes in, she just automatically does it'. It would seem, however, that the biggest hurdle for many prisoners was not actually performing in jobs but applying for them in the first place. Difficulties completing application forms were consistently mentioned as an impediment to work, though this was often overcome with social support from friends or family. Some of the strategies included: 'I immediately took it home and got me brother to help me fill it out' (Jim); 'I get someone to fill it in. I use the excuse that um, I didn't bring my glasses today, may I bring it back tomorrow fully filled in?' (Tony). In Tony's case, however, the problem was not just reading and writing the form but deciding what to write on it. He had never been to school: 'that stuffs me, you know, how am I going to tell them when I left school? You've got to lie. You can't go along to a job and say you've never been to school.' Few of the prisoners indicated they could independently complete job application forms, but the issue sometimes went beyond their literacy competence; it also related to their personal disposition. In the case of Jeffrey, for example, while he had trouble completing the form, he was determined to persevere as best he could:

> I'll just do it there, struggle through it, and what I don't understand I just, when I finish, like when he says, 'have you done it yet?' I'll say, 'not yet, I'm not sure on this that and the other.' We just go through it together then.

Jeffrey recounted that in his family he was always told to be independent:

> Well, you can't depend on nobody. My father, he's always said you've got to do it yourself. I have a hard time, I don't care. I just do my best, and if my best ain't good enough, well, unlucky.

In the general community separate from the world of work, support from others was often cited in undertaking a range of literacy practices. For example, prisoners referred to assistance from siblings to explain life insurance details, and neighbours and even the Salvation Army provided assistance with bills and social security forms. Support from spouses was especially significant, but with this support came occasional frustrations and tensions within families. Stephen, for example, while he always left reading and writing tasks for his wife to complete, had never revealed to her the full extent of his literacy difficulties. He was embarrassed that she would perceive him as 'backward':

> Well, I told her I wasn't real good at 'em, and she used to just do it automatically. She doesn't say anything, but, you know, she's only just kind of realised that, um,

how backward I am. I've never said to her, well, you know, I can't read and write. When a letter or something comes, I just leave it to her. Sometimes she gets the shits over it.

Similarly, Michael left all reading and writing to his wife and it affected how he behaved within his family:

> Even to take the kids to the doctor I leave to her because, you know, you get asked something, well, how do you spell it? Sometimes me wife, we might have, we get on really well, but from time to time we have an argument. She says, well why don't you take it over (home management), you know, if you think I'm not doing it right?

For these prisoners, their lack of literacy affected them in a personal way in their day-to-day interactions with others. Stephen, for example, was always wary of any social situations that might expose his literacy problems, and he provided the example of playing card games like 'Trivial Pursuit': 'Anything that looks like it might be something where I might have to read, suddenly I'll walk out of the room.' Tony explained that he was always living with a secret and that 'most friends of mine outside have no idea'. For Michael, it always meant 'backing off' in his interactions with others in case he was put on the spot with a literacy task.

Prisoner orientations and social networks

This chapter began with contemporary (and unchanged over recent decades) dominant perspectives on (il)literacy and prisoners, indicating that crime was linked with illiteracy, and that prisoner illiteracy rates were considerably higher than those found in the general population. The qualitative research data presented in this chapter, however, indicate an alternative, more complex picture. While all the prisoners in the research self-reported as low literate, they nevertheless displayed agency and utilized a range of social strategies to manage the literacy practices in their lives, such that it would be inaccurate to suggest they could not function in their everyday lives, either in prison or on the outside. Some prisoners may have struggled at times, and clearly there were occasional tensions and frustrations, but they nevertheless managed their lives. In many cases, this required support from others, though not always as some were determined to 'struggle through' on their own. In the following paragraphs, two brief case studies of prisoners are featured to indicate that the attitudes or 'orientations' to literacy differed markedly among the prisoners interviewed.

Some of them appeared to be in accord with the 'personal orientation' type that Levine (1986: 120) described as

> [a] sense of shame and failure has been deeply internalised and generalised so that it occupies a central place in their self conceptions. Illiteracy may be the central problem in their lives or, more likely, it has interacted with other difficulties and assumed unrealistic and perhaps neurotic proportions.

Michael appeared to fit this 'personal orientation' type. He was thirty-eight at the time of the research, married with six children, and prior to imprisonment he lived in a NSW country town. He felt acute embarrassment at his low literacy, and in his social interactions he was always defensive, 'backing off' in case he was put on the spot with a literacy-related task. He described himself as 'a bit nervous, and really, too old to be so dumb'. He blamed the school system for his literacy problems, claiming that 'when you drop behind the rest there's nobody left to pick you up'. His employment history was limited to unskilled farm work, though at the time of his criminal conviction, he was an invalid pensioner with a back ailment. While Michael received important assistance from his wife at home, he felt that lack of literacy was a burden he had carried through life, and it had 'backfired' on him yet again with his current criminal charges. As he explained, he had been convicted for growing marijuana plants (he said it was for his personal use to ease back pain), but because the police found a large sum of money in his home, he potentially faced a further sentence for drug dealing:

> Now they say the money that they found is illegal or stolen, so it's backfiring again. They say, well, marijuana and that (the money) go together, and they charged me with dealing in marijuana, which they proved I wasn't, but I've still got to appear in court on a goods and custody that's me own money.

Literacy played a key role in this because Michael claimed he only kept his money at home because taking it to a bank involved literacy practices that were too embarrassing for him to confront. His previous banking experience had involved queueing with other people and then being asked to fill in a form: 'you know, looked over me shoulder and, how the hell, you know, how do I spell this?' Michael claimed about the role of literacy in his life: 'It's nearly a conviction not being able to spell, you know, nearly a sentence when you leave school and can't spell.'

Quite different to Michael's orientation to literacy, however, was Jeffrey, who was largely unaffected by the stigma of low literacy. He could be seen to fit towards the opposite end of the spectrum in the type that Levine (1986) referred to as 'instrumentally oriented'. Jeffrey was 30 at the time of the interview and had spent his childhood in Balmain, then a working-class area of Sydney. Of his formative schooling years, Jeffrey said he did not hate his schooling; rather, he just did not care. He maintained that as the 'class thug' he had high informal status with his peers and had no need to learn to read:

> I was the class thug, you know, and what I said goes in the classroom sorta. Even further than this, you know, when they used to see me coming at the canteen, they used to give me their pies and sausage rolls and that, anything, just don't clip me. In them days Balmain was a pretty rough area and you sorta learnt to fight before you learnt to fuckin read. Reading's not going to help you fuckin stop your face getting kicked in.

He was unconcerned at having been in a low academic stream at school, and he never had to do any academic work:

> I didn't used to have to do anything, you know. Someone else would do me homework. I'd just give me book to some cunt in the yard. He'll take it home and do it, no worries. Jeff said, that's good enough. That's the way it was.

In his working life, Jeffrey claimed he had little problem in working and performing well in a range of waterfront jobs: 'I can do all the jobs in the (Ship) Painters and Dockers union. I can do crane chasing, the works, you know.'

Unlike Michael, Jeffrey had a strong sense of self-esteem, and while he was frustrated at times not being able to express his thoughts in writing ('it just pisses me off'), he refused to be defined by his low literacy:

> I think at the moment, my personality, just the way I am upfront, will get me through. I think people that hide it (their literacy problems), and get embarrassed, just ain't sure with, they're not happy with what they are, whereas I'm happy, you know. I've been brought up in a rough street, but me missus always says to me, I'm a fuckin marshmallow, you know, inside I'm a very soft human being.

When Jeffrey experienced difficulties with literacy practices, his first strategy was to 'struggle through' on his own, and if that did not work, he would seek assistance from someone else. The process was instrumental, unproblematic and very much on his terms. He would dictate what he wanted written and would ask for help only with the technicalities of grammar and spelling. He accepted and took full responsibility for his poor literacy skills and his life circumstances:

> I'm what you call it, illiterate, permanent illiterate, that's the word isn't it? I blame me. There's nobody else. Same as me being in jail right now, I can't blame nobody but meself. They (teachers) tried. I was just a fuckin hopeless case. Rebellious from the word go.

Michael and Jeffrey were just two of the eighteen prisoners interviewed for this research, and each member of this prisoner group had different accounts of the role of literacy in their lives, the value they ascribed to it, and how it affected their functioning in their everyday lives. But there were some strong commonalities also, beyond being prisoners and low literate. They had all experienced working-class childhoods, including living in low socio-economic areas (including rural NSW and urban Balmain, which ironically today is highly gentrified), low formal schooling levels, and low-skilled work. Another significant commonality across the research group was assistance provided by others with everyday literacy practices. The extent of this assistance varied according to a number of factors, including the type of literacy events and the personal dispositions of the prisoner, but nevertheless, every prisoner indicated that literacy support from others played a role in their lives. Other people acting as mediators to provide literacy support, as indicated earlier in this chapter, has long been recognized in the academic literature (Baynham, 1995; Fingeret, 1983; Papen, 2010), but rarely does it seem to be acknowledged or highlighted in discussions about adult literacy levels, either in the general community or in prisons. The term 'functional illiteracy' is still used, as demonstrated by the prison literacy references cited at the beginning of this chapter, but what the research in this chapter has demonstrated is that in their everyday lives, 'functioning' for each low-literate prisoner included support from others. In other words, there was a disconnect between the literacy/illiteracy statistics used by dominant groups, including prison professionals and related groups, and the real lives, that is, the situated social practices of prisoners (Wilson, 2000, 2004). Statistics on literacy abilities are provided on the erroneous assumption that adults should be autonomous beings in relation to how they function with literacy practices. The role played by others as literacy mediators was a key finding I took from this prison research, and it has informed much of my later literacy research studies as the following chapters in this book will demonstrate. As Papen (2009, 2010) indicates (see Chapter 9), literacy can be 'distributed', by which she means it is not simply a property or an attribute of an individual, but that it is 'shared knowledge and expertise' that resides in an individual's social network.

The perceived link between illiteracy/low literacy and crime, which, as the early part of this chapter indicated, occupies the interests of many educators, prison bureaucrats and criminologists, was not explored in the research and prisoners were not asked about their criminal convictions. In explaining how they lived their everyday lives, however, particularly in the general community before they were imprisoned, some prisoners did indicate that low literacy had caused difficulties in their lives, and in turn this could be related to their criminal convictions. One prisoner, Tony, for example, lamented that his low literacy meant that he was limited to menial jobs, which he claims led to crime:

> I've been to jail quite a few times. It's always basically six months here, five months there, and it's always stealing for money to survive, because, you know, I get bored with a job because I don't want to wash dishes. I just feel that this is so boring, I know I could do more.

Tony explained that he had an expressive flair for interior decorating that provided him with occasional affirmation from his peers, but while it was something he said he would love to do as a job, he had no opportunity to become qualified. In Tony's case, however, it could be argued that the issue was not lack of literacy per se but lack of education. He had lived with his father as a child, and for reasons Tony did not understand, he was never sent to school. Tony was the only prisoner in the research study with no schooling at all, but of the other prisoners, only one had reached Year 10 (the school leaving level at the time), and most left at thirteen or fourteen years of age. Criminal behaviour appeared more likely to relate to lack of education and poverty of life circumstances generally than with the specific lack of literacy abilities. Another prisoner, Harry, a construction worker, claimed that improving literacy would make no difference to his work and no difference to criminal behaviour: 'If you're going to break the law, you'll break the law, and you're gonna come back to jail again. It's not going to stand on the reading and writing basis.'

Concluding comments

This chapter has outlined two contrasting perspectives on prisoners and literacy. On the one hand, there is a dominant, deficit discourse which, for more than forty years, has presented a picture of high percentages of illiterate prisoners who struggle to function in society. This discourse has sought to make a causal link between illiteracy and crime, indicating that literacy/education programmes in prison have a rehabilitative role to play. An alternative perspective on prisoners is presented when attempts are made to provide the subjective perspectives of prisoners, particularly those who identify themselves as lacking in literacy abilities. The issue of functioning, in both prison life and in the outside community, is complex and based largely on social relations. These prisoners managed their everyday lives largely by drawing on social networks of support. In prison, this mainly involved support from fellow prisoners, though the circumstances varied for individual prisoners. In the general community outside prison, a range of other social networks were drawn upon, particularly involving spouses and friends. The idea that low literacy was in some generic way linked with crime was highly problematic to argue from the perspectives of the prisoners. While low literacy did present as a problem to be overcome in the lives of some prisoners, it is difficult to view any of these prisoners as non-functioning members of society based on their literacy abilities. As the accounts of their lives in this chapter have demonstrated, most of these prisoners had experienced difficult working-class backgrounds. They experienced multiple disadvantages relating to social class, including poor educational opportunities, and generally limited life opportunities due to impoverished backgrounds. These structural factors were likely to rate highly as factors responsible for criminal activities.

This study of prisoners was undertaken in the 1980s, but it provided me with early insights into the role of literacy in people's everyday lives, particularly the lives of working-class adults, that have persisted in my research studies over the decades that followed. It indicated that literacy is inextricably linked to social context and that most people experiencing literacy difficulties live within social networks that provide much of the support they need to manage their everyday lives.

3

Long-Term Unemployed People and Literacy

I didn't really want to come, I just wanted a job.
(Tony, fifty, commenting on his participation in
a jobseeker literacy programme)

No, not going to make any difference, no.
(Mary, fifty, an Italian-born jobseeker commenting on
her job prospects as the result of attending a jobseeker literacy programme)

Oh, you know what they're like, Newstart, you got no sort of say in it. Because if you sort of say no, they just cut you off the allowance straight away.
(Wayne, twenty-two, commenting on the consequences
of resisting being sent to a jobseeker literacy programme)

Literacy programmes for the unemployed

The above comments and the interview data provided in this chapter are drawn from my doctoral thesis (Black, 2001: 132–77) which explored in part the perspectives of unemployed people sent to a federal government-funded jobseeker literacy programme. Unemployed people seeking to improve their literacy abilities have always featured in Australian adult literacy programmes (Black and Sim, 1990; Dymock, 1982), but since 1991, they have become a national priority group with designated federal government-funded literacy programmes. These programmes began following the Australian Language and Literacy Policy (ALLP) which stated that '[j]obseekers with fundamental literacy difficulties will in future be sent to TAFE and adult community education providers for assistance' (Department of Employment, Education and Training [DEET], 1991: 8). Henceforth, jobseeker (the new euphemism for the unemployed) literacy programmes, which also included language and numeracy, have been funded by the federal government continuously to the present time. During this thirty-year period, the programme has undergone several iterations, beginning as the Special Intervention Programme (SIP) in 1991, then becoming the Literacy and Numeracy Training (LANT) programme in 1998, followed by the Language, Literacy and Numeracy Programme (LLNP) from 2002, and finally, the Skills for Education and Employment (SEE) programme from 2013 to the present time. In this chapter, the focus is on jobseekers who attended a NSW TAFE college as part of the SIP during 1993. Drawing on my research with these jobseekers (Black, 2001), the aim is to present their perspectives on the role that literacy played in their working lives and as registered jobseekers sent to a literacy programme. As background to this qualitative data, I begin by outlining the historical context of jobseeker literacy programmes in the early 1990s, drawing on research literature relating to this era.

The early 1990s were a reformist era with federal Labor government interventions in the field of adult literacy and social welfare provision. In 1993, the year of my research, Australia was in an economic recession, famously described by Prime Minister Keating as 'the recession we had to have' (Carroll, 2010: 70). Unemployment reached a peak of 12.2 per cent (Committee on Employment Opportunities, 1993), the highest since the Great Depression of the 1930s. The long-term unemployed, those unemployed for a year or more, became a major public policy issue for governments, comprising around 37 per cent of the total unemployed (Committee on Employment Opportunities, 1993). This was also an era in which the federal Labor government, with the support of peak organizations, including business, industry and unions, embraced skills formation (Australian Council of Trade Unions [ACTU]/Trade Development Council [TDC], 1987; Dawkins and Holding, 1987) and introduced major reforms to industrial awards and vocational education and training in order to develop the competitiveness of the Australian economy. Literacy was seen to be a key element of these skills and national training reforms, and the ALLP in 1991 indicated how literacy as human capital could contribute to the national economy (DEET, 1991; Lo Bianco and Wickert, 2001). The ALLP essentially signalled the shift in orientation from literacy viewed as a 'right' to literacy as a 'resource' (Lo Bianco, 1993), and within this new orientation, literacy was, according to one contemporary government publication, 'just like farmland or goldmines to be developed and used to help the country grow and prosper' (DEET, 1992a: 1).

The ALLP stated that '[t]here is a strong relationship between low levels of literacy and high levels of unemployment and other forms of social disadvantage' (DEET, 1991: 1). Another federal government publication around this time claimed that 'low literacy forces many people to become welfare recipients' (DEET, 1992b: 9). In light of these statements, in particular during a recession with high unemployment, it was hardly surprising that the federal Labor government would introduce literacy for jobseekers as one of its key programme initiatives in the ALLP (the other major programme targeted was workplace literacy). I have referred to these links between low literacy and unemployment as the 'literacy = jobs axiom' (Black, 1995a, 2001) in recognition of the acceptance and power of the human capital argument that improving literacy levels leads to improved employment outcomes. In the decades since the ALLP, many researchers have used statistical analyses based on large-scale OECD international literacy surveys to demonstrate links between literacy levels and employment outcomes, including incomes (Chesters, Ryan and Sinning, 2013; Miller and Chiswick, 1997; Shomos, 2010; Shomos and Forbes, 2014). As outlined in the introduction to this book, these links, promoted particularly by dominant industry and skills groups, provided the rationale for the current national policy on literacy, the National Foundation Skills Strategy for Adults (SCOTESE, 2012). They also mirror to a large extent the illiteracy/crime links explained in the previous chapter.

Nearly thirty years on from the first jobseeker literacy programmes introduced in Australia under a federal Labor government, dominant perspectives on the links between literacy and (un)employment are largely unchanged, regardless of the political party in power. Currently at the federal government level, these links remain of significant concern. For example, the recent federal parliamentary committee that examined 'Adult literacy and its importance' (House of Representatives, 2022) included in its first term of reference the relationship between adult literacy (and numeracy and problem-solving) and 'individuals living in households that have experienced intergenerational unemployment'. Its second term of reference related to the effects of literacy (and numeracy) on an individual's labour force participation and wages. Many of the submissions to the enquiry, quite predictably, featured statements that were directly comparable to those linking low literacy and unemployment in the ALLP thirty years earlier. The submission (No. 86) by the federal government's Department of Education, Skills and Employment (2021: 20), for example, included the following: 'Without the necessary literacy skills to participate in upskilling and retraining programmes, long-term structural unemployment in Australia is likely to rise.' There were many other similar-worded submissions from institutions and individuals, though significantly for this chapter's focus on jobseekers in designated literacy programmes, the peak professional association for adult literacy educators, the Australian Council for Adult Literacy (2021: 14), stated that while unemployed people are more likely to have low literacy 'programmes ostensibly designed to assist these people into employment and higher wages have to date had little impact on either unemployment levels or the prevalence of low wages'. The submission added that this was because 'individual literacy levels are only one of many factors which play a role in the continued reproduction of social inequality'. This more complex, and indeed political perspective on jobseeker literacy programmes, will be considered later in this chapter with a review of the literature and an examination of how it relates to the individual perspectives of jobseekers on a literacy programme. First, though, it is necessary to outline the unemployment contexts that gave rise to jobseeker literacy programmes.

The first jobseeker literacy programmes (the SIP) were introduced from 1991 at a time when government-commissioned reports indicated fears about the growth in the number of long-term unemployed, and even the 'very long term' unemployed (people unemployed for more than two years, see Committee on Employment Opportunities, 1993). Social welfare agencies warned of the permanent social dislocation for many disadvantaged people, and the possibility of an alienated underclass developing with little or no hope of finding work (Australian Council of Social Service (ACOSS), 1994). Unemployment was disproportionately affecting working-class groups, so-called 'blue collar' workers, partly as the manufacturing sector's share of the economy was declining (Clark, Geer and Underhill, 1996). It also disproportionately affected different demographic groups, including males in younger (15–29) and older (mid-forties and above) age categories, people without any post-school qualifications, and migrants from countries where English was not the main language spoken (Committee on Employment Opportunities, 1993).

Reciprocal obligation and jobseeker literacy programmes

Traditionally, the federal government assisted the unemployed with financial benefits (known colloquially as the 'dole'), but from 1991, the federal government implemented an 'Active Employment Strategy' which replaced unemployment benefits with a Jobsearch allowance in the first year of unemployment and a Newstart allowance for those unemployed for more than one year. Under Newstart, case managers in the Commonwealth Employment Service (CES) interviewed their long-term unemployed 'clients' at regular intervals and assessed them for skills and training with the aim of shifting them from welfare dependency to job preparation and eventual employment (DEET, 1992b). Significantly, these welfare reforms included the concept of 'reciprocal obligation', which meant that if the government was providing income support and training programmes, 'it is only fair that clients take up any reasonable offer of assistance and do whatever they can to improve their employment prospects' (DEET, 1992b: 17–18). If CES clients breached their reciprocal obligations, the CES was given the authority to cancel their Jobsearch and Newstart allowances. These reforms represented a major shift in government attitudes towards the unemployed, and 'reciprocal obligation' in later years was extended in scope to become 'mutual obligation' in 1997 under the conservative government of Prime Minister John Howard. Australian federal governments subsequently have maintained this policy of 'welfare conditionality' in which welfare recipients are required to behave in prescribed ways in order to access financial benefits, with possible enforcement through benefit sanctions (Watts and Fitzpatrick, 2018).

The idea that jobseekers may be coerced into participating in an education or training course was new in the early 1990s and it was unclear how jobseekers who participated in the programmes would respond. One report on disadvantaged jobseekers provided some early indications of discontent, particularly for some of the older jobseekers who felt that the labour market programmes they participated in were not useful as a source of jobs. They wanted 'jobs, not courses' (National Board of Employment, Education and Training, 1992: 44). This issue will be followed up in the interview data provided later in this chapter indicating how a group of participants in an SIP programme responded to these new unemployment conditions. Some background data on participants' perspectives in jobseeker literacy programmes can be obtained from the government's own evaluation of the programme (DEET, 1996). This evaluation included interviews with programme participants and concluded that most were satisfied with the SIP and believed that it improved their English language or literacy skills. But many participants also preferred simply to have any job, and there was acknowledgement that for a 'small minority' of participants the programme did not meet their needs and they were not motivated to attend. Participants differed in their attitudes both to their unemployed status and the role of SIP programmes. ESL participants, for example, who had often worked previously in higher skilled occupations, viewed English language difficulties as the main reason they were unemployed, and they were more motivated to participate in a SIP programme. Literacy participants on the other hand, with previous 'lower' occupational jobs, often cited lack of jobs as the main reason for being unemployed and literacy training was not perceived to be as important for employment (DEET, 1996).

In the years since the first SIP there have been several more evaluations of federal government-funded jobseeker literacy programmes (Rahmani, Crozier and Pollack, 2002; ACIL Allen Consulting, 2015; Department of Education, Science and Training [DEST], 2005), and all these evaluations have included the views of programme participants obtained mainly through structured interviews, telephone surveys and focus groups. These data have been used primarily for statistical analyses of jobseeker and other stakeholder perspectives. However, these government-funded evaluations have found it difficult to be definitive about a one-way cause and effect between literacy (and language and numeracy) gains from the programmes and improved employment outcomes due to the complexities and many variables involved, and thus the evaluations are often framed in terms of the 'likelihood' (DEST, 2005) or 'expectation' (ACIL Allen Consulting, 2015) that participants will experience successful employment outcomes. Overall, these official evaluations have been positive, and the continued federal government funding of jobseeker programmes over a period of thirty years reflects this. These official evaluations have essentially strengthened dominant perspectives on the links between literacy and the economy, in keeping with the human capital orientations of the OECD and its international literacy and numeracy surveys (OECD, 2013, 2017; OECD and Human Resources Development Canada, 1997; OECD and Statistics Canada, 1995; OECD and Statistics Canada, 2000; Statistics Canada and OECD, 2005).

Shifting the blame and the literacy=jobs axiom

Jobseeker literacy programmes and the human capital rationale that underpins them have been viewed less favourably from the perspectives of a number of critical educators commenting around the time of the ALLP in the early 1990s. Adopting a macro political economy perspective, critical educators have argued that by focusing the public's attention to educational problems, particularly lack of literacy, governments and other dominant groups have effectively shifted attention away from the real reason for recessions and high unemployment, the crisis in capitalism. Thus, as Apple (1987: viii) explains:

> The structural problems of poverty, of the de-skilling and elimination of jobs, of capital flight, of systemic racism and sexism, problems that are 'naturally' generated out of our current economic and political arrangements, are distanced from our discussions.

Street (1995: 125) similarly explains that by viewing literacy in the standard, 'autonomous' way, it becomes

> a symbolic key to many of the society's gravest problems ... issues of poverty and unemployment can be turned into questions about why individuals failed to learn literacy at school, or continue to refuse remedial attention as adults, thus diverting blame from institutions to individuals, from power structures to personal morality.

Shifting the blame for unemployment to people lacking literacy skills appeared to work effectively and has been briefly discussed in the introduction to this book. Daily newspaper articles on unemployment in the early 1990s, for example, ran in-depth stories on Australia's underclass and the 'cycle of illiteracy' thus promoting causal links between lack of literacy and unemployment. In more recent times, overseas critiques of employability programmes that usually involve literacy provision and target young people highlight that the 'real impact' of these programmes is to prepare people for a lifetime of marginalization in low-paid jobs and cycles of unemployment, while ensuring they lack the agency to question the status quo (Atkins, 2013). These young students are not only considered 'at risk' but increasingly are constructed as 'the risk' (Brine, 2006b: 649). In other words, disaffected and potentially unruly working-class people, especially in times of high unemployment and difficult economic times, are effectively regulated and controlled through participation in these programmes. At a local community level, this can be inferred from a case study of a steel town in the north of England, Consett, in the 1980s, where the main steel works closed down causing extensive local unemployment. One of the key programme responses from the British Steel Corporation (BSC) was to provide financial incentives for retrenched workers to participate in adult basic education courses (Holmes and Storrie, 1985). The link to jobs, however, was tenuous, as one retrenched worker indicated clearly:

> Of course the blokes are just doing the retraining course for the money. Everybody concerned knows that, but there's a big pretence from the institutions that they are retraining for work. The BSC have said they wouldn't consider putting anyone on a course if there wasn't the prospect of a job at the end of it and if there's any doubt about the validity courses, they ask the computer at Consett dole. Jesus, you don't have to ask a bloody computer where the work is at Consett, there isn't any.
>
> (Holmes and Storrie, 1985: 61)

The human capital argument that participation in a literacy programme will result in improved economic conditions, including better employment prospects and improved wages, has long been argued to be a myth (Graff, 1979; Lankshear and Lawler, 1987). The real benefit for employers is often seen to be in non-cognitive skills, with programme participants developing a range of work dispositions and traits seen to increase both their productive capacities and compliance with workplace practices. Assessing people for their literacy levels viewed in this way can serve to 'screen' people either in or out of workplace roles (Rubenson, 1989; Wickert and Baynham, 1994). Street (1990: 6) for example, stated that some employers 'have the somewhat mythical belief that employees who have learnt literacy are less antagonistic to new technology, computers etc.'

One of the main arguments promoting the need for improving the literacy skills of unemployed people in the early 1990s was the 'higher order' skills required with new technology and workplace practices in 'leading-edge', post-Fordist workplaces (Levett and Lankshear, 1994). Against this, however, educators have argued that post-Fordist and Fordist workplaces continued to co-exist and that the real growth areas of employment were in low-paid, relatively unskilled and repetitive trade and service sectors (Apple, 1999; Luke, 1992). Unemployment, therefore, particularly during a recession, could be seen as less the result of a widening skills gap and more a widening jobs gap (Hart, 1992).

Conceptually, literacy has always been hegemonic (Black, 1995b). It is believable, common sense to most people that higher levels of literacy are needed for successful employment outcomes, and those people who are both unemployed and low literate tend to accept this reasoning and blame themselves for their current work status. Unemployed people thus 'fall for the policy line ... the sleight of hand' of the policy equation (or axiom) that 'literacy=jobs' (Falk, 2001: 218). Obtaining jobs in the tight market conditions of the 1990s recession was highly problematic for many people, and those jobs that were available required more than just literacy skills. As Falk (2001: 217) argued, '[b]asic skills by themselves are simply not enough' and obtaining a job was often a matter of who you knew, that is, access to important social networks referred to as social capital. Falk (2001: 213) argued that a successful social welfare policy related to the unemployed 'must address both human and social capital elements'.

In the UK in the wake of the Skills for Life strategy (Department for Education and Employment [DfEE], 1999), similar 'jobseeker literacy programmes' were introduced, also with 'conditionality', the potential loss of welfare benefits. These programmes were critiqued by some researchers on the grounds that reluctant participants were unlikely to engage with learning and would become increasingly resistant learners. O'Grady and Atkin (2006: 277) argued, based on the reproduction theory of Bourdieu (Bourdieu and Passeron, 1990), that this literacy strategy represented 'an apparatus of symbolic violence' inflicted on programme participants.

These perspectives on jobseeker literacy programmes outlined in the above paragraphs are minority perspectives found in the academic works of critical educators. These educators analyse how power in capitalist society represents primarily the interests of governments and dominant groups and, through the operation of programmes such as the jobseeker programmes, are unlikely to work in the interests of working-class people. Unsurprisingly, these critical education perspectives are not acknowledged in government and other dominant group publications on the human capital links between literacy and the economy. There is great reluctance to complicate or sully the 'literacy=jobs axiom'.

The research study

During 1993 I was a head teacher of an adult literacy section in a TAFE college that worked in conjunction with the CES to deliver jobseeker programmes under the SIP. The programme did not displace existing TAFE adult literacy programmes at the time; rather, it was additional, a jobs-oriented programme added to traditional social justice programmes. This 'duality' of discourses (Sanguinetti, 2007) was a feature of adult literacy programmes in TAFE in the early 1990s which saw the beginnings of what has become a total shift to human capital dominance in the contemporary era (Black, 2018). In 1993, the SIP was new for TAFE colleges and for the CES, and particularly for both organizations, the 'reciprocal obligations' element of government social welfare policy meant that for the first time there could be a degree of coercion behind participation in a literacy programme. From the TAFE college perspective, reluctant learners now had to be confronted in adult literacy programmes. Until this time they had always participated voluntarily as a matter of personal choice.

My research study with jobseekers, undertaken as part of my doctoral thesis, was combined with my regular work as a head teacher of adult literacy, though some interviews were conducted outside regular college hours and also during TAFE vacation holidays. Interviews took place mainly within the TAFE college, though some were conducted in the students' homes. A total of twenty-seven SIP students were interviewed for the research: sixteen male (59 per cent), eleven female (41 per cent). I refer to them in this chapter as SIP 'students' (and sometimes participants) given my perspective as an educator, rather than 'clients', the preferred term used by the CES. Over half the students (fourteen, 52 per cent) were over forty years of age, and there were more students (nineteen, 70 per cent) born in countries where English was not the main language spoken, including Lebanon (five students), Italy (three) and the Philippines (two). Levels of formal education were mostly low, with only one of the Australian-born students having reached Year 10. The only student to have reached Year 12 level was a former teacher from Chile. Some students had received only primary school education, including students from Cambodia, Italy, Lebanon, and Portugal. Unsurprisingly, in view of the literature cited in this chapter, most of the students had previously been involved in relatively unskilled work. Previous jobs cited by the students included assembly work, builder, cleaner, dressmaker (two), driver, labourer, machinist, pre-school assistant, process work, railway work, sales work, shop cashier, unskilled (four). Two of the students said they were trained teachers but not in Australia (previously when they lived in Chile and Egypt respectively).

The interviews focused not on aspects of pedagogy and classroom content, but on the broader attitudes of students to participating in the SIP, on being referred by the CES to undertake the programme. After all, these students were participating in a literacy programme primarily because they were registered unemployed. The interviews also explored students' previous employment backgrounds and their perspectives on the role that literacy played in this and in their opportunities for employment resulting from participating in the programme. All student names in this chapter are pseudonyms.

Accommodating the literacy programme

All the SIP students were asked about their referral to the TAFE programme; whose decision was this, and did they agree with it? According to CES procedures, the referral was meant to be 'in consultation' between CES staff officers and individual clients. I begin with those students who accommodated the wishes of the CES, and by implication, the discourse that sees a direct link between improved literacy levels and jobs.

Most of the students (sixteen, 60 per cent) said they were happy to be referred to the TAFE programme, and nearly all of these students were born overseas where English was not their first language. Theresa, forty-one, from the Philippines and less than two years in Australia, said it was actually her suggestion to attend the programme because she felt she lacked spoken English skills: 'my talking, how I communicate to people'. Francisco, also forty-one, a secondary school teacher from Chile, similarly saw the programme as 'my opportunity for learn the language'. One of the students, Angelica, fifty-five, an Italian who had lived in Australia for more than thirty years, took the initiative to enrol in a TAFE literacy class just prior to being interviewed by the CES, thus anticipating referral by the CES. Some of the students said that they had long wished to attend an English language/literacy course, and they looked forward to participating in the programme. Rosa, thirty-nine, a Portuguese woman who had lived in Australia for twenty years working mainly as a cleaner, claimed: 'they didn't push me to come or anything'.

Three Australian-born students also accommodated referral to a literacy programme, but in each case it was conditional. Peter, for example, was twenty-two and keen to develop a career in diving. Previously he had difficulties passing the 'masters' course in diving because it required a lot of reading and multiple-choice answers. He maintained he would only attend the literacy programme if it had one-to-one tuition, something he had experienced and benefited from previously in Brisbane. David, thirty-two, with a retail industry background, was initially happy to participate, but he left after a couple of months to do a hospitality course because he believed it had stronger links with getting a job. Greg, twenty-seven, was having trouble completing a horticulture course, and he has happy initially to be referred to a literacy programme. He left the programme soon after though and made it clear that it was his decision and responsibility: 'I've sent myself here, and if I leave, I'll leave, you know. That's their problem, and it's my business what I do.' Later in the interview when prompted about the possible consequences with the CES he commented:

> They'd say it would affect my benefits, you know. You've got no choice, sort of, or I'll lose my money. But they couldn't do that. They'd probably do it, but they'd have to put me back on, once I start complaining, going on like.

Greg clearly believed he had some agency when it came to his discussions with the CES.

Resisting the literacy programme

There were nine respondents who indicated in the interviews that they were not entirely willing participants in the process of being referred to a literacy programme. Their circumstances were all different, but a common thread was being talked around by CES officers into participating. Don, for example, Australian born, and at sixty-three years of age with little chance of ever working again, seemed to have been quite easily swayed: 'They asked me that and I said no at first. And we was talking there, talking, and she asked me again, and I said yeah, all right.' Similarly, Tony, Australian-born and fifty-years of age, said he was talked into it, reluctantly: 'The fact that I needed help, and I thought, oh well, I didn't really want to come, I just wanted a job.' In these comments and others from the jobseekers, there was a clear power imbalance that enabled CES staff to persuade their reluctant clients to participate in a literacy programme. Superficially there may have been a degree of mutual consultation in the process, but ultimately CES officers had the power, in the form of denying the jobseeker allowance, to enforce their will. Wayne, a 22-year-old Australian-born jobseeker made this clear: 'Oh, you know what they're like, Newstart, you got no sort of say in it. Because if you sort of say no, they just cut you off the allowance straight away.'

For some of the SIP students there had been a long history of conflict with the CES over their unemployed status, and in two cases it involved their medical conditions, with both students claiming language and/or literacy played no part in being unemployed. Nevertheless, they were both sent to the SIP under the threat of losing their jobseeker allowance. Mahmoud, forty-four years of age and born in Lebanon, had not worked for the past thirteen years. He said he had a dust allergy which prevented him from working:

> No, no, I told you, no problem for learn English, because I work ten years in (name of company). Boss told me do this, do this, understand? No need talk with machine. CES think me a bludger, I'm not sick. I told them many, many times, too many times, nobody feel like I feel. Stop money, stop money.

In the case of George, thirty-nine years of age and also from Lebanon, he had a back injury from an accident working on the railways. He had an injury compensation case pending, which he claimed would preclude any company from employing him. He questioned the CES decision to refer him to the SIP: 'I say what you want to send me to school for? Why?' In fact, after attending the programme for several sessions, he left.

A distinction has so far been made of those jobseekers who were happy and willing to participate a literacy programme and those who felt pressured to do so and resisted the wishes of the CES. There were a range of individual factors operating to affect the participatory dispositions of these unemployed people, but one of the themes from the interviews was greater congruence between the perspectives of those born overseas who spoke English as an additional language and those of the CES. This should not be a surprising finding, as Auerbach (1994: 10) at the annual ACAL conference in Perth in 1994 contended:

> One of the biggest myths that ESL learners hold on to is that English is the solution to their problems, that the reason they have low status jobs is that their English isn't good enough and if only it were better, everything would be fine.

Seva, a 54-year-old woman from Sri Lanka, appeared to be one of those believing this myth. She stated: 'They (CES) believe that I am get jobs after the, if I can study something more. They and I believe I can find a suitable job.' Seva had been a dressmaker in Sri Lanka and had lived in Australia for a little over a year. Many of these older jobseekers had never received a formal education in English, having entered the workforce soon after migrating to Australia. While they generally did not make a distinction between improving their spoken and written English, it was the former they focused on in terms of obtaining jobs. This was in accord with the findings of the first SIP evaluation (DEET, 1996) that ESL students were more motivated to participate in the SIP. For many, it was their opportunity to catch up on their previous lost education. Australian-born jobseekers, on the other hand, especially younger ones, participated mainly if they could see direct relevance to improving their vocational qualifications and/or obtaining a job.

Previous jobs – what role did literacy play?

In this section, I examine jobseeker perspectives on the relationship between literacy and jobs based on their previous work experiences. For most of the SIP students, however, unlike the above beliefs about the power of literacy, it was clear that lack of literacy skills had not prevented them from obtaining jobs in the past. Mary, for example, Italian born and fifty years of age, explained how she worked from the time she arrived in Australia: 'Second day we coming here we started to work. No English, nothing. We just eh, you know, we just show with the hands, we have a job.' Initially communicating with gestures appeared sufficient for Mary to begin factory work which she continued to do for several years before staying at home to bring up her young children. Later, she recommenced work as a hospital cleaner which she continued to do for sixteen years, before giving it up to look after her sick husband. Asked if reading and writing were necessary in her cleaning work, she replied: 'No, no, that time no, everybody help that time. Just do the number.' In terms of how participating in the SIP would help her job prospects, she commented: 'No, not going to make any difference, no.'

Some of the others in the interview group had been self-employed, but despite language and literacy difficulties, they managed their jobs unproblematically, often with assistance from their spouses. Pablo, for example, thirty-four years of age and from Lebanon, managed a takeaway food shop. Most of the work was routine, and if there was something that required literacy skills, his wife was always there next to him to provide assistance. In the case of Mario, forty-one years of age and Italian born, he had successfully established himself as a building subcontractor for many years. He acknowledged that he had literacy problems, but only occasionally did it affect his work, as for example, with producing written quotes for building work. He said he would take the quote home and seek assistance from his wife in writing the quote.

For many of these unemployed people, their previous work was relatively unskilled and routine, and literacy-related work tasks (and those related to language and numeracy) were usually learnt on the job and played only a minor role in effective job performance. If these tasks were difficult or more complex, invariably there was assistance provided by fellow workers. Zara, twenty-seven years of age and born in Lebanon, provided an example in her factory work. She began as a process worker and was then promoted to line leader which involved some degree of paperwork. She said she had some minor difficulties: 'I have a couple of things mistake, you know, by the spelling,' but she did the job effectively, often with the help of co-workers: 'I was having friends there always they give me help so they was good friends with me.' For most of the jobseekers in the study, work was rarely undertaken in isolation, and workers collaborated and helped each other. Sometimes it was help provided by spouses (as in family-run businesses); often it was co-workers on an assembly line. These social networks of support were integral to performing well on the job.

Most of the jobseekers recognized that the main reason they were unemployed was because there were not enough jobs – it was a recession. Mario, the building subcontractor, demonstrated this, explaining that one employer he had known for more than twenty years had at one stage more than forty regular workers, but due to the recession

> he's going to retrench them all, and he's going to employ them as subbies (subcontractors), like, whenever there's work, he'll ring up, oh yeah, a job, do you want to go do it? I mean, that's not the way to go, but what can you do? You've gotta make the wages to pay the people. Everybody's got problems.

The absence of jobs and the oversupply of unemployed people seeking work caused some jobseekers to feel exploited in their attempts to obtain work. Tony, at fifty years of age, was sent by the CES for cafeteria jobs that required little more skill than the ability to turn on the dishwasher. He recounted one recent experience in which he undertook a 'trial' of more than an hour of work which involved washing dishes, mopping the floor and cleaning the toilet, only then to be told he would not be employed.

There were some jobseekers, especially those seeking work that went beyond the routine and the unskilled, who indicated that their poor literacy skills had held them back in trying to obtain the necessary qualifications. Greg, for example, as mentioned earlier, said he had problems completing a TAFE horticulture course due largely to literacy. He commented: 'it's all botanical names of, you know, the Latin words'. Before his interest in horticulture, he had tried a welding course at TAFE, but despite passing all the practical work ('the teacher said I was the best weld there'), for three years in a row he failed to pass the theory exam. There were other jobseekers, too, whose aspirations appeared to have been thwarted by poor literacy. Theresa, forty-one years of age and from the Philippines, was doing part-time work in a nursing home. However, she really wanted to work in childcare, and this required completing a childcare course that she thought was beyond her level of literacy skills.

Concluding comments

It was clear from the experiences recounted by the jobseekers in this research study that there was nothing definitive about the role of literacy and unemployment. Most jobseekers had previously experienced lengthy periods of work in largely routine and unskilled jobs that involved few literacy practices. And if assistance with literacy was required, invariably it was provided by work colleagues and, in some work contexts, spouses. These findings were in accord with views expressed by prisoners in the previous chapter commenting on their working lives and the role of social networks of support. There were always exceptions, however, with some jobseekers born overseas and speaking English as an additional language, who believed that their lack of spoken and written English contributed directly to being unemployed. Other workers were also clearly impeded in their attempts to obtain vocational qualifications due to their lack of literacy. But overall, the jobseeker perspectives outlined in this chapter challenged the dominant policy discourse of the SIP in the early 1990s that directly linked low literacy with unemployment. This policy discourse was promoted in each successive evaluation of the jobseeker literacy programmes and remains today the dominant perspective of governments. The effect of the SIP and subsequent jobseeker literacy programmes, nevertheless, has always been to blame unemployed people for their lack of literacy skills and to effectively shift attention away from the structural determinants of unemployment. In the case of the SIP, this blame was clearly misplaced, and the real reason for unemployment at the time of this research was the recession – there were just not enough jobs, and disproportionately these were jobs in manufacturing and other 'blue collar' trade areas. It was working-class people who undertook these jobs who felt the major brunt of unemployment in 'the recession we had to have'.

A feature of the unemployed gleaned from their perspectives in this chapter was their lack of power. They had lost their jobs in a recession usually through no fault of their own, and as registered jobseekers, ultimately, they had little say in the decision by the CES to send them to a literacy programme. All they really wanted was a job, but in the official process of trying to get one, sometimes unwillingly they were sent to a TAFE college to improve their literacy skills. As one of the TAFE literacy teachers on this early SIP course explained, 'none of them knew why they were there. CES just pulled them in and said "come in you've got to have an interview about your reading and writing." They had no idea'.

Jobseeker literacy programmes could be seen to serve the interests of several stakeholders but in a way that lacked efficacy in terms of people getting jobs (Baker, 2013: 12). They served the CES with its surplus of long-term unemployed people on their books and few jobs to offer them. The CES could send many of them off to a TAFE college with the claim that they were preparing them for work. TAFE colleges were also well served. While initially reticent to accept reluctant learners, they were nevertheless happy to accept government funding to bolster their services and their budgets. The federal government was also happy to claim that they were doing something positive to ease long-term unemployment. In the process, attention was focused on people's lack of literacy skills and away from the need to make major structural adjustments to the economy that might really make a difference to unemployment. The one group of stakeholders whose interests were not necessarily served, at least not in terms of obtaining jobs, were the SIP students themselves. The relative lack of power of these unemployed people to resist the demands of dominant government organizations appeared to accord with the conclusions of a study of similar literacy programmes for the unemployed in the UK, in which it was claimed that the programmes imposed symbolic violence on the participants (O'Grady and Atkin, 2006).

4

Local Council Workers and Literacy

I'm not much in the reading and writing, but I know how to start a shovel.
(Phil, forty-two, council construction worker)

To lay a bit of concrete you lay a bit of concrete. You can train to be a computer operator and all this because they're updating, but concrete doesn't get updated. You can't change techniques in that. Pour it in, level it off.
(Terry, thirty-nine, council construction worker)

I honestly believe we could all be taught on the job. They'd have to have someone, right, you go out with that gang, you stay there for a fortnight, you learn the way that they do this, this, and this.
(Michael, sixty-four, construction worker reflecting on workplace training programmes)

Introduction

The above comments from local council workers and the interview data provided in this chapter are drawn from my doctoral thesis (Black, 2001: 178–234). The focus in this chapter is on the role of literacy in the working lives of groups of outdoor workers in a local council. These are the maintenance and construction workers who repair and construct concrete footpaths throughout the local council area and maintain and repair the local drains. As with the previous chapter on the unemployed, this chapter deals with events and the prevailing literature at a particular historical juncture, in this case the mid-late 1990s, a period of rapid transformation in workplace practices and cultures. The chapter examines the role that literacy was seen to play in the working lives of these council workers as they were required to shift from their traditional work in 'gangs' to members of 'competitive teams' in workplace cultural changes that have been referred to more broadly as the 'new work order' (Gee, Hull and Lankshear, 1996). The role of literacy is less prominent than in the previous chapter on literacy programmes for the unemployed. In this chapter, literacy is examined more in terms of how the workers can adapt to new workplace practices, that is, literacy in the context of working 'smarter'.

In my role as a head teacher of adult basic education in a TAFE college, I was afforded the opportunity during the early months of 1996 to participate in a 'return to industry' initiative designed to enable TAFE teachers to better understand the world of work that many vocational education students would be entering. This return to industry programme incorporated a research component that formed part of my doctoral thesis. It included travelling daily with work gangs in their council trucks, observing their work practices and interviewing individual workers during 'downtimes' (e.g. while the workers waited for concrete footpaths to dry). These were difficult times for the maintenance and construction workers as they were being asked to change how they organized and undertook much of their work. They were low-paid, local government employees undertaking physically demanding manual labour in traditional working-class jobs. Now they were being told to work differently or potentially lose their jobs to private contractors. The research focused on how these workers experienced the changes and the underlying role that literacy played. After all, it was recognized that local council outdoor workers generally had low levels of formal education and were likely to experience problems with literacy. Before outlining the research data, however, it is necessary to provide a brief background picture of the changing nature of work during this time, and in particular, how it was affecting local councils.

The new work order

The 1990s were a time of rapid changes in the nature of capitalism and contemporary educators applied different labels to these changes, including capitalist reorganization (Foley, 1994), fast capitalism (Gee and Lankshear, 1995) and new capitalism (Gee, Hull and Lankshear, 1996). The essential feature of this new capitalism was heightened global competition involving continuous efforts to capture new markets beyond the saturated markets for mass products. New specialized global markets required increased flexibility in production techniques (Harvey, 1990; Neef, Siesfeld and Cefola, 1998). Intense (hyper) competition ensured production costs had to be kept to a minimum, and enterprises continually restructured their workplaces with the introduction of new technology and workplace practices designed to maximize the efficiency and productivity of workers.

This 'new work order' demanded a new relationship between capital and labour. The old Fordist model of mass production essentially employed workers 'from the neck down'. Post-Fordist workplaces, on the other hand, sought 'knowledge workers' who would think more about their work, work smarter and take greater responsibility for their work (Buggy, 1991). Instead of being told what to do by supervisors, workers would organize their own work, often as part of a self-managed team:

> Workers will be transformed into committed 'partners' who engage in meaningful work, fully understand and control their jobs, supervise themselves, and actively seek to improve their performance through communicating clearly their knowledge and needs.
>
> (Gee, Hull and Lankshear, 1996: 29)

A key element of this new workplace culture was collaborative teamwork, and industry training manuals at the time explained that teams replaced the 'top-down' decision-making processes of management, and all workers in this flatter structure needed to be flexible and responsive to workplace needs (e.g. National Food Industry Training Council Ltd, 1995). Quality and production control and team leadership were to be shared among all workers and were enacted through regular team meetings. Literacy was seen to play an integral role in the new team-oriented workplaces (Mawer, 1999), and according to Hart-Landsberg and Reder (1995: 1031) in a detailed study of one manufacturing company in the United States, literacy practices and teamwork were 'inextricably linked'. Literacy practices, for example, played a key role in the communication and documentation required in team meetings and in undertaking new workplace tasks such as understanding goals, goal-setting, calculations and reports (Gee, Hull and Lankshear, 1996). If individual workers lacked the ability to engage with these literacy practices, there was the potential to hinder the effectiveness of teams. On the other hand, as Hart-Landsberg and Reder (1995: 1035) noted, '[a]ll (team) players have a built-in incentive – their own success – to teach the one who needs to learn'.

According to Gee, Hull and Lankshear (1996), the 'greatest challenge' facing enterprises with the introduction of these new workplace practices was managing the cultural identity shift on the part of workers, not only to work 'smarter' but to be motivated and committed to the values of the enterprise. Workers were now expected to find meaning in their work, and it could at times require them to work harder and for longer hours. There was the danger of cynicism in workers, with the sense that they were being 'duped' into working harder without necessarily any additional reward.

At the time of this chapter's study in the local council, several ethnographic case studies had been undertaken of new workplace cultures, and in particular, the role of literacy (Darrah, 1996; Gowen, 1992, 1994, 1996; Hart Landsberg and Reder, 1995; Hull, 1993; Tannock, 1997). These studies explored the attitudes and dispositions of workers to workplace cultures and the power dynamics associated with new skills generally and literacy practices in particular. As discussed briefly in the earlier chapters, these studies have been referred to as 'new literacy studies' which focus on how people use literacy (or literacies) in various social contexts. They illustrated how local managerial power was exerted over workers within the context of new workplace practices and concerns over the literacy deficiencies of workers.

Reforming local councils

Local councils are the third tier of government in Australia (after federal and state), and the research featured in this chapter was undertaken at a local council in NSW in 1996. At the time, local councils were in the process of significant microeconomic reform which began in the late 1980s. Referred to by one researcher as the 'rediscovery of capitalism' (Jones, 1989: 9), local councils were being reformed following local government acts which stipulated higher degrees of public accountability, and the National Competition Policy (Hilmer, 1993) which exposed councils to the 'competitive marketplace'. Local councils in NSW were granted greater autonomy and enterprise powers, and by adopting a structural efficiency model of governance, they applied many private sector business practices and became more entrepreneurial (Aulich, 1999; Dollery and Marshall, 1997; Marshall, Witherby and Dollery, 1999). In some local councils at the time, selected services were 'contracted out' to private operators. In other councils, there were examples of 'business units' being created in order to make some areas of council work not only more efficient but profitable or, at the very least, self-funded. The following case study features the introduction of the 'business unit' concept in one section of a local council in NSW.

A case study of maintenance and construction workers

Whether it was at the behest of the council management hierarchy or his own personal ambitions and enterprising spirit was unclear, but the manager of the maintenance and construction section in this council was resolved to reform his work section along the business unit lines mentioned above. The research in this chapter was undertaken during the trial period of the introduction of these reforms as the manager put into practice the concept of 'competitive teams'. In some ways, he could be seen to be acting in accordance with the entrepreneurial leadership style now promoted for Australian corporate managers generally (Karpin, 1995) and particularly public sector managers (Osborne and Gaebler, 1993).

The research data feature the perspectives and experiences of the manager of the maintenance and construction section, fifteen of the workers and the two supervisors. All were male. The manager, David, was thirty-five years of age, university educated and had worked in the council for five years. The fifteen workers had quite different backgrounds. They were an older cohort with an average age of forty-eight years. Three were in their sixties, and the youngest were twenty-nine and thirty respectively. Two of the fifteen workers were engineers and had a tertiary-level 'advanced certificate' qualification obtained overseas, while of the other thirteen workers, only two had reached Year 10 level of schooling, the two youngest workers. Most of the workers had been in the council a long time (average eleven years), and one of them for twenty-nine years. One of the supervisors, Tony, was thirty-five years of age, had Year 10 level schooling and had been in the council for seven years. The other supervisor, Eric, was sixty-two years of age, had Year 8 level schooling and had been in the council for twenty years. The manager, both supervisors and most of the workers were Australian born. Only the two engineers and two other workers were born overseas where English was not their first language.

Competitive teams were introduced on the basis that it was essential to ward off the inevitable privatization of this area of council's work. Unless the council could 'get its act together' (manager, David's comment) and become competitive with outside contractors, then jobs would be threatened. David thus argued that he was acting in the interests of workers to save their jobs. During this trial period, only some of the teams would become competitive, while the others would remain traditional gangs. Competitive team leaders would keep accurate records of costings for each job undertaken. These team leaders had been chosen following written applications and interviews, and they received additional pay in recognition of their increased responsibilities. Membership of the teams was voluntary from the existing workforce. In an effort to ensure the success of competitive teams, several sessions were conducted of an obligatory training programme for all maintenance and construction workers in work time in the council depot's training room.

Competitive teams: A contested concept

For the manager and the supervisors, competitive teams were about being more efficient, understanding unit costings and working smarter with a view to 'win' against private contractors. Team members, however, viewed it differently. They saw it more as competition between their own teams. Two competitive teams had been established, both working on concreting stretches of footpaths. One of the teams comprised the team leader, Mark, the youngest man there at twenty-nine, and two other team members in their early forties. The other team comprised leader Richard, fifty-nine, and two team members (fifty-five and sixty-four years respectively). Perhaps unsurprisingly, the younger team could pour more concrete in a day, causing tensions with the older team. Richard commented: 'I shouldn't have to compete against Mark. I've got enough worries of me own without worrying how fast Mark's going.' Implicit in Richard's comments was fear that 'benchmarks' for concrete pours might become inflated and difficult to maintain for all teams.

The concept of 'teams' was also problematic for the workers who remained in the traditional 'gangs'. They believed they had always worked together in a way indistinguishable from teams. They had, for example, always communicated together as one ganger (gang leader) commented: 'they're not left in the dark. It's very difficult not to talk work at work'. On the other hand, other gang members commented that the nature of the work, primarily hard and manual, was such that little communication was necessary: 'We just get in and do it, there's no discussing. We know what we've got to do.' For several of the workers, therefore, the move to teams appeared to make little difference to how they interacted with each other on the job. This contrasted with the manager and his supervisors who understood teams to mean a new way of thinking, a new workplace culture and worker identity.

Knowledge workers: Thinking differently

Beginning with the perspectives of the manager, David, he explained that members of teams needed to think more about the organization of their work instead of the traditional reliance on supervisors: 'We want them to come to us to say, we require a backhoe on this particular day for these amount of hours, we require this material, we require a certain number of labourers.' The younger supervisor, Tony, elaborated on this, stating that with the costings 'now we tell them how much money they've got to spend on the job, and they do their costing each day. They know how they are going, so they can see the bigger picture'. Workers also needed to be better skilled, with Tony referring to the need to be 'teched up' because they were thinking about putting computers in the trucks. Additionally, workers would need the skills to negotiate directly with the public and quote their own work instead of referring it to others: 'while they're doing their job someone will come up and say we need a driveway done. They'll quote the driveway there and then. Normally the engineer would do that' (Tony).

A key feature of these new workplace practices was greater flexibility in how jobs were undertaken, which was a significant change in terms of working conditions for this type of manual work where workers had always started and finished their day at pre-set times (usually 7.00 a.m.–3.00 p.m.). David wanted workers to have the flexibility to adapt to the conditions of the site and possibly stay on for extra time to complete a job as opposed to going back there the next day.

Another major cultural shift which David explained was the need for workers to be 'happier' at work. He claimed that some workers were starting to think more about their work 'but a lot of them just, still have to work because they've got to'. Later in the interview he explained that 'the incentive is to be happier at work, to want to come to work and to want to give their best at work'. This applied to him in his work as the manager, and he wanted 'to try and get them to do that. I want them to be part of their own decision-making process, their teams. It's the old theory, if they're happy they'll show more interests, they'll come up with good ideas'. These comments appeared to mimic the new work order playbook about finding meaning and commitment in work (Gee, Hull and Lankshear, 1996). The problem in this case was that the traditional manual labour undertaken by these maintenance and construction workers, by its very nature, was alienating. Even the usually on-side supervisor Tony understood that workers were unlikely to experience happiness at work. Rather, their motivation was more likely to be along the lines of 'Instead of thinking I only get paid to do the job, what they've got to start thinking is, I might get extra if we do the job better, and I might keep my job if we do the job better' – in other words, extrinsic motivation of the most basic kind – extra money and keeping their job.

The implementation of these workplace changes was seen to depend largely on the team leaders, the 'linchpins' according to David. He realized that team leaders might 'pick the team up'. As with traditional shop stewards in manufacturing companies, team leaders could be seen to be at the interface between the two cultures of management and workers (Virgona, 1994). By winning over team leaders, it was hoped the workers could be brought into line with the managerial discourse. For this reason, team leaders were specially selected by formal interviews and paid more money.

The council as a 'protected' community

Before considering in more depth the skills required in the new competitive teams, including literacy, some background needs to be provided on various perspectives of council maintenance and construction work because they have a bearing on the attitudes of these workers to their work. Researchers have noted a general community perspective that working in local councils is 'protected' from the tough, private commercial world of work (Jones, 1989: 4). Tony, the supervisor, picked up on this commenting:

> They've been in this protected environment in the council for so long. Get in the real world mate, you can't live your lap of luxury all the time. You've got to get out there and be competitive.

Even one of the workers commented: 'I've done my hard work, I just come here to slow down a bit,' indicating that the council work was preferable to working the long hours and weekend work required by some private contractors. In some ways, it was considered secure work insofar as the workers' jobs were not subject to the usual ebbs and flows of the private market. The nature of laying stretches of concrete footpaths also encouraged occasional negative community perceptions because inevitably there were 'down-times' when workers were standing around waiting for concrete to dry. From the workers' perspective, and supported by the older supervisor, Eric, this could be justified on the grounds that 'if you go away and the concrete goes off, you can lose it and you've got to start again'. But the general community perception could be that they were 'bludging' (i.e. avoiding work) during these times, an unfortunate by-product of always being, as one worker noted, 'under the eye of everybody'.

The role of literacy (and numeracy)

The manager, David, explained that the team workers needed to communicate well with the general public and with other team workers for both social and technical reasons: 'you know, why is this traffic scheme going through the area? In the same conversation, this is why we are using concrete'. He also stated the need for all team members to have 'a reasonably high level of literacy'. In fact, there had been some initial discussions about the possibility of providing a workplace literacy programme at the council primarily to improve the literacy levels of the workers. One of the supervisors, Tony, was asked about the new skills required of the workers. His response was to claim: 'Well, they need probably to be more literate.' But he then went on to explain that the issue was more about numeracy, basic calculating on the job, though the council provided calculators for this. He also explained that it was the team leader who was responsible for calculations and undertook most of this work, not individual team members. Literacy-related tasks (events) were in fact difficult to identify in the work of the teams, though there was one important task, writing incident reports, required for example when the team ruptured a power cable or water pipe during an excavation. These reports, however, did not fall within the responsibility of the team leader; instead they were written by the cost clerk at the depot: 'Ralph generally writes nearly all of them automatically. Ralph's the cost clerk, but he's in charge of all the incident reports.' What this interview with the supervisor indicated therefore about the skills demands of the new teamwork was that while literacy was highlighted to be important, basic numeracy/calculating was more the issue, and even then, team leaders were mainly responsible, not the workers in the team. And in the case of an important literacy task such as writing an incident report, this was taken out of the hands of the team leader completely.

From observations of the teams at work it became apparent that, in relation to literacy practices, most team members only had to sign their time sheet in their everyday work. The basic work of these council workers had not changed, and it had little to do with literacy or numeracy. As one worker, Terry, thirty-nine, commented:

> To lay a pipe, you lay a pipe. To lay a bit of concrete you lay a bit of concrete. You can train to be a computer operator and all this because they're updating, but concrete doesn't get updated. You can't change techniques in that. Pour it in, level it off.

Occasionally there were noticeboard announcements and newsletters to read at the depot, but if there were issues of real importance, they would be discussed generally among the workers as they went about their work, so the ability to read them independently was rarely a problem.

Numeracy was more of an issue, particularly calculating concrete pours, but this would be done by the team leader, and besides, as the more experienced supervisor, Eric, explained, it was something workers became familiar with on the job:

> Well, most of the older gangers just measure, calculate in your mind. Around 100mm (depth), you've got to multiply the width by the length, give us three by four is twelve, that's 1.2 (cubic metres), that's four inches (100mm in depth). You learn that.

This was an example of performance-driven numeracy, that is, numeracy practices in the workplace that were learnt 'in practice', as opposed to academic mathematics in which the underlying theoretical concepts needed to be understood (Baker, 1998).

It was clear from talking to members of the teams that some of them considered they had problems with literacy and numeracy in a 'schooled' sense because, after all, they generally had low levels of formal education, with most having left school at Year 8. But they had no difficulties managing the literacy and numeracy practices required for their work.

With the construction teams that worked on larger projects such as roundabouts and laneways, it could be argued that literacy and numeracy demands were more complex, especially in making sense of detailed construction plans. But this only applied to the team leaders who took the major responsibility for calculations and literacy practices. There were two construction teams, and both were led by engineers, and as indicated earlier, both had tertiary qualifications.

It should be noted that our findings in relation to literacy and the work of these local council workers were at odds with the findings of other studies of local council workers (see Black and Yasukawa, 2011a). At the time of our study, another TAFE team in an adjacent council adopted a more 'orthodox' approach to assessing literacy in the workplace (Schultz, 1997) in which workers were interviewed individually at the council's training room and asked to demonstrate their literacy skills by reading and comprehending a memo and completing an accident report form. Almost half the workers were found to have literacy deficiencies and literacy support was recommended to accompany their council training. Some workers, 'those not functionally literate', were referred to a literacy specialist (Black and Yasukawa, 2011a: 225). The real difference between the two studies was that we adopted a social practice approach based on ethnographic-style research, while the other study adopted a skills approach based on testing and normative criteria. We would argue that only our ethnographic-style study accurately reflected how workers managed the everyday literacy practices of their council work (Black and Yasukawa, 2011a).

Contradictions at work

It has become apparent already in this chapter, even before providing detailed perspectives from the workers, that there were contradictions in various perspectives on how this type of work in the council was organized and practised. The term 'competitive teams' was contested, with the manager and supervisor talking about competition with external private contractors, while team leaders were more concerned about internal competition with fellow teams. The manager, in particular, conceptualized a new knowledge worker and for competitive teams to become self-directed with workers deriving meaning from their work to the extent that they would be happy workers, prepared to go 'over the top' for the council. This happiness aspect, however, was fanciful and indicated the cultural distance between him and the workers. The manager appeared to be imbued, almost at a theoretical level, with the discourse of the new work order. As a research chapter on learning at work indicated at the time: 'Managers' learning is increasingly influenced by what management gurus say it should be' (Beckett, 1999: 83). In this line of heavy, physical work, extrinsic reward in the form of increased pay was far more likely to be significant to workers than feelings of happiness at the end of the day.

There were also clear contradictions about the role of literacy in which the manager's and supervisor's claims about the need for higher levels of literacy appeared unfounded. There were similarities with Gowen's (1996) contemporary research in a manufacturing company in the United States in which the physical work required few 'texts'. Workers did not refer to repair manuals; instead, problems were solved by talking with fellow workers.

Disenchantment, cynicism and resistance

From the workers' perspective, the manager's focus on 'working smarter' was seen to be about working harder. Most of the work of the competitive teams was on constructing lengths of footpaths that could be measured and costed accurately. This work was continuous, with large concrete pours each morning, followed by afternoons setting up for concrete pours the next day. This work was more intense and regimented compared to their previous work (before competitive teams were introduced), which often entailed driving around the suburbs checking drains. To provide an additional historical context, older members of the teams could recount a time when there were 140 construction and maintenance workers in the council, while now there were less than forty, essentially doing the same work. The workers felt they were being pressured to do more, but they lacked the incentive to do so.

One area of contention was that only the team leaders were paid more in competitive teams. For the manager this was an issue of team leadership, but for the workers in these teams, it was seen differently, as one worker indicated:

> That's the trouble, they don't want to reward you for anything. More out of you and nothing reward, no incentive. It's bribery as far as I'm concerned, bribe one man to get the best out of the rest.

Lack of monetary reward was the single most significant grievance for the workers, and this was recognized by team leaders who were reluctant to push their teams too hard. One team leader, Sergio, fifty-six, commented: 'Blokes here still get the same money, that's why I can't push them to work hard. (They) say get fucked. Council don't give them nothing.' Some workers even suggested how it could be different, a system where they might have the financial incentive to work harder:

> Now if they said to us do that job, say $40,000, and we do it for 35. If they took $2,500 and gave us $2,500 as a bonus, that means we'd all be a lot keener to do it. But the council wouldn't entertain the idea.

Only paying the team leaders additional money had given way to some petty jealousies within the teams. One worker said that 'the whingers are there, see what he's getting. Some get pay rises, others don't. The system is just wrong'.

Coupled with the belief that the council was making them work harder was the view that the council's priorities were wrong and that basic services like maintaining footpaths and the drainage system were declining. A key part of the new work order involved workers identifying with and committing to the values of the enterprise, but in the case of the council workers this was problematic. They could see the deterioration in the local drains and gutters, but with a reduced workforce they felt powerless. As one worker claimed:

> Once upon a time it would get fixed up, but now it's just left there until someone complains about it. There's thousands of yards of this to be done around the area, you know, they'll never get on top of it.

These workers were genuinely concerned at the decline in these basic services, and many lived locally themselves, as ratepayers in the area. They could see their council rates going upwards, while their work on footpaths and gutters was undervalued. They resented the values of the council that were reflected in other priorities in so-called 'welfare delivery' services such as childcare, and they resented that the council was now being run as a business: 'you can't run a council as a business, because somewhere along the line someone suffers. They're not supposed to be profit-making, cut this, cut this here'. For the workers in this study, their work had a 'use value' in the community, while the direction of the council was to view their work as a 'commodity' that potentially, through privatization, could be undertaken for profit.

Adding to worker cynicism was the issue of remuneration, the fact that the growing number of managers in council's administration was receiving 'astronomical' pay rises, while the workers received little reward and were expected to be happy at work. As one worker Robert, forty-three, stated:

> David says to us, I enjoy my job, but at $90,000 a year we'd enjoy it a lot bloody more too. Like, we take home, $20,000 I've earned so far this year. I'm not much better than a person living on the dole, and then I come here and cop this.

The training programme and literacy/numeracy

To assist the introduction of competitive teams, a series of training sessions were conducted for all the workers. The sessions were held in the afternoons during work time in the depot's training room. Approximately fifteen workers attended each session, and they were obligatory. The manager conducted the sessions, along with his supervisors and a private training consultant. The aim of the training programme, according to David, the manager, was to ensure everyone knew 'where we're heading and why we're heading there'. It could be seen as a 'softening' process to break down worker resistance to working differently, to win them over, or in discourse terms, to 'colonise them' (Virgona, 1994: 133). The supervisor, Tony, acknowledged that not all workers were happy to be there in the training programme: 'Some of the older guys don't like it, but they're almost forced into the training. If they want to sit there and twiddle their thumbs, then so be it.' The older supervisor, Eric, claimed that some workers did not see the training as relevant to their work:

> They're there to do the drains, the roads and paths and that's what they're supposed to do. To come in for half a day is not doing it. That's two drains we didn't do or one concrete they didn't pour. They're quite against it.

While some of the workers, especially younger ones, indicated they were happy to participate in the training sessions, the majority were either ambivalent or opposed. 'A waste of time and money,' said one worker. The sessions comprised a mixture of activities, including videos of restructured teamwork in action, exercises relating to constructing driveways and similar types of jobs, and some group discussions. A number of objections were raised by the workers in my interviews with them. Some saw little relevance in theoretical exercises about constructing driveways that failed to take account of the many variables that affect this work in practice (such as tree roots interfering with the work). One traditional gang leader, Robert, forty-three, claimed he was already consultative in his team and failed to see the benefits of supposed 'team' efforts. Others were opposed to videos featuring US assembly lines: 'Americans, Yanks, you must do this.' This appeared to be similar to British manufacturing company employees resisting 'Yankee bullshit' and 'propaganda' (Collinson, 1994: 32).

Perhaps unsurprisingly given the low levels of formal schooling experienced by most workers, there was a reluctance to be back in a classroom setting where they had previously not been very successful. Robert, a ganger, said he felt 'belittled' by the sessions: 'You know, I feel like a school kid again. And the nature of the way it's taught to us in a sense, then I feel like, you know, here we are in a classroom.' There was also the fear that literacy deficiencies would be exposed in this more formal learning environment. The situation was reminiscent of Gowen's (1996: 23) research in a manufacturing company:

> Any introduction of print-based education and training is also seen by many front-line workers as an unnecessary intrusion that would interfere with the rich oral communication they use effectively and with great skill.

Certainly, there were some workers who acknowledged literacy difficulties in the training room, but it did not necessarily transfer as a difficulty in their regular work in the council. As one worker, Phil, forty-two, stated: 'I'm not much in the reading and writing, but I know how to start a shovel.' Phil acknowledged that he had difficulties with literacy but believed he did a good job at work for the council, and literacy had not affected him in his working life: 'Well, I get by on jobs here, like, I can lay bricks, got me truck licence through here. I can do whatever I find in my life that I need to be able to do.'

Other workers had basic difficulties with numeracy. One worker, Ken, sixty-one, stated he was 'not for figures, so, I just switch off'. These men and others were reluctant learners in the training programme, but the men were not against training at work, only this kind of formal classroom training. They were prepared to suggest the type of training they really wanted:

> I honestly believe we could all be taught on the job. They'd have to have someone, right, you go out with that gang, you stay there for a fortnight, you learn the way that they do this, this, and this. (Michael, sixty-four)

This was precisely how Tim, thirty, had learnt new concreting skills. Although he had been in the council for seven years, he had recently been placed with a new ganger:

> Well, I could give you on a personal level with Robert. He's taught me more in the space of two weeks than I've been on the council. Maybe they should have training people on the job when the start because there's a right way and a wrong way to do concrete.

These comments suggested that training on the job was favoured by these workers and could be seen more as a form of apprenticeship or what some researchers have referred to as 'situated learning' or learning in informal communities of practice (Lave, 2011, 2019; Lave and Wenger, 1991; Wenger, 1998). The formal training programme these workers were undertaking in the depot's training room, by contrast, alienated them. Presentations by the manager and the training consultant involving video clips and step-by-step PowerPoint displays represented the prevailing industrial training culture of the corporate world (Virgona, 1994) that were perceived by the workers to be far removed from the realities of their everyday work. The training programme was always intended to be a one-way flow of information from a management perspective, a transmissive mode designed to inform workers of the broader industrial climate and the need for them to change.

Conclusion: Literacy as a managerial code

This chapter has detailed workplace relations and cultures operating in one area of a local council and has indicated the divergent interests of both management and workers. It has featured contrasting views on the realities of this workplace. From the perspective of the manager, and to a degree his two supervisors, there was a vision of establishing a workplace culture founded on the 'new work order' expounded in prevailing 'fast capitalist' management texts (i.e. knowledge workers, working smarter, more flexibly). The perspectives of the workers on the other hand, or at least most of them, formed part of an 'old culture' based on the lived, conflict-oriented experiences of workers borne out of a history of exploitation and struggles with management. These were hard working but poorly paid working-class men whose 'old culture' work practices were being devalued by management. This is where literacy had a role to play. The manager and one of the supervisors mentioned that workers lacked the literacy skills needed in the new workplace culture, and preliminary discussions had begun about the possibility of introducing a literacy programme for the workers. These views were in accord with the prevailing literacy 'crisis' discourse in Australian workplaces (Black and Yasukawa, 2011a). Good literacy skills were seen to equate with a competent workforce, especially one needed to take up the challenge of working differently in a highly competitive workplace environment. The problem, however, was that our study of the everyday work practices of these maintenance workers indicated few examples of specific literacy practices needed in this type of work. Numeracy practices appeared more prevalent, but as one of the supervisors commented, it was mainly the team leader, and not the team members, who was responsible for calculations involved, for example, in determining orders for concrete pours. And besides, these types of routine numeracy practices were learnt quite easily by the workers on the job. The references to literacy could be seen, in effect, to be a code used by management to indicate that many workers lacked the skills, and indeed the social identities, to change and adapt to a new workplace culture that required workers to be more committed to their work and, in essence, to work harder for no additional monetary reward. Many of the workers recognized that management was simply attempting to extract more of their surplus labour, and therefore they privately resisted attempts at changing them. Lack of literacy was a dismissive way for managers to indicate that workers were deficient in the new roles expected of them. And yet, as the perspectives of the workers in this chapter demonstrated, literacy was not seen to play any significant role in how they performed their jobs, and neither did they feel deficient as workers. As one of the workers, Phil, stated, he could do everything in his work, and life generally, that he wanted to do, and this had little to do with his literacy abilities.

5

Production Workers and Literacy

Everyone here has got an excellent understanding of the computers; it's just that English is not their first language.
                                (Margaret, workplace trainer at Hearing Solutions)

There is no I. I always remind them every day in the meeting, there's no I; it's we, we as a team. If there's a problem, if you cannot read, please don't be shy, ask me or ask somebody.
                                (Anthony, a team leader at Hearing Solutions)

Introduction: Workplace literacy programmes

This chapter continues the theme of literacy at work with the focus on production workers. The above comments by production workers and the interview data in this chapter are drawn from data collected in an NCVER-funded research project during 2011–2013 and published in a range of reports and articles (Black, Yasukawa and Brown, 2013, 2014, 2015; Brown, Yasukawa and Black, 2014; Yasukawa, 2018; Yasukawa, Brown and Black, 2013, 2014). The research examined the literacy and numeracy 'crisis' as it related to production work in several manufacturing companies that were at various stages of introducing 'lean' production practices. The perspectives of the production workers, along with their supervisors, managers and workplace trainers, are outlined in this chapter.

Workplace literacy programmes first began in Australia in the 1970s and 1980s, and they invariably featured production workers because many of these workers, especially overseas-born migrants, were perceived to lack basic language and literacy skills (Bean, 1994; Newcombe, 1994). As briefly discussed in the introductory chapter of this book, heightened concerns over the economic implications of low levels of language and literacy in workplaces developed in Australia mainly from the time of the Australian Language and Literacy Policy (ALLP; see DEET, 1991). Henceforth, the human capital rationale for improving these skills has dominated policy and practice with the federal government's promotion of jobseeker and workplace language and literacy programmes. The manufacturing sector was a particular focus for workplace educators (Joyce, 1992; Prince, 1992) as the sector was experiencing revolutionary changes in technology and workplace cultures and the traditional unskilled/semi-skilled manufacturing workforce was perceived to be lacking in the LLN skills required in this new work order (Gee, Hull and Lankshear, 1996). National surveys of adult literacy abilities consistently highlighted the low literacy levels of Australian adults considered 'unskilled' and/or employed in the manufacturing sector (ABS, 1997, 2008a; Wickert, 1989).

At the time of our research study, concerns about low levels of adult literacy (and language and numeracy, LLN) in Australia, and particularly in workplaces, reached their zenith with the publication of the National Foundation Skills Strategy for Adults (SCOTESE, 2012). The National Strategy claimed, based on the ALL survey data, that 40 per cent of workers had a level of literacy and numeracy below that needed to meet the complex demands of work and life in modern economies. The deficit views expressed in the National Strategy and from its associated stakeholders represented the 'crisis' in Australian literacy and numeracy levels that we sought to address in our research study. It resembled the literacy and numeracy crisis in workplaces identified in other countries such as the UK (Department for Education and Employment, 1999; Hoddinott, 2000).

Manufacturing companies and LLN

Underpinning much of the industry discourse in the National Strategy were concerns about the effects of low literacy and numeracy in manufacturing enterprises (Industry Skills Council [ISC], 2011). As various skills organizations indicated, manufacturing had changed in recent times: 'Rapid changes in technology have triggered the creation of new business models, systems and processes that require considerable, and ongoing, upskilling of the workforce' (ISC, 2011: 2). According to this industry skills perspective, there was now the need for 'high-level skills to provide a competitive edge through design, product development, specialist expertise, technology and supply chain skills' (ISC, 2011: 38).

The technological changes and new ways of working in the manufacturing sector have been termed 'lean production' or, alternatively in many Australian workplace contexts, 'competitive manufacturing' or 'competitive systems and practices' (AIG/UTS, 2012). As described in our NCVER research report (Black, Yasukawa and Brown, 2013: 9–10), lean production describes a highly influential form of workplace organization which derives largely from Japanese production methods (Monden, 1994). The aim is efficiency, and it involves the ongoing reduction of resources (people, equipment), surplus production, stock and waste. It is often characterized by a 'just-in-time' approach, producing parts in the right quantity and at the right time, and high technology and seamless production stages. It usually involves small teams of multi-skilled workers who take increased responsibility for meeting production targets. Drawing on the knowledge of the teams to provide insights and suggestions for greater efficiencies, the aim is continuous improvement (Nicholas, 2011; Womack, Jones and Ross, 1990). Increasingly in Australian manufacturing the application of lean principles was seen to be 'at the heart of modern enterprises' (Manufacturing Skills Australia, 2012: 57), which was reflected in the increasing number of companies delivering the 'competitive manufacturing' courses developed by the peak manufacturing organization, Manufacturing Skills Australia. The impact of lean changes on workers was considered significant, as they were expected to radically change their work practices, cooperate in teams, promote a common vision of the company, actively participate as problem-solvers and engage in continuous training (Olivella, Cuatrecasas and Gavilan, 2008).

The dominant government and industry perspective was that workers did not have sufficient literacy and numeracy skills to engage with this advanced technological work. These perspectives on the low literacy and numeracy skills of workers, expressed in the National Strategy and by allied industry stakeholders (ISC, 2011; Productivity Commission, 2010; SCOTESE, 2012; Skills Australia, 2010), were based primarily on the ALL survey data (ABS, 2008a) and also surveys of the perspectives of employers (AIG, 2010, 2012). These stakeholders were 'singing off the same hymn sheet' (Black and Yasukawa, 2016), with the basic argument that improving literacy and numeracy skills was essential to increase the productivity, competitiveness and wealth of individual enterprises and the nation as a whole. Only occasionally did the argument become more complex. For example, research at this time indicated that many migrant workers whose first language was not English were employed in low-skilled jobs that required few literacy skills (Ryan and Sinning, 2012).

Conceptualizations of literacy in workplaces

Perspectives on literacy and numeracy in workplaces differ according to how these skills are conceptualized. The dominant government and industry perspective outlined above assumes that literacy and numeracy skills can be generalized across different contexts and that increases in these 'core' skill levels will automatically have economic benefits (Canning, 2007). This is a 'human capital' or 'technical' approach to workplace literacy and numeracy (Wolf and Evans, 2011). It involves generic skills that can be assessed nationally through standardized measures such as the Australian Core Skills Framework (ACSF) or internationally through comparative large-scale survey data developed by the OECD (IALS, ALL, PIAAC), and in the case of the Global South, by UNESCO's Literacy Assessment and Monitoring Programme (LAMP; see UNESCO Institute for Statistics, 2009). As explained in earlier chapters, however, literacy can also be conceptualized as social practices or situated (Barton, Hamilton and Ivanič, 2000), as can numeracy (Baker, 1998; Yasukawa et al., 2018). That is, literacy and numeracy practices can be examined in terms of what they mean and how they are used and valued in local contexts by different individuals or groups. This approach has been termed 'ideological' because it reveals and highlights the power and politics of literacy and numeracy (Street, 1984; Yasukawa et al., 2018). It involves qualitative methodologies, mainly ethnographic studies of literacy and numeracy practices in social contexts. At the time in Australia, there were limited studies of literacy and numeracy as social practices in workplaces (Black, 2004; Castleton, 2002; Kell, 2005), but there were an increasing number of studies overseas and particularly those involving 'high performance' manufacturing companies (Belfiore et al., 2004; Gee, Hull and Lankshear, 1996; Hart-Landsberg and Reder, 1995; Hull, Jury and Zacher, 2007; Jackson and Slade, 2008). In these ethnographic studies, links between the low literacy and numeracy skills of workers and their workplace performance were found to be complex and involved changing and contested worker identities and managerial power. Importantly, these studies provided detailed subjective perspectives of workers, what they were experiencing and learning, and how their perspectives may have differed from those with more power within organizations. These studies and others gave voice to workers that were rarely explored or heard in more dominant workplace literacy studies (see Foley, 1999; Livingstone and Sawchuk, 2005; Sawchuk, 2003).

A final point to be made in this review of the literature on workplace literacy is that ethnographic studies were not the only types of research that have contested the dominant skills crisis discourse. In the UK, for example, there were academic studies undertaken at the height of concerns about literacy in workplaces using longitudinal, quantitative methods. The findings indicated that literacy levels were not necessarily a major concern for many employers, and that improvements in basic skills had little employment effects, at least not in the short term (Ananiadou, Jenkins and Wolf, 2004; Meadows and Metcalf, 2008; Wolf et al., 2010). Later UK research has indicated that in some low-paid occupations in retail and residential care, the demand for literacy and numeracy is quite limited, calling into question the need for workplace programmes to address these skills (Higgins, 2017).

Early experiences of workplace literacy programmes

I was introduced to the complexities and politics of workplace literacy in the early 1990s, when, as a head teacher of ABE in a TAFE college, I had the opportunity to observe workplace literacy programmes in action. I recall the enthusiasm for workplace literacy programmes at the time, particularly from TAFE managers and a wide range of stakeholder executives who set about determining the operating principles for such programmes (NSW Government Workplace Literacy Taskforce, 1990). Workplace literacy programmes were the new frontier, and they were encouraged as part of the new enterprising culture in a TAFE system that had recently been restructured along business lines (Scott, 1990). While maintaining their social justice role in providing community literacy programmes, adult literacy teachers and managers were now expected to seek commercial opportunities with industry and were encouraged by the federal government's Workplace English Language and Literacy (WELL) funding which subsidized workplace literacy programmes.

My first experience of WELL programmes in the mid-1990s was with a small company that manufactured socks, in a programme that resulted from a referral from the Industry Training Advisory Board (ITAB) which represented the textile, clothing and footwear sector. The problem the company wanted resolved was the relatively high number of costly mistakes made by workers in processing orders for the socks it manufactured. This problem was seen to be due to the poor literacy and numeracy skills of the predominantly female migrant workers whose first language was not English. A WELL programme was subsequently established, and a TAFE literacy teacher from my ABE section was assigned to work with the company. Some of the complexities of a workplace programme for even a small textile company with a seemingly straightforward workplace problem soon became apparent. For a start, who was the teacher responsible to? Whose agenda was she working to? Adult literacy teachers in TAFE community literacy programmes had long worked according to the principle of the 'primacy' of the individual student in a needs-based programme jointly negotiated between teacher and student (Black and Bee, 2018b; Osmond, 2021; White, 1983). But the primacy of student (worker) needs was problematic in a workplace programme in which supervisors and management in the company had recognized there was a literacy/numeracy problem and sought the assistance of the literacy provider. Company management had a major stakeholder interest, especially as the company was paying for the programme (though part of the WELL programme was subsidized by the federal government). There were in fact multiple programme stakeholders – the company management and supervisors, the TAFE college, the federal government (i.e. WELL), the ITAB that referred the company to the TAFE college, and of course, the workers who were perceived to be the source of the problem.

Contradictions and dilemmas for the literacy teacher quickly became apparent when she interviewed the workers individually and could find no evidence of literacy or numeracy deficiencies that would negatively affect their work performance. While the workers had little formal education and, in a normative sense, lacked English literacy skills, the workplace was organized along traditional Fordist lines, and the routine work involved few literacy or numeracy practices. Through repetition and familiarity, the workers had become competent in managing these practices. Moreover, the literacy teacher concluded that many of the mistakes made in the processing of orders were due primarily to inattention on the part of the workers because the work was so routine and mundane. The workers displayed little interest in workplace literacy training that simply confirmed practices they already knew and could perform well. Instead, in their engagement with the literacy teacher, the workers' main interest was to learn how best to educate their own children so that they in turn would not end up in poorly paid, routine jobs similar to those of their parents.

The WELL project was not documented as a research study, and the above issues were of little interest to company managers and supervisors who simply wanted their workplace problems resolved. The TAFE teacher managed to juggle competing stakeholder interests by devising a colour-coded table for use by workers to help eliminate mistakes on the production floor, while also trying to provide the workers with the information they wanted regarding the education of their children. But the programme flagged for me that workplace literacy and numeracy programmes were complex, involved competing interests, and were not just about the skill deficits of workers (see Mawer, 1999).

There were other WELL programmes in manufacturing companies that I observed in my role in TAFE, and they shared some essential features. They were predominantly management centred. That is, company managers, often based on the advice of supervisors, identified workplace productivity problems that they perceived were due to literacy and numeracy deficiencies in their workforce and initiated the WELL programme. The literacy/numeracy teachers then worked with managers/supervisor to address these deficiencies. These teachers, in effect, became an arm of management, often sharing not only the office space of managers and supervisors, but their workplace perspectives, particularly in relation to the literacy/numeracy deficiencies of the workers. The workers had no influence on how the programme was conducted, and decision-making remained 'squarely with the "experts" and the boss' (O'Connor, 1993: 200). In fact, so valued was the work of some workplace literacy 'experts' in TAFE that there were examples of company managers enticing teachers to 'jump ship' to become permanent training managers for the companies. The acquiescence of adult literacy and numeracy teachers to the human capital discourse has been noted in the research literature (Lee and Wickert, 1995), but the politics of literacy/numeracy teachers, particularly those involved in workplace programmes, have rarely been discussed as an issue (Black and Bee, 2018a). Workers' perspectives in these programmes were generally not sought beyond responding to management-prescribed literacy skills audits (Schultz, 1997). In the earliest workplace literacy programmes in the 1980s, and in some early WELL programmes, workers' interests were often represented by unions (Newcombe, 1994; Sefton, Waterhouse and Deakin, 1994), but their role in WELL programmes diminished from the mid-1990s following the election of a conservative federal government and subsequent changes in WELL regulations. In the UK and some other countries, there were examples of alternative models of workplace literacy/numeracy programmes in which unions played the dominant role, but this model had not extended to Australian programmes (Yasukawa, Brown and Black, 2012).

Two manufacturing companies

In our research of manufacturing companies funded by the NCVER, we explored multiple perspectives on the role of literacy and numeracy in production work, including those of managers, supervisors, workplace trainers and workers (e.g. Black, Yasukawa and Brown, 2013, 2014, 2015). Our research examined three manufacturing companies, though only two companies will be explained in this chapter. Both companies had recently adopted lean production methods, though to varying degrees. The research involved observing workplace practices, interacting with production workers to identify the literacy and numeracy practices in their work, and interviewing company staff at all levels to document their perspectives on the role of literacy and numeracy. We also sought perspectives on how workers experienced learning in their training programmes. We referred to our research methodology as an 'ethnographic approach', drawing on social practice models of literacy, sometimes referred to as the 'new literacy studies' (Barton, 2012; Gee, 2015; Hamilton and Ivanič, 2000; Street, 2012a). We aimed to provide 'insider' perspectives on everyday literacy and numeracy practices in several workplaces (Bloome, 2012). As the two companies were so different in terms of what they produced, their organizational structures and cultures and workplace training, they will be outlined in this chapter as separate case studies (with pseudonyms for company names and personnel).

Company 1: Insulation Products

Insulation Products was a non-unionized, medium-sized company with approximately seventy employees located on the outskirts of a state capital city. The company traditionally produced gaskets but had also progressively produced a variety of insulation products (thermal, electrical, sound). The company was unable to compete on price with major off-shore companies but could provide fast delivery of specialized quality products. It was possible, for example, for a company to require a specific gasket and then have it manufactured and delivered within hours or delivered inter-state the next morning.

We located Insulation Products as a potential research site following referral from an external organization that was providing workplace training at the company. At the time of the research, the company was introducing lean production training for groups of its production workers. A literacy and numeracy course had also been conducted at the company to assist workers assessed to be in need of these skills. As I outline later in this case study, there was the perspective within company executives that the largely overseas-born, migrant workers lacked LLN skills, and many workers performed poorly when formally assessed for these skills. Company executives viewed improved LLN skills to be important for the introduction of lean production. The research comprised multiple site visits (11) by the researchers, observations and field notes of workplace practices and training sessions, and recorded in-depth interviews with the company CEO, managers (2), personnel from vocational training providers (2), team leaders (3) and team workers (10).

The production workers and most of their direct line managers were predominantly male (there were only three female production workers) and born overseas from countries where English was not the first language spoken. Many of the workers were Indians from Fiji or Tamils from Sri Lanka. Others were born in Chile, China, India, Malta, the Netherlands and Vietnam. Many of the workers had been employed at the company for a long time, including several from between twelve and eighteen years. Most workers had completed their formal education overseas, and one was university-educated (in science/engineering) in China. The production work comprised small teams of workers in several designated work areas: machine cutting, sewing thermal blankets and stores/despatch.

Our interest in the role of literacy and numeracy was explored across three work domains: routine technical aspects (cutting, sewing etc.), lean production training and conditions of employment related to 'earning a living' (pay schedules, contracts etc.). This latter domain had rarely been analysed in workplace literacy research and was usually viewed as a separate activity system to production work (Worthen, 2008; Yasukawa, 2018).

Beginning with the top company executive, we asked the Australian-born CEO, Phil, about the role of literacy and numeracy in routine production work at his company. He believed these skills were a problem, and he went on to explain that, for example, because their products were in 'trains, trucks, and power stations', not being able to read the job card properly could have major human and financial consequences if it led to products being made incorrectly. What was surprising, however, was that his critique of his production workers went beyond their literacy or numeracy skills to the fact his company could only recruit 'less educated people':

So, we're looking – we're sort of sifting around what's left for us after the mining company take all the university graduates and the IT people take all the people who are computer wizards and things like that. The people who are going to do hands-on work pretty much falls back to your less educated people, and I suppose that's what you get.

'What you get' in this manufacturing company, according to Phil, was workers from a 'foreign' background and whose English language skills were 'not real great'. The issue of spoken English appeared to be very significant for Phil, and to counter any communication difficulties (he called them 'frustrations') affecting his workforce, Phil had instituted an 'English-only' policy in the workplace. Phil's deficit views on the language proficiencies of many of his production workers, however, were not repeated or indeed reflected in our interviews with other personnel in the company.

When the quality assurance manager, Felipe, was asked about the role of LLN in production work at the company, he provided an alternative perspective to the CEO's. Felipe was born in Chile, had qualifications in mechanical engineering and had spent the last twenty years in production work. He explained that the key workplace text, the job card, required almost no literacy or numeracy skills: 'the only thing that they have to write down in the job card is how – what time do you start, what time do you finish. With your name – that's all, nothing else' (Black, Yasukawa and Brown, 2015: 624). Job cards tended to have generic features, including customer details, types of materials, dimensions, quantities and so on, and required the signatures of the workers and supervisors to sign off. Felipe also explained that while nearly all of the cutting machines were computerized, and some of them were technologically very advanced, the skills required to operate them had little to do with LLN:

> Factory work is not a sophisticated thing. The operator even – the machines here are sophisticated but the operator basically put the material into the machine, press the button. Everything is controlled from the top. They send the programme – everything. So that's – some people here had to use a mouse and a little bit of computer. But these days, everyone has a computer at home.
>
> (Black, Yasukawa and Brown, 2015: 624)

For Felipe, the key issue for productivity was not LLN skills but the attitude of the workers. He claimed he could take anyone 'on the street' and teach them to operate the machines, provided they had the right attitude. As for the issue of spoken English, it needed to be put into the work context:

If he (worker) doesn't speak clear, here it doesn't matter because everyone doesn't speak well, or everyone have a different accent. But you have your body language that helps. So even if you don't know how to – you just – people understand.

Interviews with the production workers supported this view on spoken English at work, and some workers commented that the cutting machines made the production floor a very noisy work environment which necessitated workers wearing earplugs, and thus much of the routine communication necessitated gestures and sign language. Workers were also pragmatic in their approach to the 'English-only' policy instituted by the CEO. In one work area, stores and despatch, all three workers were Tamils, and Sharma, the warehouse manager, stated: 'Mostly we speak Tamil but if anyone come from outside or other nationality comes, then we need to speak English' (Black, Yasukawa and Brown, 2015: 621).

In our observations of work practices and in interviews with workers, numeracy practices appeared to play a greater role than literacy, particularly in the work area where various types of thermal blankets were produced. The workers tended to underplay the skills required to manage numeracy practices. Richard, for example, one of the few Australian-born workers in the company, claimed that numeracy skills were minimal in this work: 'no, most of the stuff once we know what material we've got, we basically know what the sizes are, the computer will do the rest for us'. He did mention, however, that it was necessary to know how much material was required and calculating this accurately was a key numeracy practice. Samar, the Fijian-born team leader in the sewing area, stressed the importance of efficiency and not wasting material: 'I have to do ten gaskets and that's the material. I have to work out the best possible way to cut it.' Many of the jobs required converting imperial measures to metrics, and some of the jobs required complex drawings and calculations for cutting a wide range of insulation material to fit specialized machinery. Workers explained that for some insulation material, they had to account for stretching, tension and abrasion points. This work was far from routine, and workers at times had to develop detailed drawings and calculations.

In the despatch area, literacy and numeracy practices were also apparent. Vigas, for example, a Tamil who had worked at the company for nine years, explained that there were many calculations involved in determining the transport companies needed to despatch finished products:

For the transport – how much they charge. Some transport big stuff, big pallet – cheap, right. Small one, expensive. Some transport small expensive, big cheap.

So, I know already where I got that experience, which transporter, different distance, some inter-state, local.

The knowledge and skills of the despatch team had developed over time and were not really understood by others in the company. Vigas, for example, claimed that 'sales doesn't know the transport cost, only store knows. Other department doesn't know, only store – me and Sharma knows'. This work could be considered 'hidden knowledge' gained informally in their work practices (Livingstone and Sawchuk, 2005), leading to daily efficiencies unknown by management.

To summarize our interviews and observations on LLN in the routine work at Insulation Products, it appeared that all of the production workers in the three work areas – machine cutting, thermal blanket sewing and stores/despatch – were working efficiently, undertaking a range of tasks, many of them non-routine, that involved literacy and numeracy practices of varying degrees of complexity. While English was not the first language for almost every worker, and while few had experienced formal education beyond high school in their country of birth, these factors had little or no influence on their work performance. In some cases, as with the workers in stores/despatch, workers had fairly autonomous roles and were making savings for the company that only they were aware of.

Confirmation of the work skills of the production workers and the relative non-issue of LLN was provided by the external workplace trainer, Rachel, who was providing an introductory lean production course to groups of workers. As part of Rachel's work with the company, she had undertaken what she termed a 'process map' with every production worker. It involved looking at their job, analysing how much LLN there was and determining how the workers were managing. She summarized her findings as follows:

> There's a fair bit of writing up in the warehouse but they seem to be coping with that. So, I don't think it's – there was no – we talked to management, we talked to the operators. I've talked to them about problems and where the problems were. There didn't seem to be anything coming up from people misreading or writing incomprehensibly. There's a bit on the verbal communication, but people understand that they have to work a little bit harder at that, so I don't think that was a major one. So, I think really, possibly some pronunciation stuff would support people, but people seem to be able to read their job cards. They can read the programmes to put information into, to put the design into the machines. There's really not that much call for it.
>
> (Black, Yasukawa and Brown, 2015: 623)

It would be fair to conclude, therefore, that in terms of the routine work being undertaken by the production workers at the time of this research, LLN did not present as a problem in this company. At the most, there was the view that workers might need some work on pronunciation, but this was really only a reflection of their ESL/EAL migrant worker status and had no impact on their routine workplace performance. There was no LLN 'crisis' reflected in this company's operations. However, as the literature on manufacturing indicated, production work was changing, and lean production was being promoted strongly. The issue therefore was what role would LLN play when or if the company went 'lean'?

Management at Insulation Products had an interest in introducing lean production in their company, and this was the main reason for seeking the support of an external workplace trainer. It was agreed that lean production would be introduced in incremental stages, beginning with workers on the production floor, and then possibly extended to the whole company workforce. LLN was perceived by the company's top executive to play an important role in the introduction of lean production. The CEO, Phil, when asked about the need for LLN in lean production, commented: 'Oh, big time, yes', though he clearly saw the issues primarily in terms of spoken English: 'The concept of lean is quite simple to explain in English, but just try to explain that to someone who's not really fluent in English' (Black, Yasukawa and Brown, 2014: 64).

The first stage in introducing lean production was to interview and assess the literacy and numeracy skills of the whole workforce using the national standardized assessment tool, the Australian Core Skills Framework (ACSF). Traditionally in WELL projects, only those workers assessed at or below level three (of the five levels) were eligible for workplace LLN programmes. Unsurprisingly, many of the production workers fell within this target range, including some at the lowest basic level one. It was on this basis that several 'stand-alone' LLN classes were conducted by the external trainer in work time for small groups of production workers. As the workplace trainer, Rachel explained, the LLN classes were '[j]ust to build their literacy skills up so that next year when [name of teacher] is available, she'll come in and do some basic lean principles' (Black, Yasukawa and Brown, 2014: 65). This represented a 'front-end' approach to workplace LLN – an attempt to lift the LLN skills of workers to better enable them to undertake workplace learning. From observations of one class and from interviews with workers, the LLN classes included exercises on pronunciation and spelling (e.g. 'short vowels, long vowels') and also exercises on role-play communication based on workplace roles. In the research literature, this type of workplace programme would fit within the restricted range on the expansive-restricted continuum of workplace training programmes (Derrick, 2012; Fuller and Unwin, 2004). It was a deficit model because it focused on correcting perceived deficiencies rather than developing communicative creativity and competence. It targeted only those workers assessed to be in need, focusing mainly on generic (autonomous) LLN skills and some specific workplace-related skills.

It was interesting to note that, based on the external workplace trainer's analyses of workplace functions, and the views of managers and workers, the main area of costly mistakes in the company's operations was not on the production floor but in the communication work of the sales teams located within the administration offices. According to one of the managers, the auditors had determined that 80 per cent of problems were in the sales area, and this was well known in the company. Felipe, for example, the quality assurance coordinator, claimed that often the sales people did not have sufficient technical knowledge of products, leading to miscommunication with customers. A production worker, Richard, said that most mistakes came from sales people mistyping a letter or a number on the job card. When assessed for their literacy and numeracy levels on the ACSF, personnel in the sales teams all recorded scores above level three and thus were ineligible for LLN training provided by the external training organization. It meant that the prime focus of training to improve workplace efficiencies in the company was focused on improving the skills of production workers, where few problems had been identified, while the sales teams 'where communication skills were desperately needed because that's where the problems were' (Melinda, LLN teacher) were left untouched.

According to one of the external workplace trainers (Rachel), it was not LLN skills that were holding back productivity in the company but how the work was organized, the workplace systems (or lack of):

> Lack of standardised approaches to working. There's so much more that you can do to utilise the skills and experience of all workers if you can have effective means of sharing information and letting them participate.

This was what the lean production course was designed to do, to enable all workers to engage more and participate in order to improve productivity. Rachel claimed that in the traditional Fordist structure of this particular workplace, there was little need for all workers to engage in LLN practices because 'the team leader does it'. But even with lean production methods, including regular team meetings of workers, LLN would not necessarily present as 'problems' because

[t]he language is consistent, it's contextualised to the workplace, and that language is easy to pick up because it's very familiar and it will come up every day at your team meeting or your toolbox talk. You'll know the four areas that you're being measured. You'll understand all the different language that we use for non-conformances. You'll understand the language we use for problem solving. So, it develops.

(Rachel, external workplace trainer)

In this manufacturing company, lean production was being introduced in a superficial manner because management was unsure whether the company should fully embrace lean principles. The choice to start with production workers was seen by some in the company to be a mistake. Felipe, the quality assurance manager, made the point that lean production needed to be a whole-of-company process. He claimed that at Insulation Products, it would be better to start lean training with senior management because then if it did not work with them, 'down the string it doesn't matter'. The workplace trainer, Rachel, agreed, stating that most companies she had worked with started at the top levels of management: 'we've done our top, and now we are ready for our operators and frontline management to be trained'.

The production workers who undertook the training programmes, both the stand-alone LLN classes and the introductory lean principles course, were compliant and participated well. Observations of sessions of both the LLN class and the introductory lean course indicated in fact that the workers had little idea of why they were attending or for how long, but they were generally positive about the courses. With the LLN course, Rashana, born in Fiji, said that for her it was 'like a refresher course ... when we learnt many things in English, verbs and things, where we use full stops'. She was in fact studying childcare on weekends because it was her previous vocation in Fiji, and she hoped to undertake it again in Australia. The observation of a lesson in the lean course indicated that workers engaged with the course and could identify inefficiencies in their areas of work. The problem, however, as one worker Faras noted, was that the course would only be useful if everyone came together to make it happen: 'With the cooperation of the management ... it can be done. If nobody is interested, then that will never happen.'

The final work domain to be examined for the role of LLN was workers' conditions of employment related to 'earning a living' (pay schedules, contracts etc.). We asked one worker, Ranveer, a Fijian Indian, if his wages were set by a national award. He answered: 'I don't know much about that.

What do you mean, like, national award system?' He had no idea because not one of the workers had been told about pay scales; moreover, no one on the production floor knew what other workers were receiving in wages ('we keep it personal, so we don't really know'), even though many had matching skills. Another worker, Faras, said, 'It's all done in the hush. Who gets it, who doesn't get it, nobody knows.' Fijian-born Ranveer contrasted the situation to his previous job with a large company where 'we'd just go to our union leader, the union delegate, and he does all the talking on our behalf, and the pay rise was automatic every year as per cost of living adjustments'. Insulation Products, on the other hand, was a relatively small company, and there was no union representation. Obtaining a pay rise was similarly obscure as there was no official company mechanism to apply for one. Ranveer speculated that the manager might get word from a supervisor that particular workers were working well (involving, for example, 'extra work, extra effort') which might lead to better pay, but he added: 'I'm not sure, I'm only guessing.' Faras agreed with Ranveer, commenting:

> Nobody knows to whom to ask. So maybe we need to go and ask (name of manager) who will say okay leave it to me, leave it to me for eight months, nine months. You keep on in frustration.
>
> (Black, Yasukawa and Brown, 2015: 621)

At Insulation Products, therefore, LLN was not an issue in terms of workers' understanding their employment conditions because there were literally no LLN practices to engage with.

Company 2: Hearing Solutions

The second company, Hearing Solutions, produced a variety of customized hearing aids. Like the previous case study, it was a non-unionized company located in a light industrial area on the outskirts of a state capital city. The parent company was based in Europe, and the Australian office assembled and repaired hearing aids for mainly Australian clients. We located this company following a referral from a training organization that was providing lean training at the company. Hearing Solutions was seen to have embraced a whole-of-company approach to lean production, and we were keen to explore the role of LLN in this company. The research comprised multiple site visits (6) by the researchers, observations and field notes of workplace practices and training sessions, and recorded interviews with production and other managers (4), team leaders (7), team members (5) and the external workplace trainer.

The company assembled in-the-ear (ITE) and behind-the-ear (BTE) hearing aids under different brand names. The main production work involved modelling and producing hearing aid shells (for ITE) to meet client requirements that were sent in from audiology clinics throughout Australia. Approximately ninety production workers were employed at the company, with similar numbers of males and females. Most were born overseas where English was not the main language. Main countries of birth included the Philippines, Vietnam, China and various Balkan states. Many of the workers were long-term employees, having been at the company for many years (fifteen years or more in some cases). There were seven work teams focused on separate production roles, each with a team leader and a team of between four and twelve workers.

As with Insulation Products, we aimed to examine the role of LLN in the three workplace domains of routine technical work, lean production and training, and conditions of employment. At Hearing Solutions, however, because lean principles were so embedded throughout the company's operations, it was difficult at times to separate routine work from lean aspects. Necessarily, if lean worked properly, they were one and the same. Our main focus on the lean aspects was the team meetings conducted at the beginning of each workday.

The experienced external workplace trainer, Margaret, responsible for introducing and maintaining lean production at the company, described the production work at Hearing Solutions as more 'electronic' than 'hands-on' manufacturing, and she regarded some of the work tasks as 'very highly skilled, you do need a very good understanding. You know, some of the stuff they do is just mindboggling. Some of the moulding and everything on the computer'. This did not mean that all the work tasks were complex, but her description of the work indicated that it was a high-performance company. And yet, as with the other company we researched (Insulation Products), the company recruited workers largely with low levels of formal education or work qualifications. The production manager, Ivan, who had been at the company many years, stated that their main employment criteria were 'soldering skills, good hand skills and good eyesight'. Nearly all the workers were born overseas, spoke English as a second or other language, and were either not educated beyond high school or had overseas qualifications that were not recognized in Australia.

The company provided all the training required in the production work, and it was standard for new recruits to begin with relatively low-skill jobs such as lacquering ear mouldings ('it's the same as doing your nails', according to Ivan, the production manager), and then workers were trained, mainly by team leaders, to work their way up the skills hierarchy to jobs such as computer modelling. This was an example of shared workplace practices, 'situated' informal job-based learning in which new workers learnt their job roles by doing them collectively as co-participants with other more experienced workers (Lave, 2011, 2019; Lave and Wenger, 1991; Wenger, 1998). Ivan, the production manager, commented that when he first started at the company a couple of decades ago, he was informally apprenticed in this way through all the main job roles and that now as the production manager, he had a deep understanding of how the production processes worked.

The computer modelling had quite high status on the production floor as workers sat in front of a computer screen with a dual mouse to produce individualized, three-dimensional images of ITE hearing aids based on specifications supplied by hearing aid clinics. This was quite complex, non-routine computer work often requiring creative solutions. One of the modellers, Andrew, who had worked at the company for twenty years, said, 'It makes you look good to be in front of the monitor.' Other work teams specialized in repairing and servicing hearing aids, and one small team's role was to check the operation and quality of all work undertaken prior to despatching the products to the hearing aid clinics.

When we asked about the role of LLN in these work areas, the consensus expressed throughout the company was that LLN skills, and in particular the lack of such skills, was not an issue of concern. Ivan stated that LLN was not blocking them: 'I guess we find a way around it. So, it didn't stop anyone getting training or learning something' (Black, Yasukawa and Brown, 2015: 624). If at times a worker did struggle with a job task that involved LLN practices, the solution was straightforward: 'they go and ask somebody else to help them' (Ivan). The entire workplace was team-based, and it meant that team members were always available to help others in the team. As one of the team leaders, Anthony, stated:

> Only a few of them cannot read properly, but they're intelligent people. They can learn, yeah. But I don't have a problem with that. If you show them correctly or with patience they can learn.

He added that that was how teams worked:

> There is no I. I always remind them every day in the meeting there's no I; it's we, we as a team. If there's a problem, if you cannot read, please don't be shy, ask me or ask somebody.

Anthony's comments were a clear indication that teams operated as a significant social network providing support for fellow workers.

The workers often tended to underplay the skills required in their jobs. Computer modelling, for example, was complex work and required not only the requisite computer skills but deep knowledge of hearing aids usually acquired following a lengthy experience of working in the full range of other work teams at the company. One modeller, Brian, described his work as 'just like playing a video game, basically' (Black, Yasukawa and Brown, 2015: 620), and another modeller, Mile, claimed that 'basically we don't need to use that much brain, everything is in the software'. Additional complexities to their role often arose when an audiologist had specified a hearing aid model for an ear mould that technically was too small to fit all the components – the vents, electronics, receivers and other elements. Brian explained that he then had to reject it and suggest a suitable alternative to the audiologist:

> which is interesting, because an audiologist – they do several years of study at universities and colleges and get paid huge salaries, where we don't. Yet we have to do half the thinking for them and suggest what's going to fit in there. So, it's a bit mad in that respect.

These comments were an indication, as with workers at Insulation Products, of the 'hidden knowledge' gained informally by production workers in daily work at this company (Livingstone and Sawchuk, 2005; Sawchuk, 2003). They became highly skilled and knowledgeable in their field through learning together with fellow workers, but this was not reflected in their pay packets as production workers.

The interaction that computer modellers had with audiologists and hearing aid clinics involved a number of embedded LLN practices, including informing customer service via email of problems with order specifications and occasionally communicating directly by phone with audiology clinics. Additionally in their everyday work tasks involving job cards, modellers found that before they could proceed it was necessary to read and check not only their in-house order but the attached original clinic form in order to ensure that it had been interpreted properly. This was to ensure that mistakes were not made which could then 'waste everybody's time' (Brian, modeller).

Another aspect of the computer modelling role was the impact of changing technology, with new hearing aid models being introduced 'pretty much every year'. Wilbur was a modeller who had worked for the company for nineteen years. He explained that each new model had specific features which they had to learn, and he had been sent to Denmark, along with other workers, 'six or seven' times for training. The training also went in the reverse direction – with workers from Hearing Solutions training other workers in Europe. This was highly technical work performed by experienced workers who had received little formal schooling and, in a normative sense, had low LLN skills. It corresponded with the type of work researchers have since termed Industry 4.0 (Farrell, Newman and Corbel, 2021) as work practices shifted from routine and standardized computerization (the Third Industrial Revolution) to innovative and highly customized work practices. The literacy practices (Literacy 4.0) required for this work involved not only advanced technical knowledge but the social skills to work with others to generate new knowledge. Margaret, the workplace trainer, spoke about Tai, a Vietnamese-born worker who had just been sent to Poland to train workers there. Tai had some LLN problems, especially with spoken English, but his 'technical literacy skills' and his experience and understanding of hearing aid technology overrode any such problems with spoken English. As Margaret said, 'everyone here has got an excellent understanding of the computers; it's just that English is not their first language'. It was not a barrier either to their learning or to them training other workers.

It was clear from the interviews that while some workers may have struggled individually with LLN practices when they first started at Hearing Solutions, through their informal apprenticeship learning from more experienced fellow workers, LLN difficulties in relation to workplace practices became a non-issue. They learnt LLN as they learnt their job skills; there was no distinction between the two; they were one and the same (Kell et al., 2009). Mile, for example, was Serbian and had spent a decade in the company. He said that when he first started, he specifically asked not to work with fellow Serbian-speaking workers and that this experience 'was great, wonderful for me to pick up English and give me the confidence to talk with people'. He acknowledged that his writing was 'not that good' but that he could 'always ask some other guy how to spell correctly'. In the case of Lam, who arrived in Australia as a refugee from Vietnam, she claimed, 'I just pick up' the language, and like other workers, if she did encounter LLN difficulties: 'I go ask someone else'. Furthermore, Lam felt no qualms about speaking Vietnamese at work: 'if you're working with another Vietnamese person, obviously you speak Vietnamese'. Moreover, the production manager, Ivan, claimed it was understandable, and indeed desirable, that 'someone from the same ethnic group is able to explain in their native language. It minimizes the problem'. In other words, communication was widened on the production floor, and linguistic diversity was productive (Cope and Kalantzis, 1997); it was not viewed as a problem. This was quite unlike the situation in the other company we researched, Insulation Products, where there was an 'English-only' policy on the production floor.

Lean production was also understood and introduced quite differently at Hearing Solutions. It was a whole-of-company approach, as the production manager, Ivan, made clear:

> It has to be from top to bottom. If the management doesn't believe lean and is not involved, it doesn't work; simple as that. Everybody has to be in it, and you have to constantly remind people it's not just another initiative which will die in twelve months or six months or two years. Lean is continuous process. There is no end to that, so you live in it.

Every production worker in the company had undertaken the in-house certificate course in lean production, and every team leader was at the time of the research undertaking the more advanced diploma course. This training was provided by the one external workplace trainer, Margaret, but unlike the training at Insulation Products, there was a general absence of 'classroom' training. Margaret said she did not even refer to it as training, as she worked with the workers 'on the floor' in their teams. The training was very much 'hands-on' and visual rather than theoretical and textbook-based. Prior to the course commencing, Margaret explained that there was some discussion about the need for translators due to English language difficulties, but this soon became a non-issue as there was always someone in the work teams 'that can sort of do a quick interpretation'. Margaret also focused a lot on visual aspects, graphs for example, to support lean practices.

One of the key lean changes to workplace practices was the team meetings held at the beginning of work each day in which all team members were expected to contribute. After initially being led by the team leaders, team members then led the meetings on a rotational basis. By the visual use of graphs on large whiteboards, the focus was usually on the previous day's production output and various aspects of problem-solving ('we're in the red guys, how come?' (Margaret)) that would improve the efficiency of the team.

Production managers expressed the many positive changes that resulted from these team meetings. Ivan, for example, stated:

> Through the lean process, we actually manage to get many, many more people involved. Even people who never spoke at the meetings had to present things, had to be part of that, and they are doing it. So that's a great change.

Another manager, Derek, commented that workers were contributing in ways that had big implications for the company, even for assisting their overseas productions:

> Sometimes you get brilliant suggestions on how to do things – and, you know, some of the things that I show to people in other countries and all that, that's come from them here.
>
> (Black, Yasukawa and Brown, 2015: 618)

Team leaders and team members appeared to have accepted, indeed embraced, lean production. One of the team leaders, Novak, indicated some initial reluctance with daily team meetings, but he soon realized that the regular communication within his team was effective in remedying mistakes: 'Rather than going and waiting for mistakes to happen and then go and fix it, so trying actually to prevent things that shouldn't happen, let's not let them happen.' Some team members felt that team meetings had helped them in their personal interactions with others, increasing their sense of agency. Vietnamese-born Huong, for example, was observed actively leading a team meeting. She stated, 'In the past I'm shy, but now I'm not really that kind of person outside. If I got opportunity, I will take it.'

LLN skills were not cited as issues of any concern in the team meetings. Having the confidence to lead meetings might have been expected to be an issue, given the workers' diverse language backgrounds, but less than perfect English grammar and pronunciation were not recognized as problems because almost everyone was in a similar position as overseas-born migrants. And besides, the focus was on technical aspects of work which all were familiar with: 'they understand it. They're around it all day long in their area. They know how much we've received. They know how many errors. They know … ' (Michelle, team leader). The visual documentation, particularly graphs, reduced any difficulties with literacy. The main numeracy practice involved the calculations that were presented in graphs at the team meetings, but these calculations were common and predictable.

The lean training at Hearing Solutions featured many elements of an 'expansive' model of workplace learning (Fuller and Unwin, 2004). For example, it operated across the whole company at all levels; it linked directly to workplace 'communities of practice'; it was knowledge-based with times allocated for discussion and reflection; it featured a strong vision of workplace learning – as Ivan stated: 'Lean is continuous process. There is no end to that, so you live in it'; formal qualifications were awarded that were transferable to other workplace contexts; the technical skills of the workers were highly valued (to the extent that some were sent to Europe to share their skills), teamwork was valued and there was a focus on innovation.

The final work domain for LLN to be considered in this chapter is employment conditions, and in this, Hearing Solutions again contrasted sharply to the situation at Insulation Products. All workers at Hearing Solutions were provided with written documentation on their working conditions at the time of their recruitment, and surprisingly for a production workforce, flexitime was an option. An administration manager at the company explained that workers could start work between 7.00 a.m. and 9.00 a.m. and leave from 3.30 p.m. onwards. She claimed this was one reason the company had a high worker retention rate.

With the all-important pay schedules, the production manager, Ivan, explained that all workers fell within the national metal trade industry award, and there were five levels of pay. The problem, however, was that so many workers had experienced a lengthy employment history with the company that 90 per cent of them were on the highest pay scale. He said there was nothing more he could offer workers to reward them for additional skills and work performance beyond a small allowance 'to show them that we care, and we appreciate what they're doing'. Only one of the workers commented about pay. Novak, a team leader, explained that he had worked for the company for fourteen years and in that time had undertaken a wide range of work roles. He had reached his pay limit and commented: 'The only thing that is missing is probably financial stuff. If they would pay a little bit more it would be better.'

Concluding comments

The two manufacturing companies examined in this chapter have provided insights into a range of perspectives on the role of LLN in production work. At the beginning of this chapter, I outlined the literacy 'crisis' discourse in workplaces and the human capital argument that improvements in literacy (and language and numeracy – LLN) will result in improved productivity. This LLN crisis was not reflected in either of the two companies in this research study. In both companies, there was little evidence that lack of LLN, as measured by standardized tests, was a factor of any significance for productivity. The CEO at Insulation Products made negative comments about the lack of English language proficiency of his overseas-born production workforce that appeared to accord with dominant policy discourses and popular deficit stereotypes (see Hunter,

2012; Hunter and Cooke, 2014), but his views were not reflected in the interviews with managers, workers and external educators at the company. The workforces of both companies comprised mainly migrant workers whose first language was not English. In both companies, these workers were highly proficient in their work roles, but in the case of Insulation Products, the quantification of LLN through the application of a standardized assessment (the ACSF) had the effect of identifying some workers as deficient in LLN skills (Gibb, 2015). But importantly, this had no bearing on their proficiency as workers. At the high-performance Hearing Solutions, the workers were highly skilled and had acquired these skills largely through informal on-the-job learning with experienced co-workers. As recognized in many 'blue collar' working-class jobs, there was a 'cognitive richness' evident in the skills of these production workers that could not be measured and acknowledged through standardized testing regimes (Rose, 2004).

The two manufacturing companies had different approaches to workplace LLN and the introduction of lean production. At Insulation Products, workplace learning has been described as 'restrictive'. It was underpinned by a deficit perspective with the belief, based on a formal assessment of their LLN skills, that the production workers lacked the LLN skills to successfully learn and work in a 'lean production' workplace. Workers assessed as lacking LLN were required to participate in a front-end 'upskilling' LLN programme. At Hearing Solutions, all production workers were involved in a whole-of-company approach to lean production. No one was assessed for their LLN skills, and everyone participated and completed the lean production courses and received formal recognition (certificates, diplomas). The course was structured in a way to minimize formal learning in training rooms, with most learning undertaken on the production floor as part of regular work routines. Informal support was provided by co-workers, team leaders in particular, to any workers who required it. This type of workplace learning and the culture that fosters it has been termed 'expansive' (Fuller and Unwin, 2004). The workplace cultures of the two companies and their location along the restricted–expansive continuum were reflected to some degree in the employment conditions of the workers. At Insulation Products, no workers were aware of how their pay rates were determined or how they could progress within the company, while at Hearing Solutions, these conditions were formalized within national industry awards and employment conditions were documented and provided to all workers.

In the literature on workplace learning, 'expansive' learning contexts are viewed predominantly as progressive and 'good'. In the case of workplace learning at Hearing Solutions, workers described their learning experiences almost universally in a positive light and this chapter has reported this learning within a consensual, team-based learning framework. However, as critical educators such as Avis (2010) indicate, workplace learning can be viewed in a more critical sociopolitical context set within the capitalist order in which it has to be recognized that the prime motivation for workplace learning generally (and at Hearing Solutions in particular) is to make the company's operations more efficient and profitable. As a consequence, workplace learning of this type with its focus on teamwork and continuous improvement in workplace practices can be seen to intensify the work process for the workers. According to Avis (2010: 183), workplace learning viewed from this critical perspective is concerned primarily 'to discipline labour so as to develop appropriate forms of subjective dispositions which facilitate the production of surpluses'. Thus, team-based workplace learning with its newly empowered knowledge workers can be viewed as 'soft-touch hegemony' (Gee, Hull and Lankshear, 1996: 23). Workers may believe they are working in a new 'enchanted' workplace (Gee and Lankshear, 1995), but the purpose is always to maximize surpluses.

6

Adult Literacy Students and Literacy

Talking to other people and seeing other people the same as I am, the same problems, and all different nationalities in the class and age. One was fifteen and all ages, and we got on well. That surprised me.
(Ken, adult literacy student)

I never shame because I don't know this language.
(Hajira, an adult literacy student born in Afghanistan)

In this chapter, the focus is on adult literacy students – who they are, how they experience literacy education, and their perspectives on the role and value of literacy in their everyday lives. These are adults who have acknowledged that they have a literacy problem affecting their lives, or at the very least, they have a wish to improve their literacy abilities and have decided to do something about it by attending a community adult literacy programme. For the most part, the research data presented in this chapter are based on students who attended TAFE adult literacy programmes, and the research was undertaken as an extension of my professional work in the TAFE adult literacy field.

Illiterate adults and deficit ideology

At the time of my first engagement with the adult literacy field in the early 1980s, there was a fast-developing international research focus on the perspectives of adult literacy students and how lack of literacy affected their lives. Particularly significant were some qualitative studies undertaken in the UK in the wake of the 'Right to Read' campaign of the 1970s (Charnley and Jones, 1980; Jones and Charnley, 1978; Levine, 1980; Mace, 1979) and also some studies in the United States (Eberle and Robinson, 1980; Mezirow, Darkenwald and Knox, 1975). Their research methods included in-depth interviews which influenced me at the time in my own approach to researching literacy in prisons, as outlined in Chapter 2. The representation of adult literacy students in these studies varied, but it was predominantly one of individual deficit in an era, especially in North America, where there were major concerns about the high rates and effects of illiteracy in society (Hunter and Harman, 1979; Kozol, 1980). In one study of adult literacy programmes, 'illiterate' adults were described as 'desperately hobbled in trying to cope with everyday life' and they were found 'disproportionately at the dirty end of every index of social well being' (Mezirow, Darkenwald and Knox, 1975: 37–8). This theme of literacy deficits significantly affecting people's capacity to function in their everyday lives, especially poorer, working-class people, has continued through the decades in Australia to be a defining feature of the field, often reinforced by popular media constructions of illiterate adults (Wickert, 1993). Government-sponsored reports in Australia have contributed to these perceptions of the personal inadequacies and costs to individuals and to society of people lacking literacy skills (Hartley, 1989; House of Representatives, 1991).

Moving forward several decades to contemporary Australia, and there are indications that this popular representation of low-literate adults being 'desperately hobbled' in their everyday lives continues to prevail in the general community. For example, many of the public submissions to the recent federal parliamentary enquiry into 'Adult literacy and its importance' (House of Representatives, 2022) highlighted cases of literacy teachers/tutors describing how their adult students struggled to function with everyday life. Students were portrayed as living precarious lives and 'prevented … from enjoying the most basic things in life' (see Chapter 1 of this book). Another example is the recent three-part television series on adult literacy, *Lost for Words*, broadcast nationally in Australia by SBS (2021a), which supports, and indeed builds, narratives of individual deficit as it focuses on the lives of adult literacy learners. The series, referred to by SBS as an 'observational documentary', follows the lives of eight selected students in an adult literacy course, highlighting their inabilities and personal shame in trying to undertake everyday events such as reading a train timetable or a menu or food recipe. The series charts their progress in the adult literacy course, showing how they manage to overcome adversity and shame. This representation of adult literacy students appears to fit the characterization of 'heroic victims', with the focus on 'who or what can undo the victimisation of the learners, the triumph of individual effort, and the redemptive power of literacy to heal emotional injury and trauma' (Belzer and Pickard, 2015: 6). This emotive portrayal of adult literacy students provided the marketing appeal of the TV programme.

Australian policy documents since the early 1990s (DEET, 1991; SCOTESE, 2012) can be seen to have played a role in extending and broadening deficit perceptions of low-literate adults to employment contexts. Much as Hamilton and Pitt (2011) demonstrated in relation to key UK policy texts on adult literacy, these Australian policy texts viewed literacy skills increasingly as human capital, and low-literate adults were represented, particularly by governments and dominant business and skills groups, as unproductive workers, and with a greater chance of being unemployed. Within this human capital thesis, low-literate adults may be characterized as 'broken cogs' (Belzer and Pickard, 2015: 7) insofar as a 'repair' is possible if the right strategies are applied. In the case of the National Strategy, it was 'to encourage, inspire and empower individuals to develop the courage and confidence to improve their foundation skills' (SCOTESE, 2012: 11).

The first Australian research studies of adult literacy students began in Victoria in the 1970s (Council of Adult Education, 1974), and in the 1980s, several influential qualitative studies were undertaken which examined the lives of adult literacy students (Grant, 1985, 1987). These incorporated case studies of adult literacy students and explored how their literacy abilities and attitudes towards literacy education were influenced by their schooling experiences, family lives, and sense of self, including their anxieties and fears. These studies eschewed the contemporary focus on 'illiteracy' rates and deficit and viewed literacy instead as a relative concept, 'not the attainment of a particular level of mastery' (Grant, 1987: 11). The main aim was to gain greater understanding of the needs and perspectives of adult literacy students.

Ethnographic research and the new literacy studies

Ethnographic research approaches have been promoted for researching classrooms and for representing programme participants' perspectives (Hamilton, 1999), and these approaches have been integral to the work of new literacy studies (NLS) researchers, deepening our understandings of the lives of adult literacy students. Beginning with pioneering studies in the early 1980s (Cook-Gumperz, 2006; Heath, 1983; Street, 1984), the focus has been on examining literacy practices in communities and how people engage with them in their everyday lives (e.g. Barton and Hamilton, 2012; Barton, Hamilton and Ivanič, 2000; Baynham, 1995; Gee, 1990). These studies of literacy as social practices were not necessarily fully fledged ethnographies; rather, they drew on 'ethnographic tools' (such as observation notes and open-ended and semi-structured/informal interviews) and thereby adopted an ethnographic 'stance' (Hamilton, 1999: 432) or 'style' (Street, 2012b).

Several of these studies in the UK have examined the role of literacy in the lives of adult literacy students (Barton et al., 2007; Duckworth, 2013; Ivanič et al., 2006) presenting the subjective perspectives of the students. These studies were undertaken over several years and provided important longitudinal data on how students' lives had changed over time (Appleby and Barton, 2009; Hodge, Barton and Pearce, 2008). Some of the overall findings from these studies included the following: many students brought with them a broad range of literacy skills often unrelated to the curriculum; the majority of students had negative schooling experiences and some had backgrounds that included violence and trauma; students had different reasons for participating in programmes and experienced a range of constraints; feelings and emotions shaped people's experiences of learning; students had a range of life aspirations common to most people (including a safe, settled life, good home etc.); and students had many roles, responsibilities and commitments, often causing them to dip in and out of learning (Barton, 2009).

Study 1: Adult literacy students and the learning experience

My initial research with adult literacy students began in the late 1980s when ABE provision in TAFE was growing rapidly, but little was documented about the students, particularly in NSW (compared for example, with Victoria). The research study was funded by the federal government as part of a suite of funding initiatives under the National Policy on Languages (Lo Bianco, 1987). Undertaken in conjunction with a work colleague (Black and Sim, 1990), the study was local and qualitative and involved interviewing sixty-eight former students from an adult literacy programme in a TAFE college and an evening college in a Sydney suburb. The students' comments provided in this section are drawn exclusively from this research study. All the students in the study had attended the adult literacy programme part-time (usually two sessions per week of three hours each), either day or night, and the classes comprised small group tuition (usually a 6:1 ratio of students to teachers). As with all adult literacy programmes at the time, there were no course fees, and attendance was voluntary. College enrolment records were used to contact students, initially by telephone, to seek their participation in an interview to explore their reflections on their

ABE learning experience. Interviews were semi-structured and recorded, and questions focused on why they participated in the ABE programme, what their expectations and experiences were, and why they left the programme.

One of the common misperceptions about adult literacy students has always been that the students are Australian born and/or native English speakers, as for example with most students who participated in earlier Melbourne adult literacy programmes (Council of Adult Education, 1974; Grant, 1985, 1987; Grant and Hayles, 1981). Our small study indicated, however, at least in respect of the two colleges in Sydney that the majority of students (65 per cent) came from backgrounds where English was not the first language spoken. Thus, many students were participating not because they had failed to acquire literacy skills previously, usually as school, but because it was an additional language for them, and they had never been taught English literacy. The diversity of languages and cultures was a reflection of the multicultural composition of the catchment areas of the two colleges and was quite typical of many other suburbs in Sydney. The students' main nationalities of birth included Italy, Greece, Lebanon and Sri Lanka, followed by a wide range of other countries. Other demographic data included similar percentages of male/female participants (i.e. 47/53 per cent respectively); most students were under forty years of age (59 per cent), and almost half of the students (47 per cent) indicated they were unemployed at the time they participated. While detailed data on socio-economic status were not collected from the students, as with most students in adult literacy programmes, these students were predominantly working class. The Sydney catchment areas of the two colleges featured working-class suburbs (though rapidly becoming gentrified), where many people engaged in relatively lower-skilled and poorly paid jobs.

Motivations to participate in the adult literacy programme varied across the student group. Approximately half mentioned employment-related reasons, including wanting to improve their job prospects ('well, I don't want to spend the rest of my life in a factory' (Luis)) and wanting to be able to make written applications for jobs. Others expressed the desire to improve their literacy skills irrespective of job factors and more to improve themselves and their own feelings of well-being ('I want to be able to do things, sort of without asking someone else to help me' (Mary)). With some students it was a life circumstance, such as a marriage breakdown, that motivated them to enrol ('I was alone in the house ... and I thought I've never been to school in this country, and I saw the pamphlet in the letterbox' (Seva)). Others expressed the view that they wanted to help their own children's education, or they were encouraged to participate by others, often family members. This wide range of motivations to participate was not unusual and resonated with the findings of other contemporary adult literacy studies (Brennan, Clark and Dymock, 1989; Charnley and Jones, 1980).

While some students said they expected the literacy programme to be like attending school for the first time with an emphasis on the 'ABC', along with a didactic approach ('Here, write this out' (Stephen)), and even being 'picked on' (Maria), their actual experiences of classes were often a pleasant contrast. For many students, it was the individualized care and attention of the teacher that they appreciated. One student, Maria, stated: 'They respected what I said and what I did. They gave you freedom of choice.' Another student, Afat, explained: 'I feel they are very close to the person. You don't feel they are just teacher.' Firouz explained that while he had left the class because there were too many people in it, the teacher continued to encourage him to return: 'She writes the letters to me, "why don't you come?" And she write "I hope you don't be sick." She was very kind.' Not all students, however, were so impressed with the teachers or their teaching, particularly those who seemed to have an expectation of a more formal schooling experience. One student claimed the teachers talk too much and do not set writing assignments, and another student (Connie) said her mistakes 'were just set aside, they weren't pointed to what I expected'.

One aspect of the classes, how they related with other students, was commented on very favourably by most students. One student, Pedro, commented, 'We were like a family.' Another student, Australian-born Ken, commented:

> Talking to other people and seeing other people the same as I am, the same problems, and all different nationalities in the class and age. One was fifteen and all ages, and we got on well. That surprised me.

The cooperative spirit, the group 'we' feeling, an aspect of social capital explained later in this chapter, was strong and was appreciated by many students. Comments included: 'everyone shared ideas' (John); 'others help you. It was a good atmosphere' (James); 'They wouldn't let you work on your own, it'd be like the whole class. You'd be hearing other people's ideas ... found that pretty good' (Dennis).

It was evident from the interviews that while there were some consistent themes, such as appreciating caring teachers and enjoying the company of other students in groups, these adult students had differing and complex social and educational needs. Group interaction, for example, was important for many, but some students found they received insufficient individual attention, especially if the group was quite large. One student, Phillip, said, 'I just didn't think enough time was spent with me. I've got to have someone over my shoulder.' Similarly, Dimitri felt frustrated at the lack of individual attention: 'I felt like I'm losing my time there. You just feel hopeless you know, when time goes by and you're sitting there.' Lesson content and structure also received varying responses. The more relaxed, relatively unstructured lessons were suited to many of the students, such as Chris, who commented that 'it was more flexible, like it wasn't planned. I think the course was nice, I enjoyed it', while others were critical, stating that they wanted 'grammatical' work, 'dictation' and 'a set system'. There was also the issue of spoken English, with some students expecting more work on English pronunciation, while others were critical that 'migrants needed a lot of help just with their speaking'.

The study supported to a large extent the findings of other qualitative adult literacy studies at the time, particularly in relation to the key student outcome from participating in the course – increased personal confidence (Brennan, Clark and Dymock, 1989; Charnley and Jones, 1980; Darkenwald and Valentine, 1985; Grant, 1987). This was a consistent outcome, even for students who participated for only a short period of time. One student, Leslie, for example, stated, 'I feel better in myself,' and other students spoke of now having the confidence to go out more ('and no one's going to be staring at me' (Maria)), and being more actively engaged in activities such as reading aloud publicly without fear and being more independent.

As the study focused on *former* adult literacy students, those who had left the programme, we were interested in exploring why they left the programme. Some of the reasons cited have already been indicated, including classroom factors such as inappropriate placements in the course, with some students needing spoken English (ESOL – English for Speakers of Other Languages), while others felt they were at too high a literacy level to benefit from the course. One more advanced-level student said she felt she was 'infringing on their time, and I sort of dropped out'. Insufficient individual attention in a class with too many students was also cited as reason for leaving. A complex range of non-classroom reasons also featured. Many cited employment-related reasons, such as the interference of shift work, and not enough time (one student claimed he worked sixty hours per week). Others cited family circumstances (childcare, for example), and other factors included preparing for a wedding, family bereavement, helping children with schoolwork ('They need more qualifications more than me' (Asuman)) and a range of health reasons. Quite a few of the students maintained their absence from the class was temporary only and that they intended to return when their circumstances improved. These reasons for leaving resonated with findings from a Canadian study (Malicky and Norman, 1996) and UK studies mentioned earlier (Barton, 2009), which indicated students had many roles, responsibilities and commitments in their lives that caused them to dip in and out of learning. Predominantly, the students in our study were from working-class backgrounds, and finding the time to attend an adult literacy course had to be juggled with competing priorities, especially long and often physically demanding work hours (cf. Malicky and Norman, 1996). One of the students, Theresa, commented on her attendance at a night class: 'If you've been working all day, you are really wrecked. Three hours too long.'

Study 2: Multilingual students in an adult literacy class

My second study of adult literacy students undertaken some years later comprised interview data collected for my doctoral thesis (Black, 2001: 116–31). It included collaboration with a teaching colleague (Black and Thorp, 1997) and focused on six students who comprised the cohort of an adult literacy class in a TAFE college in Sydney. As with the previous study, these adult literacy classes were part-time and fee-exempt, and in the case of the class we examined, attendance was for two mornings each week. The study was small scale and drew heavily on the principles and methods of the NLS. My research collaborator (Kay Thorp) was also the teacher of the class, and she had in-depth knowledge of her students and their educational needs. We jointly interviewed each of the students with a largely informal/semi-structured format. Our focus was not on aspects of pedagogy but on the students' backgrounds and how literacy affected their lives. We were particularly interested in exploring their everyday lives and the intersection of the languages other than English and their use of English literacy. As indicated earlier in this chapter, a characteristic of adult literacy classes in many TAFE colleges in Sydney was the multilingual composition of the classes. In our study of one adult literacy class, all the six students were born overseas in countries where English was not the main language spoken. This was not uncommon for many other adult literacy classes in this college, and the issue of the pedagogical overlap between the fields of ABE and ESOL was beginning to be explored at this time by academic researchers (Davison, Taylor and Hatcher, 1994; Hammond et al., 1992).

The role of literacy practices in multilingual communities has been a feature of many NLS, and they provided a model for how to approach our study of adult literacy students. Baynham (1988), for example, indicated the richness and variety of literacies in linguistically diverse communities where people may be bi- or multi-literate. Pertinent to our study, he indicated that an understanding of how these communities used different languages and literacies could help to counteract 'deficit model thinking':

> The individual who struggles with reading and writing in a literacy group may be the same individual who teaches Qur'anic school, or who organizes Saturday schooling for children in his/her community.
>
> (Baynham, 1988: 62)

There were many other sociocultural studies of literacies in multilingual communities published in this era (e.g. Hamilton, Barton and Ivanič, 1994; Martin-Jones and Jones, 2000; Street, 1984, 1993), but rarely did they feature Australian research or contexts (later exceptions included Cruickshank, 2006; Kral, 2012).

There were six students in our study, all from the same adult literacy class, and each had very different backgrounds and reasons for participating in the class. Briefly, the students' profiles were as follows:

Youssef was a refugee from Afghanistan in his late thirties. He had been living with his wife and young son in Australia for eight years. He had some tertiary qualifications in engineering but had worked in a factory since arriving in Australia. His aim was to upgrade his literacy skills for employment purposes.

Mei Ping was in her late fifties. She was born to Chinese parents and lived her early life in Indonesia. She later went to university in China. She had been in Australia for nine years after migrating from Hong Kong. Her aim was to be able to write stories in English for her grandchildren.

Maria was a widow in her late fifties. She was born and married in Lebanon but had been in Australia for over thirty years. Her aim was to improve her English literacy in order to take on everyday tasks previously undertaken by her husband.

Nawal was in her forties and was born and married in Lebanon. She had been in Australia for twenty-two years. Her aim was to improve her English literacy in order to become employable and socially independent.

Mariam was in her thirties and born and married in Iran. She had been in Australia for seven years. Her aim was to look for a job when her youngest child completed school.

Lily was in her forties. She was born in China, lived in Hong Kong as a child, and had been in Australia for twenty-three years. She lived with her Cantonese-speaking husband in Sydney, and her aim was to improve her reading and speaking in English.

Linguistic diversity was a feature in the lives of all the students, but particularly for one student, Mei Ping. She explained that in her early childhood in Indonesia, her home language was Chaozhou (or Teochew), an eastern Chinese dialect, though 'in the marketplace' she spoke Hokkien (a related Chinese dialect). As an Indonesian resident, she learnt Indonesian and also Mandarin because she was educated in a Chinese-speaking school. In the early 1950s, she and her brother were sent by their parents to Nanking, where she completed her schooling and went to university. During this five-year period, she learnt Russian, as China and the Soviet Union at the time were in close alliance. She then married a man whose first language was Shanghainese, and she described learning the language as she brought up her children in Shanghainese. Later in the mid-1970s, the whole family moved to Hong Kong, where she spoke Shanghainese at home and Cantonese in the local community. In her everyday life now in Sydney with her family and friendship networks, she shifted mainly between Shanghainese, Chaozhou, Cantonese, and Mandarin, and of course, English which she practised with her grandchildren and was learning at the TAFE college. In total, Mei Ping had learnt seven languages involving three different written scripts, though one of these, Russian, she said she had not used since the 1950s. Mei Ping's linguistic life trajectory was exceptional, but it was not entirely unusual for multilingual students attending adult literacy classes in Sydney. Her case provided an alternative perspective to the usual adult literacy story of 'deficit' and non-functioning outlined earlier in this chapter.

For the other members of the literacy class, in addition to learning English, Youssef spoke Farsi (Persian) and Pashto, Mariam spoke Farsi and read a little Arabic, Lily spoke Cantonese and some Mandarin, and both Nawal and Maria spoke Lebanese Arabic. All were competent spoken and written users of their languages except for Nawal and Maria, both of whom had limited and disrupted schooling in Lebanon, and their Arabic literacy skills were restricted. In the case of Nawal, she acknowledged that our interview with her was the first time she had admitted to anyone (outside family) that she was illiterate in Arabic.

In their everyday lives, the students often shifted language codes in spoken and written forms depending on the demands of the situation (Baynham, 1993; Martin-Jones and Jones, 2000; Wardhaugh, 1992). Youssef provided a good example of code switching. At school in Afghanistan, Youssef learnt to write in both Farsi and Pashto. At home now in Australia, his communication with his wife was in Pashto, but when he wrote to people in Afghanistan, he did so mainly in Farsi (Persian), though occasionally in Pashto to those not educated in Farsi. Interestingly, with the unstable political situation in Afghanistan at the time (in 1997), he had to address his letters in English to an informal network of people in Pakistan, who would then transit the letter to Afghanistan. His wife did not understand Farsi having received only a limited formal education in Afghanistan, and the language of the home was Pashto. With his young children (aged three and six), Youssef said he would teach them to write in Pashto when they were older, but 'their first language will be English'. In his home environment, he had few books in Farsi or Pashto. With events like birthdays and weddings, he explained that cards and formal statements of well wishing were usually written and distributed by a well-educated community member with expertise in such writing. At times in Sydney when he became sick, language and literacy practices in English were largely redundant because he visited a Farsi-speaking doctor. In his work in a factory, he said there were no literacy practices and all the other workers spoke languages other than English.

The role of other people as literacy mediators in support networks was important for all the students, even for Mei Ping with her repertoire of languages. She indicated, for example, that if she was required to write a formal letter in English, she would request help from one of her daughters currently studying at university in Sydney. Cantonese-speaking Lily did not always have the same type of family support available, and she relied on her Chinese neighbour and the use of an interpreter service and a social worker. Youssef said he received literacy support from within the quite extensive Afghan community network in Sydney. He also received help from a clerk where he worked, a Yugoslav man: 'he is a really good person not he help only me, but he help everybody … any forms'. Maria, Nawal and Mariam all had children, some at university, who could provide support in English if required.

Several students did experience some difficulties and dilemmas relating to languages and literacies within their families. Nawal and Mariam, for example, deferred to their spouses with many literacy practices such as writing notes to their children's school and excursion forms because they did not feel as competent in English literacy. Sometimes they were subjected to ridicule at home with family members 'laughing' at them because they lacked English language skills. Often it was the husband who had acquired the dominant English skills through his work, while they, though very resourceful, were relatively isolated in the local community.

Potential difficulties in some families arose as children developed different language competencies to their parents. In the case of Lily, for example, she and her husband spoke Cantonese and were literate in Chinese, but not English, while their children spoke Cantonese and English, but were literate only in

English. Mariam recounted a situation in which she wanted to leave a message for her thirteen-year-old daughter. If she wrote in Farsi, she knew her daughter would have difficulties reading it, but to write it in English was a problem for Mariam. It was a balancing act for Mariam at home between encouraging her daughters to learn Farsi, while trying to develop her own competence in English.

Most of the students managed their lives quite comfortably using their native languages, and if needed, they had social networks to assist them with literacy practices in English. Maria and Nawal, however, lacked formal education in their first language, Arabic, and were unable to use it in their everyday literacy practices. Maria said she wrote 'half Arabic half English' but lacked formal competence in both. When she tried to write notes in English she claimed, 'My daughter, she laugh on me.' For Maria, learning English literacy skills was valued highly: 'I wish I could, like a miracle, I could write it so easily.'

This small study served to highlight the role of multilingual literacies in the lives of an adult literacy student group. It provided a counter to the dominant perspectives outlined at the beginning of the chapter about adult literacy students being non-functioning members of the community. For most of the students in this one adult literacy class, acquiring literacy skills in English provided an extra dimension of languages to their lives that may have assisted their everyday living. If they felt their own abilities in English were inadequate for some literacy practices, they would have the ready support of others to assist them. Only if they lacked formal competence in their first or native languages did it seem that the acquisition of English literacy would become a major factor in their lives.

Study 3: Adult literacy students and social capital

In the two studies of adult literacy students outlined so far in this chapter, supportive social networks have played a role. In the first study, the comment 'we were like a family' to describe the literacy student group was telling of the role of a new social network for participants, and in the second study, each of the students could access literacy support networks, often involving family members, but not always. Youssef, for example, had someone at work who assisted him with literacy practices, indicating the important role that a literacy support person or mediator could play (Baynham, 1993; Baynham and Lobanga Masing, 2000). The third study in this chapter takes this issue of social networks further by examining the role of social capital for students in adult literacy programmes.

The study, which began in 2005 and was funded by the NCVER, focused on examining the social capital outcomes for students attending adult literacy and numeracy courses. I worked on the study with two other researchers (Balatti and Black, 2011; Balatti, Black and Falk, 2006, 2007; Black, Balatti and Falk, 2006), and we each drew on cohorts of students and their teachers for in-depth interviews from different parts of Australia (Sydney, Townsville and Darwin). In this chapter, I will focus on findings from interviews I conducted with a group of adult literacy students in a Sydney adult literacy programme, along with some comments from the adult literacy teachers (eight were interviewed). In total, twenty students were interviewed from a range of adult literacy classes in a TAFE college, selected on their availability and consent to be interviewed. All the students were born overseas in countries where English was not the main language. Fourteen (70 per cent) were female, and six were male. Most were older students (average 53 years, range 39–73). These demographic trends were no surprise as during the time of our study, a survey was undertaken of an adult literacy programme in one metropolitan TAFE college in which it was found that 95 per cent of students (N = 150) were born overseas in countries where English was not the main language, and most students (82 per cent) were female (Black, McGregor and Lucchinelli, 2006: 13). In our social capital study, the students' countries of birth included China (8), Hong Kong (5), Afghanistan (3), Iran (2), Myanmar (1) and Columbia (1).

The research focus on social capital outcomes from adult literacy courses was new at the time (though a study in Scotland was undertaken at around the same time, see Tett and Maclachlan, 2007). By social capital, we meant 'networks, together with shared norms, values and understandings which facilitate cooperation within or amongst groups' (Australian Bureau of Statistics, 2004: 4). This was the definition our funding organization requested that we apply in our study. Our aim was to explore changes in aspects of student networks resulting from their participation in adult literacy and numeracy courses (Balatti, Black and Falk, 2006). Social capital has been viewed as important for cohesive and healthy societies (Putnam, 2000), and prior to our study, it had been shown to play a role in adult education contexts leading to socio-economic benefits and community development (Balatti and Falk, 2002; Falk, Golding and Balatti, 2000; Field, 2003; Kilpatrick, Field and Falk, 2003). Social capital also had the potential in the field of adult literacy education to be recognized as an additional dimension to programme outcomes. From the early 1990s, these outcomes had been viewed in policy documents largely in relation to human capital (DEET, 1991), measured according to international (OECD and Statistics

Canada, 1995, 2000) and national reporting indicators (Coates et al., 1996). Non-cognitive or dispositional outcomes from participating in adult literacy programmes had long been held to relate to an individual's improved self-confidence and sense of self (Charnley and Jones, 1980; Grant, 1987), but these outcomes, at least in a policy sense, held reduced sway with the rising dominance of human capital discourses. Potentially, there was scope in the study to indicate both human and social capital outcomes, and that together they might interact for improved socio-economic well-being (OECD, 2001).

The understanding of social capital that we applied from the ABS (2004) was multidimensional. It featured not only changes in students' *network types* (i.e. bonding, bridging and linking ties) but other dimensions such as *network qualities*, including people's changing levels of trust and sense of efficacy; *network structures*, including changes in the size of the network and the nature of membership; and *network transactions*, including the sharing of support and knowledge within networks (Balatti, Black and Falk, 2006).

Most of the students participated in small-group adult literacy classes with up to eight students and the classes were conducted within the traditional student needs-based pedagogy (Black and Bee, 2018b; Osmond, 2021). Some classes had more students (15–18) and were taught by two teachers in a team-teaching arrangement. In the process of participating in the adult literacy programme, the students were entering into new social networks. These included networks with other students, with individual teachers, and with the formal network of the classroom as a whole. Students working and relating with other students in the class was often a key network. While all the students had diverse cultural and linguistic backgrounds, they also shared commonalities as students in a class, including the bond of wishing to improve their English literacy abilities. Their stated aim was usually expressed as 'to improve my English' and this related to both their spoken and written English. The teachers were employed primarily to teach English literacy and not ESOL, but the students were unconcerned at the pedagogical differences, and in practice the classes included an emphasis on spoken English (Hammond et al., 1992). The adult literacy programme was a shared opportunity for students to engage in an English-speaking learning context where they could improve both their spoken and written English.

Friendships developed between students that often extended beyond the classroom, and there were many instances cited in the interviews of students meeting with other students for shopping and social visits to each other's homes. In some cases, they shared common languages and cultures, as with Barbara (fifty-five years) and Jill (forty-nine years). They were both Cantonese-speaking former Hong Kong residents and they went to the gym together several times a week. Their living circumstances, however, were different insofar as Barbara worked part-time as a dental technician, while Jill was not working and lived with her daughter (26) and son (10) at home in Sydney. Her husband worked in Hong Kong and only returned home during school term breaks. Jill said she sometimes felt lonely in Sydney and Barbara had become her 'best friend'.

Social isolation and loneliness at home were features of some of the other students' lives. Mya, fifty-four years, for example, like Jill, was living in Sydney with her daughter (at university) and son (13, at school), while her husband was working overseas. She had qualifications as an accountant from Myanmar but felt she needed to improve her English before she could work in any capacity in Australia. Narek, fifty-two years, was another example of social isolation. Born in Iran and speaking Armenian, he had previously worked in a factory but was now unemployed and living at home with his elderly mother. He said he had a 'zero' social life and valued the opportunity to mix with other students to practise his English. So anxious was he for social interaction and the opportunity to practise English that sometimes he even made an excuse to engage in conversation with bank staff 'for some loan or something ... they took one hour you know'.

In addition to individual friendship networks developing among the students, the class group was also an important network with its own set of norms. A teacher demonstrated this with a story of a recalcitrant student (a rarity in adult literacy classes) in a night class. The student was the only one in the group who was not working during the day, and he was very demanding of the teacher, wanting her complete attention to the detriment of time spent with others in the class. He was also quite rude and aggressive to other students, and yet despite this, according to the teacher, 'they were fitting in with him, they were accommodating him and his demands'. The teacher finally confronted the student in private and, with reference to an official statement on college students' rights and responsibilities, explained how his attitude and actions were intimidating for other students, and unfair to them. He was then absent for the next lesson, but the following week he was back, and the teacher explained: 'The others were very, very good to him, they all rallied round and deliberately included him in things and deliberately spoke to him.' In subsequent lessons the teacher claimed:

> There was a dramatic turn-around. He's getting on with another fellow and chatting in the break ... He actually moved from one end of the table down into the group because the others were speaking a little bit softly, and he moved down to hear it. I couldn't believe it.

This story was an illustration of compliance with shared group norms, and how they were established and maintained by both the teacher and the students (for a social network analysis, see Balatti, Black and Falk, 2006: 35–6).

The relationship an individual student had with the teacher comprised an additional, separate social network, and in many cases, they were examples of trust involving private communication between the individual student and teacher. They were often enacted in informal, private spaces such as during class breaks or after the formal lesson had concluded. For example, one of the teachers described how she started to connect on a more personal level with an Afghan woman in her class: 'Oh, she was looking really unhappy one day, and just when everybody had left, and she was the last to leave, and so I just spoke to her then' (Black and Bee, 2018b: 192). What the teacher learnt was that the student was living in an abusive household with her brother-in-law and mother-in-law: 'he was just checking on every movement … she was virtually like a prisoner and so were the children'. The teacher maintained the relationship with the student as a trusted confidante, during which time the student moved out of the abusive household. Sometime later, when the student had progressed to a different class, the teacher continued to show concern for the student: 'I just say how's your family going, and she says everything is so good'.

Another example of a trusting network developing between teacher and student was provided by a teacher who applied the teaching strategy of letter writing, ostensibly as a means to improve students' literacy skills. Students would write to her on a regular basis, and she would reply individually to them by letter. One of her students wrote that she wanted to bring her mother's ashes from Hong Kong to her home in Sydney and did not know how to do this. As the teacher stated, 'she would never have said that in class'. It was a deeply personal issue for the student and was a demonstration of trust in the teacher. After the teacher enquired and contacted the relevant government departments for information to relay to the student in writing, the student, months later, wrote to the teacher to inform her that 'her mother's ashes were on the way out, and she could have them rest in the Buddhist temple where she went' (Balatti, Black and Falk, 2006: 34). As these two examples have demonstrated, teachers were a rich resource for students in ways apart from their expertise as literacy teachers. Students had the opportunity to get to know teachers well and could draw on their knowledge, skills and networks.

The classroom network was the site of formal pedagogy where teachers and students as a group interacted together. Except that in the case of adult literacy classrooms, the aim was often to provide a relatively informal learning environment where the teacher was not assumed to be the source of authority and knowledge; rather, these were shared between teachers and students (Black and Bee, 2018b; Lee and Wickert, 1995). Lesson content, for example, was often initiated from students and was based on their interests, aspirations and everyday living: 'In other words, in this network, students have full membership by simply being themselves' (Balatti, Black and Falk, 2006: 36).

We concluded in our study that the adult literacy course-related networks to which students became members served as 'a practice field and they are bridges' (Balatti, Black and Falk, 2006: 36). As a 'practice field' there were multiple examples provided in the interviews. One student in a night class, for example, spoke of being bullied at work – he had moved up a promotional level and other workers were unhappy about it. The other students in the class were very supportive of the student ('people just said to him, hang in there'), and the teacher then featured bullying as a discussion topic in the class. In time, the bullying stopped with the student more cognizant of how to deal with it in the workplace. Following on from the bullying topic, another night student in the same class, who worked as a housecleaner, spoke about her employer who had been criticizing her work, telling her: 'I am not doing it well, I should be doing this, and I should be doing that, and I don't know whether to stand up to her or not.' This also became a class discussion ('we talked about what you can do'), and according to the teacher, the student subsequently responded to her employer in a way that seemed effective:

> she said: 'but you didn't ask me to do this … you are not happy with what I am doing, but you don't tell me beforehand what you want to me to do,' so she actually confronted her employer, quite nicely.

In both of the above examples, individual students were supported by the classroom network of teacher and peers, and they were given the opportunity to discuss and learn how to manage various social practices in their everyday working lives. Many other examples were provided of students learning how to navigate the social practices of everyday living. In some cases, they involved role-playing in the classroom as students practised making phone calls for various appointments, how to write absentee letters to teachers, and how to engage in person with the teachers of their children. One student, Linda, forty-four years of age and from China, explained how she could now explain to her son's teacher that her son needed ESL tuition. Another student complained in person to the teacher of her six-year-old daughter that a boy in the class had kicked her daughter.

With many of these social practices, students learnt not only the appropriate language and literacy norms but how to be more assertive to develop a sense of efficacy. When a mother with self-acknowledged poor English language and literacy skills confronted an authority figure such as the schoolteacher of her child, it required agency, belief that she/he could have a personal influence on an outcome. In another example, a teacher explained how her classroom activities had influenced the agency of one of her students in the way that her student interacted with her doctor:

> We've been doing quite a bit on health because they find that a very threatening area of their life and one them experienced one of the problems we looked at in the newspaper articles, and that was the first time she had opened up and she said this is true, because this happened to me, and my doctor said it's going to take six months to get that out of my system. And that actually helped her because she went back to the doctor and talked to him and said why is this not working for me? That was something she had not done before. She had not questioned the doctor in what he had said was wrong with her.

Beyond their role as a practice field, classroom networks worked as 'bridges' to link students to other networks and institutions. For example, one student sought to donate blood after a lesson involving the topic in class. Other students participated in the 'Clean Up Australia' campaign. In one lesson, the health benefits of dancing were discussed, and as a result, unbeknown to the teacher or the students, a student originally from Hong Kong took up modern dancing seriously and joined several different dancing groups. Months later in a class discussion on hobbies, he spoke about his dancing, and the class, including teacher, practised dance moves in the classroom and later travelled to a dance club for a lesson. Two students subsequently started dancing lessons.

The network comprising the formal classroom may also be extended to incorporate a feature of many adult literacy programmes – excursions and external visits. There were many such visits for students to a wide array of institutions and locations, including law courts, art galleries, museums, restaurants, farms, zoos, and scenic areas, including beaches. Thus, students were introduced to institutions, networks and cultural practices that hitherto had been beyond their own networks and experiences. Teachers also encouraged students to volunteer in the local community and links were established with community-run organizations. This was appropriate for many students who were in a post-work life phase, but it also provided opportunities for other students to gain paid work. One initiative linked to a community volunteer organization saw some students volunteer in a childcare programme which subsequently led to paid roles. Other students volunteered for activities such as 'meals on wheels' and visits to aged care centres (Black, Lucchinelli and Flynn, 2006).

When we first planned for our study of adult literacy and numeracy students, we were unsure that we would find evidence of social capital outcomes. Our study findings, however, indicated quite the contrary, as this chapter has demonstrated. The various networks involving students and teachers provided a new and safe environment in which to play out new aspects of identity and to practise new skills. The resources developed included new attitudes and beliefs about self and others, new ways of interaction and new links and connections (Balatti, Black and Falk, 2006).

Concluding comments

This chapter began with stereotypical perspectives of adult literacy students as deficient, non-functioning adults in the community, 'desperately hobbled' in their everyday lives. While this was a perspective promoted in 1970s research, it was suggested that the same perspective prevails half a century later in contemporary Australia, as demonstrated by a recent television documentary series on adult literacy and also by many of the public submissions to the recent federal government enquiry into 'Adult literacy and its importance'. At the conclusion of this chapter, however, a quite different perspective on adult literacy students has been presented by seeking and documenting their perspectives on the role of literacy in their lives. These students were almost exclusively from culturally and linguistically diverse communities in Sydney and they typified the adult literacy student population in many urban TAFE colleges in and around Sydney. The students did not fit the stereotypical deficit label. They were engaged, multilingual members of Australian society, who, through participating in an adult literacy course, were actively seeking membership of a broad range of networks in Australian society that would add to their socio-economic well-being. Many of these students were well credentialed within their own cultural and linguistic groups. According to one characterization of adult literacy students in the research literature, these students could be termed 'competent comrade', that is, 'dedicated, motivated, engaged, self-reliant, and resilient learners' (Belzer and Pickard, 2015: 9). These students did not experience the type of personal shame and stigma reflected for example by the 'heroic victims' in the *Lost for*

Words TV documentary. Moreover, one of the participants in our social capital study, Hajira, a thirty-nine years of age, Afghan woman who had formerly spent eight years as a lawyer in Afghanistan, commented explicitly that 'I never shame because I don't know this language'. She was now desperately trying to improve both her spoken and written English, and at the time of the research she was in the process of planning a new career (in childcare). Many other students were engaged and contributed constructively in local communities with paid and unpaid voluntary roles.

7

Marginalized Young People and Literacy

You're not screamed at, like, you're not feeling pressured completely. I think a lot of people perform a lot better because they are not being jumped on every ten minutes.
    (Sophie, seventeen, commenting on her experiences of the TAFE course)

Like, now I can do my own taxes and do my own banking because I actually understand what I'm doing. And I couldn't spell, I was the worst speller, and I can spell lots of words, (and) just speaking properly.
    (Chloe, eighteen, commenting on outcomes from the TAFE course)

Introduction: Marginalized young people

This chapter examines the role of literacy in the lives of a group of young people, all teenagers (with one exception) and early school leavers. The interviews with the young people were undertaken as part of an NCVER-funded project on social capital outcomes from adult literacy and numeracy courses (Balatti, Black and Falk, 2006), and later published in a journal article (Black, Balatti and Falk, 2010). Most of the young people had left school because they disliked teachers or the regulatory school system, and they had a 'second-chance' education through their enrolment in a TAFE pre-vocational 'enabling course' (Ross and Gray, 2005) that essentially assisted them to obtain the qualification that they would have achieved had they completed Year 10 at school. This qualification was the School Certificate, and the TAFE equivalent course they were enrolled in was the Certificate in General and Vocational Education (CGVE). In an important sense, this TAFE course was their attempt to compensate for having left school early without the School Certificate. It represented 'unfinished business', a chance to prove to themselves and others that they could return to education and succeed (Munns and McFadden, 2000). The research project was undertaken in 2005–6, and it should be noted that a few years later in 2010–11, with the raising of the school leaving age from fifteen to seventeen, the School Certificate was discontinued by the NSW Department of Education and replaced with a Record of School Achievement (RoSA).

Commonly, the term 'at risk' is used to describe young people disengaged from school (e.g. Hancock and Zubrick, 2015). In this chapter, I have used the term 'marginalized' young people in preference following the argument that 'at risk' suggests personal deficiencies in young people, that they are the 'problem' that represents a risk to themselves and society, and they are in some way in need of 'fixing'. There have been fears that young people lacking academic skills and leaving school early will become unproductive members of society as NEETs (not in employment, education or training; see OECD, 2013: 70–80). While the 'at risk' label suggests young people are the ones who are the problem, this perspective ignores what may be wrong with schooling (Smyth and McInerney, 2013). 'Marginalized', on the other hand, indicates inequalities faced by young people through their relationship with schooling and society generally (te Riele, 2006, 2007; Wyn and White, 1997).

The students differed quite markedly from the adult literacy students featured in the previous chapter. These were young people transitioning from school to vocational education and employment (Wyn, 2006), except that for some students, following their TAFE course, they intended to return to the school system to undertake their Higher School Certificate (university entrance level). These young people, as early school leavers, are usually viewed by dominant society in deficit terms and often labelled troublemakers due to the conflicts they were involved in, often with teachers while at school. It has been argued that students leaving school early, either through being 'eased out' or 'pushed out', depended largely on how they accommodated 'relational power':

> [I]t is largely because of the way the relational space within schools and educational policies is being constructed (or foreclosed) for them in ways that young people feel are inconsistent with the identities they are pursuing for themselves.
>
> (Smyth and McInerney, 2013: 44)

Schools can be places of inclusion for students who are prepared to conform to middle-class cultural norms, but places of exclusion for students whose identities are not consistent with these norms, particularly those portrayed as deviant and often from working-class backgrounds. The dominant view is that these 'deviant' students are the problem, 'and not the social institution of schooling or the middle-class values that underpin it' (Smyth and McInerney, 2013: 44). Smyth and McInerney (2013) provided in-depth case studies of young people in socio-economically disadvantaged areas who had left school early and were subsequently involved in 're-engagement programmes'. These 'failures' or 'no-hopers' found schools were uncaring institutions 'where learning was divorced from their own lives, emotions and aspirations' (2013: 51). But they regarded the re-engagement programmes as 'havens' where they could 'reclaim some degree of self-respect and control over their learning' (2013: 51). In conclusion, however, Smyth and McInerney (2013) indicated that while re-engagement programmes offered a more humane approach to learning by teachers working with the best of intentions, the emphasis on applied learning limited students' job prospects to 'low-skilled, insecure, and poorly paid areas of the workforce in a context where academic qualifications count the most' (2013: 51).

The above account by Smyth and McInerney resonates in many ways with the study examined in this chapter, except that the re-engagement programme, the TAFE CGVE, was not viewed by students as an applied, vocational course; rather, it was an academic course insofar as it replicated much of the Year 10 curriculum at school. As this chapter will indicate, there were some students who aspired to academic qualifications beyond Year 10 level.

Unlike in the previous chapter on adult literacy programmes, literacy is not the explicit focus in this chapter insofar as literacy (and also numeracy) was largely integrated within the CGVE course. While invariably these young students experienced low levels of literacy and numeracy according to normative testing criteria, improving their literacy and numeracy was not their primary aim. Their aim was to gain their School Certificate equivalent, and in so doing, this was a demonstration that they had achieved a level of literacy and numeracy commensurate with Year 10 school leaving. Many jobs at the time stipulated the School Certificate as the minimum educational level required.

The TAFE course featured in this chapter was taught by the adult basic education (ABE) section of the college, or rather, the AFE (Adult Foundation Education) section, a change of name common to many ABE sections in TAFE in this era. The young students were usually enrolled in TAFE literacy and numeracy course units in addition to being enrolled in CGVE study units, but literacy and numeracy were taught essentially as part of the CGVE, that is, they were integrated. Thus, the type of literacy and numeracy taught was not, as with the adult literacy students in the previous chapter, in 'stand-alone' programmes focused on everyday literacy and numeracy practices. Instead, literacy and numeracy were taught as school subjects, and in the case of literacy, a 'schooled' literacy, in line with the 'autonomous' model of literacy (Cook-Gumperz, 2006; Street, 1984, 1993; Street and Street, 1991). In this chapter, therefore, the focus on what literacy meant to people and how it affected their everyday living became, in effect, what their School Certificate (or equivalent) meant to them and how having (or not having) the qualification affected their lives.

Social capital and re-engagement with education

The research with these marginalized students was undertaken as part of a broader study funded by the NCVER which examined the social capital outcomes of adult literacy and numeracy courses (Balatti, Black and Falk, 2006). The students in this chapter comprised one of the Sydney research groups. Other research groups included the multilingual adult literacy students examined in the previous chapter and student groups located in Townsville and Darwin. This study of social capital outcomes from adult literacy and numeracy courses (details in the previous chapter) adopted the ABS (2004) definition of social capital as 'networks, together with shared norms, values and understandings which facilitate cooperation within or amongst groups' (Australian Bureau of Statistics, 2004: 4). The intention was to explore aspects of the social networks of students that resulted from their participation in the course and particularly their relations with other students and teachers. We focused on how these networks affected the students, and others, including their families. We also examined the pedagogical conditions that produced these networks.

This research was undertaken at a time of heightened interest in the role of social capital, particularly in relation to young people who were disengaged from their families, school and mainstream society. As indicated earlier in this chapter, social relationships were key to understanding why some students failed to succeed at school and left early (Smyth and McInerney, 2013). In the literature, social capital was viewed as a resource which could variously help to construct identities and provide young people with the tools to navigate transitions to further education, employment and adulthood. Different types of social networks involving bonding, bridging and linking ties influenced how young people related with others, particularly their families, peer groups and authority figures such as teachers (Barker, 2012; Bassani, 2007; Boeck, 2009; Bottrell, 2008; Holland, Reynolds and Weller, 2007; Raffo and Reeves, 2000; Shildrick and MacDonald, 2008; te Riele, 2006).

By definition, marginalized young people are peripheral to or disengaged from mainstream schooling, and for them to re-engage successfully in education and learning requires either modifications within mainstream schooling, or participation in alternative forms of schooling. Much research attention in the past decade has been focused on alternative forms of schooling or 'flexible' learning programmes designed to meet the particular learning needs of marginalized young people. Common features of such programmes identified in the research literature include the following: learning activities are 'meaningful' and relevant to young people; participation is voluntary; the learning environment is relaxed, flexible and unlike traditional schooling; learning is individualized to meet student needs; relationships between students and teaching staff are supportive, connected and respectful, and students are accepted for who they are; and links are provided to a range of other educational and vocational agencies (e.g. Bradshaw, 2001; Chodkiewicz, Widin and Yasukawa, 2010; McGinty et al., 2018; McGregor et al., 2015; Mills and McGregor, 2010; Murray and Mitchell, 2016; Smyth and McInerney, 2013; Spielhofer, Marson-Smith and Evans, 2009; te Riele, 2019). Social capital features strongly in these programmes, particularly in terms of how teachers and students connect to each other in social networks, ensuring that marginalized young people feel they 'belong' in these networks (te Riele, 2018).

The TAFE programme on which we based our research included all the features outlined above for alternative, 'flexible' programmes for marginalized young people. The programme was officially called 'CGVE flex' to differentiate it from the mainstream CGVE programme undertaken by other groups of students at the same TAFE college. All students worked on their own individualized study programme and sought assistance from teachers when they needed it. The individualized programme followed a negotiation process between teachers and students to determine which CGVE units of study students were to undertake and their learning goals and expected progress. Regular meetings were held between individual students and their assigned mentor teacher. All the study was self-paced, and students' work was assignment-based – there were no formal exams. The teaching/learning space in the TAFE college comprised three open-access classrooms in which several teachers at a time were rostered and available to help students on a one-to-one basis as required. The aim of this classroom structure was for students to take responsibility for their own learning in meeting their negotiated learning goals and to access teachers readily when needed. As explained earlier, literacy and numeracy were 'integrated' within the CGVE course subjects, with the pedagogical focus on students achieving their negotiated goals. A further aspect of the 'flexible' programme was the relative absence of rule-bound routines associated with the school system. Student participation was part-time and timetabled to attend on specific days of the week, usually three days a week. This part-time aspect of the programme meant that many of the students could also be engaged in various types of part-time work, often casualized service delivery-type jobs. It was an adult learning environment in which students were expected to take responsibility for their learning, and hence it was an environment that could accommodate students choosing when to leave the study area for short breaks. Students could enrol for the programme at any time of the year and complete the course at any time, depending on their progress.

The research study and participant profiles

A total of thirteen students and five teachers (including the head teacher of the programme) were interviewed individually for the research. These interviews were analysed and published in a research journal article (Black, Balatti and Falk, 2010), and many of the students' comments in this chapter are drawn from this journal article. All interviews were semi-structured and tape-recorded. As researchers have indicated, interviewing marginalized young people can be problematic, in part because young people may not know or necessarily trust an independent researcher (McGinty, Bursey and Babacan, 2018). In my research at this TAFE site, I was the sole researcher/interviewer, and the trust that enabled honest and reflective responses from the interviewees was to a large extent facilitated by the teaching staff on the TAFE programme. While I was a researcher, I was also a TAFE teacher from another college. Following my consultations and visits to the college, the teachers trusted me, and the students in turn trusted them. The teachers located individual students for the research and briefly explained the purpose of the interviews, and I followed that up at the beginning of each interview with my own explanation and written consents by the students. In this way, students generally appeared to be happy to talk with me about their experiences at school and in the TAFE programme.

Leaving aside one student who was twenty-three years of age, the average age of the students was sixteen (four students were fifteen). Six were male; seven were female. While the study was small scale, it contributed to what has been termed the 'dearth' of studies that have focused on what young people say about their education, 'and particularly those who have been disenfranchised by their educational experiences' (McGinty, Bursey and Babacan, 2018: 63). All the students in the study fell within this 'disenfranchised' category, deprived of completing school, and they all expressed negative perspectives on their previous schooling experiences. Their alienation and subsequent disconnection from school were often accompanied by low socio-economic backgrounds and familial dislocations, though it needs to be stated that the catchment area of the TAFE college was an area of Sydney not considered socio-economically disadvantaged. While youth and a dislike of school to the extent they could no longer attend were common to all students, their individual backgrounds and life circumstance were diverse, as the following vignettes of just four students illustrate.

Adam, seventeen, had left school two years previously at the beginning of Year 10 because, in his words, he 'got sick of it'. He then enrolled in the TAFE CGVE 'flex' course, but discontinued soon after because, as a self-confessed 'angry type of person', he became involved in drugs and some property damage and was 'kicked out' of home. The culmination of his antisocial activities was a court appearance and a one-night stay in a juvenile offenders' unit, which had a sobering effect on him. The juvenile justice authorities agreed that he could return home to his parents, and he subsequently rejoined the TAFE course: 'I said that I'd do TAFE, get my Year 10, and I really wanted to do it.'

Olivia, at fifteen, was one of the youngest students in the TAFE course. She had problems at home and at school: 'Well, I moved into a foster home, and school was just big trouble, I was getting in trouble, and I wasn't going.' She said her home circumstances (change of foster parents) and school had become 'just too much pressure', and some of her friends on the TAFE course encouraged her to join them: 'they just said come join, it's OK'. Her life since joining the TAFE course had turned around, having made new friends ('my entire social group changed') and progressed well in the course. She spoke now of the possibility of completing her HSC (Year 12) after she had finished the TAFE course.

Not all the students had troubled home lives, and reasons for leaving school varied. *Sophie*, seventeen, for example, had moved from her country town to Sydney, and despite being 'a straight A' student at school, she said she was 'very unsettled in my lifestyle at the time' and chose to leave school and enrol in the TAFE course. She commented that she enjoyed the flexibility of the TAFE course (allowing her to work), and unlike school, 'you're not screamed at, like, you're not feeling pressured completely. I think a lot of people perform a lot better because they are not being jumped on every ten minutes'. At the time of the interview, she was living independently (in shared accommodation with another girl) and was working long hours ('I do about fifty-five hours' per week') doing waitressing and barista work. She called this work 'an in-between thing' as she had quite definitive vocational plans following completion of the CGVE course: 'as soon as I finish this, I plan to start a Diploma in Childcare through TAFE' (Black, Balatti and Falk, 2010: 108).

Another student, *Chloe*, the second oldest student at eighteen, dropped out of school in Year 10 and joined the TAFE course two years later. She said she started to develop problems at school following a cancer diagnosis:

> So, I started to get into a lot of trouble at school with teachers because, just the discipline, like they don't all want to know your problems, it's all black and white, and it was just too difficult. I couldn't keep up with everyone 'cos I kept leaving school.

After leaving school early, *Chloe* had proven to be resourceful, volunteering in a hospital and a church, and starting her own business 'doing fairy birthday parties'. To develop her business, she felt she needed a Year 10 certificate:

> [L]ike now I can do my own taxes and do my own banking because I actually understand what I'm doing. And I couldn't spell, I was the worst speller, and I can spell lots of words, just speaking properly.

She also had high career aspirations following the CGVE, planning to enrol firstly in a real-estate management course and later to study law at university. She considered she was now a role model for other students in the TAFE course:

> Well, they knew me in school, and I was kinda troublemaker. I got in a lot of trouble, so they knew that I was, you know, wasn't very smart ... I couldn't read properly, and now they've seen all this work I've done.

These four vignettes of students indicated the diversity of the students, but what they had in common was their marginalization from school and a desire for an education (cf. McGinty, Bursey and Babacan, 2018).

Social networks

When students started the programme at TAFE, they were introduced to new social networks with new norms and values. How the students managed their role within these networks, and in particular, whether they felt they were accepted and belonged in these networks, determined whether or how they progressed in the course. The new network of fellow peers seemed particularly important.

The head teacher of the programme made the observation: 'If they don't form a friendship almost straight away, then they are not going to last' (Black, Balatti and Falk, 2010: 111). On this basis, some students did not last and left the course very early, but those who were interviewed in the research were current participants in the programme and they had made friends straight away. They indicated that making friends was quite easy, and acceptance and belonging in the peer network was not a problem, as the following two comments attest:

> 'I made friends very quickly. Everyone here are nothing like students at school. They're accepting of people, really nice'
>
> (Patrick)

> 'Actually, I made friends straight away. Oh yeah, first day. Everyone is just more, like, you know, in school they're a bit bitchy, and if you're not in the cool group, it's not ... here they're just nice, and it's just more maturity type of thing' (Georgia).
>
> (Black, Balatti and Falk, 2010: 111)

Most students when they first enrolled at TAFE did not already know other students, and for some it was a completely different social scene. Olivia, for example, said, 'I've made heaps of friends here, my entire social grouping has changed. I'm doing a lot better now because I'm not hanging about with the bad kind of people' (Black, Balatti and Falk, 2010: 111).

At least as significant as peer groups, and more so in relation to the educational outcomes for students, was the course-related network of teachers and students. This was particularly significant in view of the previous experiences that many of these students had with teachers at school where teachers were seen to be a major factor in their marginalization from school. Some of the students' comments about their former teachers at school included:

> I used to hate teachers. (Elle)
> They (teachers) treat you like you're six years old. (Patrick)
> I wasn't really agreeing with the teachers on anything. (Emily)

Teacher–student relations represented perhaps the greatest contrast between the students' previous school lives and their TAFE lives, due in part to the way that teachers interacted with students on a one-to-one basis as the students worked through their individualized learning programmes. The students spoke of their relationship with their TAFE teachers in very positive terms. Typically, one student said, 'They're just friendlier. They don't hassle you' (Elle) (Black,

Balatti and Falk, 2010: 112). Another student, in response to the question, 'What do you like best about coming to the programme?' replied: 'I would have to say the teachers. I have a good relationship with them. Everyone's friends here, everyone talks here, and I just like coming' (Georgia) (Black, Balatti and Falk, 2010: 112). These comments related to the formal pedagogical network of teachers and students in the classrooms, but there were also other less formal networks involving teachers and students in activities beyond the classrooms. For example, one of the teachers on the programme invited a student to a weekend youth group that was quite independent of the TAFE programme. On another occasion, the same teacher invited a student along to a popular music event because she had a spare ticket as her own daughter did not want to attend. In another example, one of the students involved himself in a local drama group, and at one of his performances, several of the teachers came along to watch him. Further, these informal networks of teachers and students interacting together extended beyond the Year 10 course, with teachers commenting that ex-students often called in to the TAFE programme just for a chat with the teachers.

Teachers provided insights into the nature of the course-related learning network that appeared to result in positive relations between teachers and students. A couple of the teachers mentioned the 'connection' and respect they had with individual students which may well have differed from formal school learning contexts. As one teacher explained:

> They feel, I think, because the course is individualised, we treat them as individuals, and we do respect them. I think that they feel they're a somebody here, and they didn't feel that at school. They felt they were just one of the masses, there was no flexibility. But they do feel that here. They feel that we hear what they're saying.
>
> (Black, Balatti and Falk, 2010: 112)

As another teacher explained: 'I think we act with them very naturally. But we joke, we have good laughs sometimes. We're warm ... We listen to them, to what they're saying, what they're thinking' (Black, Balatti and Falk, 2010: 112). The students appeared to respond well to this level of informality and to genuinely enjoy engaging with teachers. One of the students, Sophie, commented: 'Like, today's my day off work, but I'd rather come here than stay at home because I get to have a conversation with the teachers and have a laugh and still do my work' (Black, Balatti and Falk, 2010: 112). Another illustration of this 'connection' between teachers and students was how students responded when they met teachers in the community, such as in local shopping centres. One teacher saw this as a measure of how she knew when she had done a good job: 'The first thing is they've got a CGVE. The second thing is, they're pleasant to you, and when they're out on the street they'll say hello' (Black, Balatti and Falk, 2010: 112). Linked to this comment, and also illustrating the student–teacher connection, another teacher explained her dilemma when female students insisted on hugging her when they met in the nearby shopping mall. The issue of reciprocation was difficult for this teacher, given the official advice provided to teachers by child protection courses. She explained: 'We still hug them, but then we get nervous that we shouldn't be doing this. But I mean, if they make the move, how could you back away?' (Black, Balatti and Falk, 2010: 112).

This is not to say that every student adapted seamlessly into their new networks and their participation was a success. Those who did not make friends quickly, as indicated earlier, often left the programme early with little benefit from the programme. And inevitably there were teething problems as some students initially expected confrontation with teachers, and others, while they enjoyed the programme's social environment, found that actually re-engaging with formal study took a lot longer. One student, Georgia, said that at the beginning of the course, 'I didn't really come at all, for three months straight I didn't come'. But later she changed and started attending all the time: 'Now I got my life planned out and I kinda know what I want to do' (Black, Balatti and Falk, 2010: 113).

A key aspect of a social capital approach to pedagogy, certainly in the area of adult literacy and numeracy, is the establishment of classroom norms that ensure students feel safe to explore new learning opportunities. As the authors of the main social capital study stated, adult literacy and numeracy teachers who apply a social capital approach to their teaching establish norms with their learners that

> produce a social-emotional environment in which tolerance and good manners prevail; in which new students are welcomed; where students feel safe to take risks and share; where people listen patiently when others talk; and where being non-judgemental is paramount.
>
> (Balatti, Black and Falk, 2006: 35)

This learning environment was referred to in the previous chapter as a 'practice field' (Balatti, Black and Falk, 2006: 36) for students to play out new aspects of identity. Aspects of this 'practice field' have already been outlined in this chapter in terms of the new relationships students established with teachers that were different to their former experiences with 'authority figures' at school. As suggested in the above quotation, another important element of this learning environment was tolerance to difference, and in this TAFE programme for young people, there was a specific policy understood by all, that there was to be no 'bagging' (a colloquial term meaning to 'make fun of' or 'insult'). As a teacher explained:

> We've got all sorts of kids. We've got kids here that don't fit the mould. They might say something, but they know you don't bag anyone here, there are no put-downs. So, most of the kids feel pretty safe. Sometimes someone will say something, but if you pull them into line they know ... Oh, ok, I shouldn't have said that, because it's not fair. They know that. But they know that they're not going to be put down either.
>
> (Black, Balatti and Falk, 2010: 113)

To 'pull them into line' in this case may have involved nothing more than a reminder to them or the group as a whole that 'bagging' others was not part of the classroom norms. Another important element of classroom norms was the absence of embarrassment at requesting help from a teacher. The individualized structure of the programme assisted this process because all students were working at their own pace on their individualized programmes. As one teacher noted: 'There's no stigma attached if you're really struggling with your maths and you need one of us to sit with you' (Black, Balatti and Falk, 2010: 113). This last example and others showed that how teachers interacted and connected with students had a lot to do with the flexible, individualized programme structure in this TAFE programme, and that these two aspects went hand in hand. Teachers found they could relate informally and in a relaxed manner with students partly because they were not bound to enforce rigid rules involving, for example, dress codes, late passes and permission slips to go to the toilet, that were typically found in school-based learning environments.

The underlying pedagogical philosophy was that, within the bounds of teacher accountability, it was up to them, the students, to take greater responsibility for their own behaviour. The teacher's role was to be as supportive as possible, to encourage them and to remind them at times (sometimes often and quite directly) that they were falling behind in their goals. It was the programme structure with its focus on students working towards their individualized goals that enabled teachers to not constantly be telling students to do things, as one teacher explained:

> I don't just say, you do, because that doesn't work with these kids. That's how school was, and school didn't work, so you set yourself up for conflict. The

learning that comes from them now has to come from them wanting to learn. So, if they're outside and I go to round them up to get them in, I don't say, you've got to come. I'll say, ok, your goal is ... now, are we going to meet those goals, you've got two week's left ... ? So, it's all the time making them make the decision, take responsibility for their learning. (Black, Balatti and Falk, 2010: 113)

Programme outcomes – human and social capital

Both the students and the teachers of this TAFE CGVE course indicated positive course outcomes. These outcomes could be seen to comprise two main types of capital: human and social, and both were evident from the interviews conducted in this study. Human capital outcomes are usually associated with the acquisition of qualifications and skills which in turn can lead to improved economic benefits. One of the key course outcomes for these students was obtaining their CGVE (Year 10 equivalent) which demonstrated they had acquired a requisite level of academic skills, and in particular, literacy and numeracy. It was difficult to be definitive about this outcome for this group of students because the interviews were conducted at a time when they were working towards obtaining their CGVE. From student and teacher comments, however, it would seem that most students who undertook the programme either completed their CGVE, gained employment or were accepted into a vocational course. For many of the students interviewed, completing the CGVE was a foregone conclusion based on their progress in the course to date. Elle, for example, stated she had 'only got another two or three weeks to go', and Sophie said she would finish 'hopefully, first or second week next term'. As a reflection of the inevitability of gaining their CGVE, many students had clear plans for what they wanted to do beyond the CGVE. Some comments included:

> When I finish here, I'm going straight into the Reserves (Army) and go as far as I can in the Reserves (Patrick)
> I want to do a computer course after this (Elle)
> As soon as I finish this, I plan to start a Diploma in Childcare through TAFE (Sophie). (These quotes are cited in Black, Balatti and Falk, 2010: 108.)

Other students planned to continue their studies to the next level beyond Year 10 (the Higher School Certificate – HSC) or get an apprenticeship (plumbing and electrical were mentioned). Interestingly, and quite remarkably, considering the background of these students, it was not unusual for students to rejoin the school system for further studies, and one of the teachers said that 'quite a few' students from the previous year had gone back to school to do their HSC. One of the students interviewed had actually tried to go back to school while on the TAFE programme, and the only factor holding her back was the school insisting she repeat a year: 'Like, I want to go back to school now, but I couldn't because I wanted to be in the year that I was in' (Georgia) (Black, Balatti and Falk, 2010: 108). Going back to school after previously being disconnected from it was a surprising and significant outcome. This outcome provided an important link with other less tangible course outcomes relating to the second main type of course outcomes, social capital outcomes. For example, one of the teachers explained how a former student with a previous drug habit had obtained her Year 10 at TAFE and then returned for a social visit:

> She came in the other day in a school uniform, and I said, 'How are you going, wearing your uniform and having to be in class?' And she said, 'Nah, it's cool, it's cool. I feel good now. I know where I'm going.' So, it's like, I think they just feel better about themselves and more confident and therefore they're not as angry, therefore they're happy, and they'll take it.
>
> (Black, Balatti and Falk, 2010: 108–09)

What this anecdote appeared to demonstrate was how this student considered she had changed as a person, how she felt about herself, and as a consequence, how she related with others in her social networks. It was certainly the opinion of her former teacher, who knew her very well that this anecdote indicated a significant identity shift on the part of the student.

Quite a few other students in the interviews similarly demonstrated strong personal changes that affected how they related with others in their social networks. These changes in network qualities can be seen to fall largely within the social capital indicator referred to as 'sense of efficacy', that is, action to solve problems in the student's own life or that of others (see Balatti, Black and Falk, 2006: 17). Bandura (1995: 2) defined self-efficacy as 'the belief in one's capabilities to organize and execute the courses of action required to manage prospective situations'. In other words, it relates to a person's belief in their ability to succeed in particular situations. These young people seemed to be taking greater control of their lives and took personal responsibility for their actions and how their actions might affect others. Georgia, for example, the young girl who wanted to return to school, stated: 'I'm so different, it's not funny. I'm more mature, I'm more independent' (Black, Balatti and Falk, 2010: 109). Another student, Sophie, also expressed how she felt better about herself and her ability to take control over her life:

> I'm actually a lot more proud of myself because I know I'm doing this all on my own ... a lot more self-confident in myself to know that I can actually come and do something without being made to go and do it. It's a choice that I make and it makes me feel better.
>
> (Black, Balatti and Falk, 2010: 109)

Another student, Tom, was in a fair bit of trouble at school, and he was basically told by the school to leave. He explained how he felt he had changed on this programme: 'Well, the idea that I can actually work without [being told] ... just kind of rely on myself more to get the work done. It's up to me to get it done.' He also suggested he was not 'so aggressive' and explained that he 'did not get into that much trouble anymore either' (Black, Balatti and Falk, 2010: 109). The above quotes from interviews were indications that students had changed in their beliefs about their own personal influence on their lives, and how they were prepared to act to solve problems in their lives. In a number of cases, the course had enabled students to relate better with adults, especially teachers, and as a consequence some students obtained part-time work. Patrick, for example, had previously found it difficult to interact with adults because he felt they would treat him in the same disrespectful way that he considered he was treated at school:

> Oh, when I was at school, I figured that older people, adults who have power over me, would all be like that. But now, once I come here, I seen that they can treat you as though, treat me the way they should ... I treat them (other people) with a lot more respect, because I realise they're not all like that.
>
> (Black, Balatti and Falk, 2010: 109)

It was Patrick's new-found ability to interact with 'authority figures' which he said was a factor that enabled him to obtain part-time work as a landscaper and builder. Another student, Elle, had never been able to discuss her personal problems with adults before, but now she felt more confident to do so: 'just like counsellors and, you know, all that. Like I never used to be able to talk in general about life and, you know, problems I had' (Black, Balatti and Falk, 2010: 109). These changes to how the young people related to adults were often linked to newly developed trust. Not only were some students beginning to trust others, including 'authority figures', but others were trusting them. Patrick, for example, stated in relation to his mother: 'She's sort of more trusting of me because she knows that when I come here, I come, whereas at school she was constantly asking me what's going on sort of thing, mistrusting me' (Black, Balatti and Falk, 2010: 110). With this trust came changes in other elements of social capital. Emily, for example, commented that she was having a hard time with her parents previously 'and since I left school and came here, I've actually been able to repair those relationships; they're actually enjoying having me around the house' (Black, Balatti and Falk, 2010: 110). This was an example of a change in the nature of a network membership, in this case her family network.

One final area worth documenting in relation to the outcomes of this programme was the reverse-side perspective, the possible outcomes for some students had they not attended the programme. This was not explored specifically in the interviews, but some students did speculate on what might have been, had they not participated in the programme. Adam, for example, said: 'Oh yeah, it'd be a lot different, I'd still be smoking bongs' (Black, Balatti and Falk, 2010: 110). Tom, in a fair bit of trouble at school, stated, 'Like, I don't know, this helped me heaps, like otherwise I probably would be doing drugs or just in depression.' Patrick said, 'I don't know what I would've done because I couldn't go back to school. I'm not sure I would have even tried to do my Year 10' (Black, Balatti and Falk, 2010: 110).

Concluding comments

In light of the disconnection between these students and the school system when they enrolled in the TAFE programme, human capital outcomes in terms of Year 10 completion, planned further studies and part-time work, and social capital outcomes such as increased sense of efficacy, greater trust and generally relating better with adults and their own families, were significant. The interview data would suggest, at least for quite a number of students, a transformation in their lives. They had reconnected with learning and education systems, and they had a new sense of identity that enabled them to interact successfully with others that was in marked contrast to when they first entered the TAFE programme.

These young people were different to the adult groups featured in earlier chapters of this book insofar as their limited abilities in 'schooled' literacy (and numeracy) were incorporated into their formal education situation in not having completed their schooling to Year 10 level. The School Certificate (or rather it's equivalent, the CGVE) was their primary aim. For them, it represented their entree into mainstream society (providing access for example to further education, jobs) that was unavailable to them as school dropouts. In the process of achieving this qualification and reconnecting with learning and education, they experienced a different kind of pedagogy and a different relationship with teachers and the educational system. They had reconstructed their social networks and had created a space for learning, dialogue and confidence building.

8

Vocational Education and Training Students and Literacy

It depends, if I need help with something, I ask my boss at work, or the people at work too.
(Aleyna, sixteen, hairdressing student commenting on the assistance she receives with theory assignments)

The disadvantage of it was it was in their class time, and while they were with her, they were missing out on something.
(Laurinda, hairdressing teacher, commenting on LLN support provided to students during their hairdressing lesson time)

Everyone helps each other, we've become a little family.
(Carol, a student in an aged care course commenting on the role of fellow class members)

VET students, the literacy 'crisis' and social class

In Chapter 1 of this book, I outlined a daily newspaper story, published in the early years of my career in adult literacy education, about the 'fury over illiterate students' in TAFE courses (Black and Sim, 1989). The news story included the claim that students 'cannot read their own textbooks', and while I highlighted a political motivation for the story, the theme of vocational education and training (VET) students being hindered in their studies due to literacy difficulties has remained constant over the ensuing decades. In this chapter, I outline the perspectives of VET students on the role of literacy (and to a lesser extent, numeracy) in their studies. According to the dominant 'crisis narrative' promoted by industry and government policy, large percentages of the adult population are deficient in literacy and numeracy skills, and the issue is particularly significant for adult students undertaking VET courses (Industry Skills Council, 2011; SCOTESE, 2012; Skills Australia, 2010). According to an OECD review of Australian skills based on those falling below level two on the latest PIAAC results, 'around 17 per cent of current post-secondary VET students have low basic skills (literacy or numeracy)' (OECD, 2017: 58).

Few studies in Australia have explored the perspectives of VET students. Indeed, according to some researchers, 'learner voice is rarely sought much less heard' (Angus et al., 2013: 569). In this chapter, I draw on several case studies of the perspectives of students in VET courses. The aim is to present their 'voices' as a counter to the dominant government, business and industry perspectives that have prevailed for the past several decades (Angus et al., 2013). These case studies are drawn from several research projects I have worked on (Black, 2007, 2008a, 2008b; Black and Yasukawa, 2011b), and they indicate a wide variety of narratives as students reflect on their experiences in a range of VET disciplines and pedagogies. As this chapter demonstrates, VET is a diverse field, and it has been argued that no one-size-fits-all approach is appropriate for addressing literacy and numeracy issues (Leach et al., 2010).

The wide range of VET courses undertaken by the students who feature in this chapter include assistant in nursing (aged care), automotive vehicle servicing, beauty, electrical trades, fitness and hairdressing. Predominantly, the students were from working-class backgrounds preparing for working-class jobs. Australia's public VET institution, TAFE was established in the early 1970s 'to redress the disadvantaging impact of class and poverty' (Clemans and Seddon, 2000: 117), and reports in subsequent decades have indicated that VET students generally are from disadvantaged, low socio-economic families and communities (Crump, Connell and Seddon, 1997; Foley, 2007; Lamb, Long and Malley, 1998; National VET Equity Advisory Council, 2010). Related to the social class factor has been the lack of status accorded to TAFE in the Australian community. It has sometimes been referred to as an undervalued 'Cinderella' institution (Fooks, 1994; Rushbrook, 2010), and more commonly as providing a 'second chance' education following students' incomplete or failed schooling (Kell, 2006; Ross and Gray, 2005). As indicated in Chapter 1, in the Further Education system in the UK, which compares with the TAFE system in Australia, researchers have commented that educational provision is seen to be for 'other people's children' (Avis, 2021; Orr, 2018; Thompson, 2009).

The deficit approach to literacy and numeracy support

I begin with an anecdote that illustrates some of the issues to be discussed in this chapter. While employed as a head teacher of adult basic education in a TAFE college in the early 2000s, I received an email from one of the vocational counsellors in the college. He wrote:

> I would like to refer S (name of female student) to ABE for assessment and placement in an appropriate literacy class. S has been enrolled in the Fitness Certificate 3 but is about to withdraw because of her extremely low literacy levels. I have done brief cognitive and literacy assessments and find that while she is within the average range for cognitive potential, she is below the 5th percentile and 1st percentile for her word recognition and spelling respectively. She reports extremely disrupted and unsatisfactory primary and secondary education in her country of birth in Ireland. Could you or your staff contact her?

This email extract was first published as part of an editorial for the academic journal *Literacy and Numeracy Studies* (Black, 2009: 1). My purpose at the time in quoting the email was to demonstrate that this was *not* an example of a social practice model of literacy; moreover, it represented the antithesis, and I used it to draw the contrast between the 'autonomous' model of literacy and the 'social practice' model that featured extensively in the journal articles. In some ways, the email could be seen as a microcosm of dominant perspectives on how low literacy affected VET students and the usual institutional response. Individual students who experienced literacy difficulties in undertaking their courses needed firstly to be assessed by a professional (in this case it was a vocational counsellor) to determine their 'level' of literacy difficulties, followed by remedial treatment in the form of specialized literacy tuition. In other words, this was a deficit approach designed to target and then address an individual's problems. In the case of the fitness course student in the email, the assumption was that at a later stage, following an improvement in her literacy skills, she could recommence her vocational studies with greater success. What in fact happened with this student following her referral to ABE was that she left a phone message with the ABE section in which she cancelled an appointment and explained that she thought we would be wasting our time trying to improve her literacy skills (though she did later become an ABE student receiving one-to-one tuition).

Adult literacy and numeracy (ALN) teachers have for a long time eschewed the types of 'psychological' tests favoured by this vocational counsellor in TAFE. On several occasions over the years, I received reports from TAFE vocational counsellors, as with the case of the Fitness Certificate student, indicating that an individual vocational student was functioning at a particular reading age based on standardized tests and was in need of remedial literacy assistance. I always found it incongruous to work with an adult student who had been identified to be functioning at a reading age of a seven-year-old (or whatever age the standardized test determined). What these reports demonstrated was that some counsellors worked within outdated psychological education paradigms in which literacy was based on children's reading age norms. ALN teachers on the other hand had their own assessment measures designed specifically for the adult literacy and numeracy field, known originally as the National Reporting System (NRS; see Coates et al., 1996), and several iterations later, as the Australian Core Skills Framework (ACSF; see Brewer et al., 2008; McLean et al., 2012; McLean, Oldfield and Stevens, 2017). In effect, however, the ACSF has performed much the same deficit role as any other standardized literacy tests insofar as it determines literacy levels (there are five levels), and those who fall below a particular level (e.g. level three) are deemed to be in need of improved literacy skills and thus qualify for a remedial literacy programme.

While the ACSF has become the standard literacy/numeracy assessment measure used by ALN teachers, for many years from the mid-1980s, ALN teachers (myself included) designed their own individually tailored assessment measures, often referred to as 'screens', in order to determine who needed literacy and/or numeracy support in their vocational courses at TAFE. They were often based on the ALN teachers' understanding of the particular literacy and numeracy practices required in the different vocational disciplines. For example, curriculum subjects such as carpentry and joinery featured assessments based on the common types of calculations required in that trade. Often these assessments were administered en masse to groups of newly enrolled vocational students in TAFE. Those students identified to be in need of improved literacy/numeracy were then offered various types of support provided by the ABE sections in TAFE, including individual and/or group ALN tuition, and sometimes team teaching involving vocational and ALN teachers working together in the classroom (Black, 1996; Black and Yasukawa, 2011b, 2012, 2013a, 2013b). While these literacy and numeracy support measures were considered 'good practice' in adult literacy education (at least in the late 1980s, see Kelly, 1989; Randazzo, 1989), they were nevertheless predominantly deficit oriented, exemplified in cases where individual or small groups of students were subsequently withdrawn from their vocational classes in order to receive remedial literacy or numeracy support. Many team-teaching strategies could also be termed deficit-oriented if the main role of the ALN teacher was to provide support during lessons primarily to those students deemed to be lacking literacy/numeracy skills. Some ALN teachers have described their role as 'hovering' over these students in need while the vocational teacher addressed the student group as a whole (Black and Yasukawa, 2012, 2013a, 2013b).

Integrating literacy and numeracy support in VET

Literacy and numeracy support provided in the form of team teaching between ALN teachers and vocational teachers usually involved 'integrating' literacy and numeracy in the vocational discipline (McKenna and Fitzpatrick, 2005). In other countries such as the UK (Casey et al., 2006; Latham, 2010; Roberts et al.) and New Zealand (Leach et al., 2010) the preferred term has been 'embedding' literacy and numeracy. According to an early Australian definition, integration involved concurrently developing literacy and numeracy and vocational competencies 'as interrelated elements of the one process' (Courtenay and Mawer, 1995: 2). In other words, literacy and numeracy were taught not as separate or discrete skills but contextualized or 'situated' within the process of learning vocational skills (Black and Yasukawa, 2011b).

While team teaching within an integrated model could be seen to be deficit-oriented if it focused mainly on those students assessed to have literacy/numeracy needs, in our research we identified integrated team-teaching models that went 'beyond deficit models' (Black and Yasukawa, 2013a). In one of these, the Course in Applied Vocational Study Skills (CAVSS), developed in Western Australia (Bates, 2004), vocational and ALN teachers worked closely together, often as 'tag teachers' (i.e. alternating in their classroom delivery) in both theory and practical sessions. Students were not assessed for their levels of literacy/numeracy skills and thus no individual or group of students was targeted for their skill deficiencies. Instead, the whole class or group benefitted from learning about and improving literacy/numeracy within the vocational disciplines. We referred to this pedagogical model as 'vocational socialisation' (Black and Yasukawa, 2013a), drawing on the 'academic socialisation' model of academic support described in higher education contexts (Lea and Street, 1998, 2006). The aim of this approach was to induct the students and the ALN teachers into the disciplinary culture of the relevant vocational occupation. Essentially, they were required to 'fit in' with the vocational status quo.

Another form of 'non-deficit' literacy/numeracy support in VET was provided in a model we referred to as 'shared delivery' that involved ESL and vocational teachers working together (Black and Yasukawa, 2012). In the example we provided, groups of students in a TAFE college, who were all born overseas, were enrolled concurrently in an ESL course and a vocational course (aged care and automotive vehicle servicing were the two courses in our example). Students had similar timetabled hours in both the ESL and the vocational course. The ESL and vocational teachers worked closely together planning and delivering their respective courses and they shared equal responsibility for the same group of students. Their primary aim was to assist the students to gain employment in their chosen vocational field. The teachers did not necessarily team teach (though there were some examples of this), but they actively worked together in all aspects of the planning, delivery and content of their courses. This included some ESL teachers having their office space in the vocational teaching sections of the college. For the model to be successful, both teachers had to be open, critical and committed to changes in their respective disciplines. Accordingly, we found examples of an automotive teacher who changed his pedagogy from a 'telling, leading sort of style, to more interactive' following close collaboration with an ESL teacher. There were also examples of ESL teachers challenging aspects of vocational disciplinary knowledge, including an ESL teacher critiquing a business course that included outdated work practices. We referred to the shared delivery model as 'vocational literacies', adapting the terminology from the 'academic literacies' model identified in higher education contexts (Lea and Street, 1998, 2006). A key point of differentiation for this model was its potential for challenging and changing aspects of vocational learning disciplines as distinct from expecting students to 'fit in' with or be socialized into the vocational status quo (Black and Yasukawa, 2012, 2013a, 2013b).

The academic/vocational literacies model was based on a social practice approach to literacy which has remained largely marginal to mainstream thinking in disciplinary studies in both higher education (Lillis, 2019; Lillis and Tuck, 2016) and vocational education (Ivanič et al., 2009). The social practice approach links literacy practices to context, to how disciplinary knowledge and practices are used, and this is usually explored through ethnographic perspectives (Robinson-Pant, 2018). In the VET sector, Ivanič et al. (2009) adopted a range of ethnographic methods to research the multiple literacy practices of vocational students in their everyday lives and vocational disciplinary practices across the further education curriculum. They indicated how curriculum and assessment practices in subject areas could be changed to better resonate with the everyday literacy practices of students (see Edwards and Miller, 2011; Mannion et al., 2009). The social practice approach to literacy provides an important critical space for changing disciplinary and pedagogical practices, which is largely absent in deficit-based approaches where disciplinary practices are prescribed. In the Australian VET system, beyond our promotion of the 'shared delivery' model (Black and Yasukawa, 2012, 2013a, 2013b), the approach to literacy and numeracy support has remained predominantly deficit-based, as problems to be addressed by a range of remedial literacy/numeracy strategies.

Non-English-speaking background students in VET

My first research into the perspectives of VET students came in a study (Black, 2007, 2008b) which examined how non-English-speaking background (NESB) students fared in TAFE courses. At the time the descriptive term NESB was commonly applied in government reports but has since been largely replaced with the term 'culturally and linguistically diverse' (CALD). For consistency with my original research study, I will continue to refer to NESB students. The genesis for the study was state-wide statistical data that indicated NESB students, those vocational students who indicated on their enrolment form that they spoke a language other than English at home, performed less well in their course module completions compared to English-speaking students. The research literature at the time indicated a similar trend for NESB students generally in VET (Dumbrell, de Montfort and Finnegan, 2004: John, 2004; Miralles, 2004) though there was acknowledgement that the NESB student category encapsulated enormous variation and diversity within TAFE and VET, including variables relating to social class, age, gender, geographical location and residential status (Volkoff, 2004; Watson et al., 2000).

The study of NESB students in TAFE aimed to explore some of the factors that influenced how they performed in their vocational courses, and this mainly involved interviewing NESB students and their teachers from several courses. It seemed a reasonable assumption that if language and literacy were perceived to be problems for TAFE students generally, then for NESB students they would be even more critical. In analysing the statistical data in more detail at the TAFE institute level, it was found that NESB students fared differently according to the courses they were enrolled in. In this chapter, with permission from NSW TAFE, I draw on interview data, previously published and unpublished, that were collected as part of the research project which examined the perspectives of NESB students in TAFE (see Black, 2007, 2008b). I will focus on one VET course, hairdressing, to examine why the NESB students in this course performed relatively well in terms of their course module completions. All interviews with students and teachers were semi-structured, tape-recorded and later transcribed in full. Pseudonyms were used for all students.

Case study one: Hairdressing

Interviews were conducted in one TAFE college with a teacher and eleven students who were undertaking the hairdressing Certificate III course which qualified students to become licensed hairdressers. Enrolment data were used to select students for interview who had indicated on their enrolment form that they spoke a language other than English at home. All the students were apprentices; that is, they were employed by licensed hairdressers on a reduced training wage while they learnt their trade and attended the TAFE course for education and training one day each week. The apprenticeship usually lasted for two or three years. At the time of the research, hairdressing was listed as a skills-shortage occupation (Birrell, Healy and Kinnaird, 2007), reflecting that hairdressing in Australia did not enjoy high occupational status, due mainly to low wages and the long hours of work (Brennan-Kemmis and Ahern, 2010).

Most of the students interviewed were female (eight of the eleven), with an average age of just under eighteen years (five were sixteen, the oldest was twenty-two years of age). Languages spoken at home varied and included Arabic (3), Greek (2), Armenian, Italian, Polish, Russian, Spanish and Turkish. Most left school in Year 10 and went straight into the hairdressing apprenticeship at TAFE. Two students had completed their Higher School Certificate (Year 12) first, and several had tried various jobs. While all the students spoke a language other than English at home, all but two of the students were born in Australia, and those two arrived in Australia aged six and seven years respectively. Thus, the schooling experiences of these students would have been similar to student cohorts born in Australia and whose first language was English. According to the TAFE Institute statistics for 2005 used in the study, NESB students enrolled in hairdressing completed their course modules at a rate higher than English-speaking background students (88 per cent compared to 80 per cent; see Black, 2008b: 16). This statistical trend ran counter to the idea that NESB students performed less well in TAFE courses.

This case study is focused in particular on students' perspectives on how they managed the language, literacy and numeracy (LLN) demands of their hairdressing course. In their practical work as hairdressers, however, it was clear from most of the students' comments that they did not consider LLN to be an issue of major concern as not one of the students indicated that these skills affected their 'hands on' job performance in hairdressing salons. Their spoken English proficiency in particular was not an issue as almost all the students were born in Australia and had experienced an English language schooling. Literacy and numeracy were only perceived by them to be an issue in relation to the theory components of the hairdressing course and in completing the formal written assessment tasks for the academic requirements of the course.

Those students who indicated that the theory component of the course caused them some difficulties were predominantly younger students who left school in Year 10. Aleyna, sixteen, who spoke Arabic at home, appeared typical of these students. She claimed: 'I guess the science class gets me and the problems and the maths.' To overcome these problems with theory classes she said she sought assistance from people at her work: 'it depends, if I need help with something, I ask my boss at work, or the people at work too.' Other students who left school in Year 10 appeared to concur with this. For example, Fedir, seventeen, Ukranian-born and Polish-speaking at home, was one of the few male students in the course. He wanted to become a hairdresser for male clients but was required by the course to study 'ladies hair' which included a colouring component that was 'pure science'. He claimed, 'It's hard, and some of the vocabulary, it's hard, the theory stuff.' But Fedir, as with some other students who found the theory difficult, drew on networks of support that included fellow work colleagues and student peers, or he managed independently despite his difficulties. These younger students had often struggled academically at school. Aleyna, for example, said of her time at school: 'Well, I did my hardest at school, I just wasn't the school type.' Studying hairdressing at TAFE, however, was different to school and was indeed a 'second chance' education that allowed her and others to achieve some success. A key factor that seemed to enable these students to succeed in the course was their passion for their chosen vocation. This love of hairdressing seemed to provide sufficient motivation for them to persist with and overcome difficulties they may have had with literacy and numeracy and the theory components of the course. Russian-speaking Arina, sixteen, for example, stated, 'I did bad at school, but this is something I like, so' (Black, 2008b: 18). Other comments from the students clearly reflected their passion for hairdressing:

'It's in me, you can't take it away' (Aleyna, sixteen, Arabic-speaking)
'Mate, ever since I started, I love it. I've tried other things but nothing's better than this' (Jasar, twenty-two, Arabic-speaking)
'Ever since I was a little girl, never really wanted to do anything else' (Thea, eighteen, Greek-speaking). (These quotes are from Black, 2008b: 18.)

In some cases, this passion for hairdressing necessitated overcoming opposition from parents and other family members. Aleyna (above) for example, who said hairdressing was 'in me', experienced opposition from her mother who she said did not want her to do hairdressing. But after trying alternative work/study options, Aleyna resolved that it was to no avail: 'I worked a bit, worked around, tried to study, I just couldn't do it. I had to come back to hairdressing.' Fedir also indicated opposition from his family:

> Most of my family's all builders and my cousins are mechanics, they're not really a fan of hairdressers. They're a bit jumpy at the word hairdressers. Everyone's like, in a real trade ...
>
> (Black, 2008b: 18)

As research at the time and since has indicated, hairdressing, as with some other caring/relationship occupations (e.g. childcare), involves a high degree of 'emotional labour' (Cohen, 2010; Klope and Hedlin, 2023). It is a course and an occupation where students are expected to exhibit a high degree of personal 'passion' for their work, and students entering this and similar relationship occupations are often found to reflect stereotypical class and gender roles (Colley, 2006; Vincent and Braun, 2013).

Beyond the theory classes, the other potential area of difficulty for the hairdressing students that involved literacy numeracy was formal written assessments. But the main problem for the students was not so much the difficulty of the assessments, rather, the number of them. Fedir, for example, said, 'There's just too many assignments with hairdressing, pretty packed on together, a lot of them.' Armenian-speaking Eva, sixteen, said that when she started the course, she did not think she would be getting so many assessments: 'that's why I left school, not to get any assessments'. From the perspective of the hairdressing teacher, while she felt constrained to ease the volume of assessments required in a curriculum that was based on assessing discrete aspects of vocational competence, there was some flexibility that allowed her and other teachers to modify the assessment criteria to better meet the literacy and numeracy needs of the students. As the hairdressing teacher, Laurinda, explained, assessing the theory side of the course involving science and physiology comprised only a small component of the overall course, and she and other teachers exercised a degree of pragmatism, particularly in relation to literacy:

> The theory side is only a small component of the course. In this course they would have had to do their science, physiology. We just say, as long as we can understand it, we don't care, so they haven't got to worry about the spelling, the grammar ...
>
> (Black, 2008b: 18)

Another assessment strategy adopted by the teachers was to allow students two attempt at assignments, especially written ones. In these ways, the hairdressing teachers adapted their pedagogical practices to better meet the needs of their students. As Laurinda explained, hairdressing students were often not academically inclined, and were usually better 'hands on, because they are more see and do it'.

One final factor noted by the hairdressing teacher that contributed to the relative success of these hairdressing students in completing their course modules was the strong bonding, 'a real team thing' (Black, 2008b: 19) that featured as an important part of the culture of both the TAFE hairdressing course and work in the hairdressing salons. Students felt well supported by their classmates and by their employers and teachers. Arabic-speaking Lily, sixteen, for example, commented, '[I]f you do something really good everyone comments and stuff like that. We all get along very well. Here nobody's left on their own' (Black, 2008b: 19).

In this hairdressing section of the college, specialized support from literacy and numeracy teachers had only a limited role. A literacy/numeracy teacher had at times been requested by hairdressing teachers to provide some additional support to students with the physiology aspects of the course, but withdrawing individual students from their regular class, even for a short period of time, proved to be problematic. As the hairdressing teacher, Laurinda, indicated, 'the disadvantage of it was it was in their class time, and while they were with her, they were missing out on something'.

In summary, the main areas of the hairdressing course which presented literacy and numeracy difficulties for students were the theory components, often involving science-based subjects, and the many written assignments. While many of the students were young and had performed poorly at school, they overcame literacy and numeracy difficulties largely through a combination of their strong motivation and love/passion for hairdressing, and the strong bonding ties and teamwork support provided from their student peers, teachers and employers. It also included a pedagogical approach from teachers which to some degree adapted to the needs of the students, acknowledging that hairdressing was primarily a 'hands-on' trade.

Case study two: Aged care

The second case study features a specific category of students – unemployed, mature-aged women (over forty-five years) who were undertaking a one-semester Certificate III TAFE course in aged care. The research was undertaken as one of the case studies (Black, 2008a) for a larger study, funded by the NCVER, of the role of vocational education and training in the federal government's welfare-to-work initiative (Guenther, Falk and Arnott, 2008). Completing the TAFE certificate course qualified students to become an Assistant in Nursing (AIN), often referred to as personal carers, and students could then, if they chose to, go on to obtain formal nursing qualifications by enrolling in and completing the Certificate IV in Enrolled Nursing (EN). At the time, the Certificate III course was in the process of becoming a prerequisite for work in aged care, a field where there was (and remains) an acute shortage of workers (Jackson and Daly, 2004). There were no course fees or materials to pay for these students as it was subsidized as part of a state government initiative to encourage training for older workers. The course appeared to address the contradiction between relatively large number of unemployed, mature-aged people with the skills to work in aged care, and the great need for such labour in that employment sector (Price et al., 2004). The great majority of workers in aged care were female, and there was wide recognition that the work was low paid, low status, featured high staff turnover (Healy and Moskos, 2005; Richardson and Martin, 2004), and, like hairdressing, the work involved a strong element of 'emotional labour' (e.g. King, 2016). There was also recognition that following increased quality control and accreditation requirements in aged care work, literacy practices in the sector had increased and had become more 'textual' (Wyse and Casarotto, 2004). At the more advanced diploma level for EN, 'core skills' including literacy and numeracy have been considered integral for study and work in nursing (Ryan et al., 2016).

Ten students, the head teacher and three teachers in the aged care course were interviewed with a focus on exploring the issues faced by the students in the course and 'what works' that enabled them to achieve successful course and employment outcomes. The students did not form a separate class; rather, they were incorporated within an existing AIN course with a much younger cohort of students. All ten students were female, over forty-five years of age, and unemployed at the time. Most (six of the ten) students were born in Australia (the others were born in China, the Philippines, Iran and New Zealand).

Most of the Australian-born students had unhappy and/or limited early schooling experiences, and as a consequence, they lacked confidence in their academic abilities as TAFE students. One of the extreme examples was Julie, fifty-three, who said she went to twenty-six different schools in her childhood as her parents moved constantly due to their work. She said she had never studied in her life: 'I was always the new kid sitting up the back of the class for three or six months and then I was off to a new school again.' This was the first formal education course she had undertaken since those days. On her first day in the course, she broke down in tears and spoke with the class teacher:

> I was very emotional, lots of crying. I didn't know if I was able to cope with all the study ... I wanted her to know because, in a sense I was saying if I'm doing something wrong, be a mentor, please help me.
>
> (Black, 2008a: 48)

She explained further: 'I always felt I was lacking compared to everyone else ... these niggly doubts in me that everyone was a bit better' (Black, 2008a: 46). Another student, Margaret, in her mid-fifties, also lacked confidence in her academic abilities. She had previously worked in hospitals as a 'wardsperson' but had to give up the work following a back injury. She said she would love to become an enrolled nurse, 'but I'm not sure I've got the brains, it's all too much'. She had left school at fourteen ('I never really studied, full stop') and apart from cleaning jobs, she had spent eighteen years 'at home looking after my kids ... husband did two jobs to keep me at home'.

A commonality within the student group was their poor economic circumstances and desperation for paid work. Carol, for example, in her late forties, was divorced and living as a single mother with her eleven-year-old son. She had previously worked as a photographer, but after five years of 'being a mum' she felt she was 'out of date by the time I went back into the workforce'. As a student on the course and without an income, she had constant concerns about her everyday living costs: 'school care, extra parking for the car, petrol, transport'. She knew aged care work had a poor image and the pay was bad, but she had no family 'back-up' and few other employment options: 'glorified bum wipe ... really, but that's fine, that's all there is out there. I have no other choice, there's nothing else I can do for someone of my age'. Another student, Charlotte, in her early fifties, had previously worked in the corporate training world, but after becoming pregnant at the age of forty-two, she could no longer cope with competitive work pressures and insecure employment contracts. She wanted to become a qualified nurse but could not manage the costs involved:

> There was no way I could afford to go to university, and I can't take three years off and all the rest of it, it's just not feasible. I could never pay them back because of my age and I've got childcare cost going out every week.

Charlotte was concerned that even when she completed the AIN course, she would still struggle financially:

> [O]nly $12 an hour it just would not be enough, do you know what I mean? The only way I could bump it up would be to work all night, so that's my only concern, the money just wouldn't be quite enough to keep the house going, but that's not the fault of the course.

(Black, 2008a: 49)

These students were experiencing financial hardships, and several were struggling with family responsibilities. These factors underpinned their disposition to undertake and complete the course and their career aspirations generally. One of the students, Julie, the student mentioned previously who broke down crying because she lacked confidence in her ability to complete the course, in fact excelled in the course, achieving several distinctions. One of the TAFE teaching staff offered her a coveted one-year traineeship as an enrolled nurse, the only student out of eighty to be offered such a position. But despite being 'thrilled' to be offered it, she had to decline it because it meant living in Sydney for a year, and she would have been unable to meet her living expenses. Instead, she planned to return to the NSW north coast where it was cheaper to live.

The main focus of the course was 'hands-on personal care', including the clinical skills of nursing in areas such as occupational health and safety, manual handling and infection control. But the course also included the academic study of human biology and aged care subjects such as dementia, and 'documentation, reports, charts, things like that which most of them would not be familiar with' (Rachel, aged care teacher). Nevertheless, despite the limited and unsatisfactory schooling experiences of some of the Australian-born students, and the anxieties and lack of confidence of some about returning to formal learning, these students did not indicate problems with literacy and/or numeracy in the course. Margaret, for example, had left school at fourteen and claimed in the interview that she did not even know how to turn a computer on. But literacy was not a problem: 'I'm not bad at writing, stuff ... I'm pretty good at English'. Similarly with Patricia, who had worked for many years part-time in the local supermarket. Initially she had her doubts about succeeding in the course ('if I can't do it, I can just drop out') because she had disliked school and thought she was 'not real good at anything academically'. But writing in the course was 'no problem' for her. She recounted in fact that many years ago she had undertaken a secretarial course that involved 'manual typewriter and stuff, and shorthand that does not exist now'.

The students born overseas had varying experiences in managing the course. Leila was born in Iran and had been in Australia for fifteen years. She had studied child psychology in Iran, but her qualifications were not accepted in Australia. In recent years she had gained some experience as a dental nurse assistant. She claimed to have no problems with written course assignments. Her main problem was finding the time to study at home with three children. Carmel was from the Philippines where she had completed a bachelor of science and nursing, but she explained that this was in the early 1980s, and for the past twenty years she had lived in Australia with her husband. He now had a back ailment and was unable to work and they were struggling to manage financially. She was only doing the aged care course because there were no fees, and she was working on the days she was not attending the course. She had ESL needs and was worried about her level of spoken and written English, particularly with written reports for the course. Yan was from China and had only been in Australia for nine months. She was formerly an accountant in China, had quite extensive ESL needs, and was struggling with spoken and written English. She was doing the course primarily because an ESL teacher from her previous course suggested she might attempt it.

The teachers had a dilemma with some ESL students on the course. While the teachers were quite flexible in assisting these students with role-plays and practical work, there were certain requirements for AINs participating in the work environment:

> If you can't write out a job letter or you can't write out a resume, we don't want it so that someone does all of it for you, because in the workplace they are required to write ... If you can't then go to work and write a nursing report about what you saw, you'd be fired, so, it has to be a fair evaluation.
>
> (Annabel, head teacher)

Most students successfully completed the course. For the Australian-born women in particular, the main issue they had to overcome was their lack of confidence in themselves to do well academically. Julie was a prime example, overcoming those 'niggly doubts' about her academic abilities. She became highly motivated to succeed and claimed at the conclusion of the course: 'now it's almost like, I do feel on a level playing field now. I never felt that before ... this whole course has really opened me up as a person' (Black, 2008a: 46).

Social networks played a positive role in the study. Students spoke very favourably of their relations with the teachers ('she's absolutely brilliant' (Jennifer); 'teachers here are wonderful' (Carol) 'they are lovely' (Leila)), and the students in the course formed a close-knit group. Carol commented that 'everyone helps each other, we've become a little family'. The negative factors that influenced students in the course included their overstretched life circumstances as many struggled financially to manage family lives with childcare and transport costs. These were working-class students, and the Australian-born students indicated they had poor educational backgrounds and low levels of formal schooling. And yet literacy and numeracy were not mentioned by these students (or their teachers) as factors of any significance in terms of how well they managed the demands of the aged care course. Only two students indicated difficulties with literacy, and in both cases, they related to their ESL needs as students whose first language was not English.

Case study three: Literacy and numeracy support models in beauty, electrical trades and automotive vehicle servicing courses

This final case study considers the perspectives of groups of students on the literacy/numeracy support provided in three TAFE courses. The research was undertaken to examine the various types of literacy/numeracy support provided in vocational education and training (Black and Yasukawa, 2011b). The main focus of the study, as with other Australian studies of LLN support in VET (e.g. Bak and O'Maley, 2015), was the professional perspectives of vocational and LLN teachers who were 'working together'. Student perspectives, however, were an additional focus in the study. At the time, student perspectives on LLN support in VET had rarely featured in Australian research (later studies included Levy, Briede and Frost-Camilleri, 2021; Ryan et al., 2016), though student perspectives had featured prominently in some UK studies (Casey et al., 2006; Ivanič et al., 2009; Roberts et al., 2005).

Students' perspectives were documented in three TAFE courses: beauty, electrical trades and automotive vehicle servicing (Black and Yasukawa, 2011b: 28-30). In the case of the Certificate III beauty course, a small group of female students was interviewed. All were in their late teenage years, and for all but one of the students, English was not their first or main language spoken at home. The LLN support they received was mainly in the form of one-to-one tuition or small group tuition with the LLN teacher arranged outside of class time through prior appointments. This was a traditional 'deficit-based' LLN support model as discussed at the beginning of this chapter in which the LLN teacher worked only with those students identified as 'in need', and the support was largely provided separate to the regular beauty classroom timetable. As one student noted, 'if you don't go to see her, she won't help you' (Black and Yasukawa, 2011b: 28).

The beauty therapy work that these students were training for was very practical, and one student expressed the view that reading and writing had a very limited role:

> In the industry we have to know about skin and everything, but we don't have to sit down and do tests about it. So, it's more in beauty – it's more practical, so there's not really much reading and writing you have to do.

The difficulty for these students was passing the many written assignments and exams in the course, which some students expressed frustrations with. One student stated, 'I think too many theory exam. They should have more practical exam' (Black and Yasukawa, 2011b: 28). Another student commented. '[W]e just keep doing it. Within two weeks another theory (exam) and, you know, so on until the end of the course' (2011b: 28). These comments about exams and assessments were similar to those expressed by the hairdressing students featured in the first case study in this chapter. Quite a few of the beauty students failed the course the first time, and they simply re-did the exams until they passed. If required, the LLN teacher would sit with a student as a reader for the exams: 'they just explain the question. Like try to use another word' (2011b: 28). One student explained that '[p]racticals is fun, but, you know, the theory is, you have to put everything in writing' (2011b: 28). The role of the LLN teacher was primarily to assist students to pass the theory exams.

In the electrical trades course, the students were all young males with many having entered their apprenticeship directly after leaving school. The LLN support model was different in this course insofar as the electrical trades teacher and the LLN teacher taught together in the classroom as team teachers. The main focus of this support was on numeracy and a large part of each lesson comprised mathematical exercises, mainly the transposition of formulae. Some students continually experienced problems with academic maths, and the lessons featured considerable repetition as worksheet exercises on transposition of formulae were jointly delivered by both teachers. Two of the students interviewed had few problems with maths and they found the constant worksheet exercises repetitive and uninspiring. One of their complaints was the relative lack of practical work on the course, and while this was only the first year of the course, they had reservations that the course would help them in the workplace as electricians:

> There's a lot of formulas and stuff like that, whereas the practical side of things, I don't think there's enough. Like, if you did the whole TAFE course and then went out for a job, you'd know nothing sort of thing. It might get better or different.
>
> (Black and Yasukawa, 2011b: 29)

These students could see the value of two teachers in the classroom with one specializing in maths, especially for those students who had left school early. In particular, they enjoyed the genuine exchanges between the teachers to clarify points: 'they even converse in the middle – so each of them knows what they're talking about, which is good because it explains it to everyone' (2011b: 29). But they disliked the repetitive and prolonged focus on academic maths: 'like, we spent six weeks solid just doing transposition. We're now in second semester and some guys still can't do it properly' (2011b: 29).

The third group of students was different again to the previous two. The students were all males born overseas in countries where English was not the main language. Countries included Sudan, Afghanistan, Turkey and Vietnam. This was a 'shared delivery' course (Black and Yasukawa, 2012), and the students were enrolled in two courses concurrently – an ESL course and a Certificate II in automotive servicing. Both courses were linked closely, and the two teachers, while they taught their own respective courses, essentially worked as a team, meeting together early in the morning once a week to jointly plan their teaching programmes and share resources and ideas. The interviews with the students revealed unanimous enthusiasm for the way the course was structured, the quality of the teaching and the outcomes of the course. All students claimed strong gains in their spoken and written English skills, their automotive knowledge, and their positive attitudes to further study and/or work. Many of these students had previously been mechanics. Typically, one Sudanese student said: 'I have lot of experience, mechanics, just the English here is difficult ... I know everything about the car, just after it is difficult, you need the certificate, you need to follow the rules' (2011b: 29). These students were very anxious to obtain work in the automotive industry, mainly as mechanics, but were limited by their English language and literacy skills and their lack of Australian qualifications. Typically, another student said they started 'from beginning' with their spoken English and were now 'going better'. One said as the result of the course, 'all the parts name, how to fill job card, how to report information for the car ... do a lot of practice in workshop, transmission, cooler, everything we now become better' (2011b: 29).

The shared delivery model enabled these students to undertake an automotive course which they could not enrol in as a mainstream course because they did not have the entry requirements. One student said, '[S]o they will put you at the back of the line ... very hard to get into' (2011b: 29). The automotive vehicle servicing course was chosen as a shared delivery course because it led directly to job prospects. Because the course had been so successful, the two teachers at the time of the interviews were lobbying for the students to be allowed to enrol in the Certificate III automotive course the following year, which, if they passed, would result in them becoming trade-qualified mechanics. A small group of students was also planning to start up their own automotive servicing business.

There were a number of factors in this shared delivery model that enabled high student satisfaction and successful course outcomes. The ESL teacher focused exclusively on the spoken and written English these students would require in the automotive workforce, and her programme was jointly planned with the automotive teacher. The automotive teacher for his part shifted his programme delivery from the traditional automotive teaching model in order to accommodate the needs of these students. His pedagogy had changed with greater focus on practical work and written work as secondary, as he explained:

> To me, their learning is based more about doing, so we spend large amounts of time actually doing the job, and then talking about how we do the job, and then writing about the job, where the (traditional) apprentice programme is, we write about the job, and then we do the job. So, I've reversed the whole process.
>
> (Black and Yasukawa, 2011b: 30)

The three student groups featured in this final case study section had varying experiences of LLN and the support provided to them in their vocational courses. In the beauty course, students attended special one-to-one or small group LLN support primarily to pass the theory written exams. However, the students saw little link between the written theory work and the practice of being a beautician, and this was reflected in their relative lack of enthusiasm for the course theory and the LLN support provided. The electrical trades students, while limited to the perspectives of two students, were also largely lacking in enthusiasm because the primary focus of much of the course so far had been on seemingly endless exercises on academic maths, and in particular, transposition of formulae. These students also could not see direct links between the course theory and their later work as an electrician. The team teaching may have been beneficial in teaching academic maths, but without direct practical application, student motivation for the course was compromised. The shared delivery programme that involved enrolment in an automotive and LLN course featured highly motivated students who enjoyed their course, spoke very highly of their teachers, and were working hard to obtain employment in the automotive industry. These students saw the direct relevance of the course delivery model and their future work aspirations. Further, while they all had spoken and written English needs, the courses were interactive and drew on and respected their pre-existing knowledge as mechanics in their former home countries.

Concluding comments

This chapter began with an explanation of the dominant LLN skills crisis narrative in vocational education and training, and the deficit ideology that has underpinned most LLN support models for students. The 'voices' of students outlined in three case studies have indicated diverse perspectives on the role of LLN in VET courses. By examining LLN from the perspectives of individual students undertaking VET courses, a quite complex picture has emerged of how they managed the courses. For some students, such as those featured in the hairdressing and aged care courses, LLN were not seen to be a major factor in determining how they progressed in their courses, and their perspectives in effect undermined the idea of an LLN skills 'crisis' in VET. From a dominant 'skills' perspective, the socio-economic and educational backgrounds of students in both courses would have suggested that they would experience LLN difficulties. In the case of the hairdressing course, the students were young, often early school leavers, and they all spoke a language other than English at home. In the case of the students in the aged care course, all were unemployed at the time, and commonly they had experienced disrupted and low levels of formal schooling. The factors that contributed to the success of these students in their courses included social networks of support and individual dispositions – attitudes and motivations towards their studies. The hairdressing students, for example, had ready support from fellow students, teachers and their employers, and they really loved their vocation. The aged care students often had to overcome fear of failure resulting from previous poor schooling experiences, but they managed the academic demands of the course largely through their personal motivation to succeed, which was often predicated on their dire economic circumstances as unemployed people and support provided from the course teachers and other students. Only those students from ESL backgrounds indicated LLN difficulties. In the LLN support models provided in the beauty, electrical trades and automotive servicing courses, students expressed some dissatisfaction with deficit models that targeted individual students experiencing problems with the course theory and written exams. The shared delivery model of LLN support on the other hand was provided for a specific group of students, those with ESL needs and unable to access mainstream VET courses. These students were enthusiastic for this delivery model largely because it drew on their existing vocational skills, and they could see its direct relevance to their vocational aspirations in the automotive field.

9

Diabetes Patients and Literacy

Knowing and doing are two different things.
(Dianne, a diabetes patient commenting on her diet)

She does everything for me. Like, she pays for my bills, pays for my doctor's fee, everything.
(Ria, a diabetes patient, commenting on the assistance she receives from her niece)

Because there are so many resources you can do … they can always find someone who can do it for them. There's no barrier really.
(Agila, a diabetes educator, commenting on the role of literacy and numeracy in her patients' self-management of diabetes)

Introduction: Health literacy

This chapter draws on research data from a study that examined the role of health literacy in the everyday lives of a group of adults who were experiencing a chronic health condition, type 2 diabetes. It is an updated and revised version of a journal article that reported on the findings of the study (Black et al., 2016). Health literacy is a burgeoning concept which, while contested and broadening in scope in recent decades, has long focused on the skills and capabilities of individuals to manage their own health (Nutbeam, Levin-Zamir and Rowlands, 2018). One of the early and influential understandings of health literacy adopted by the World Health Organization was that it represented:

> [T]he cognitive and social skills which determine the motivation and ability of individuals to gain access to, understand and use information in ways which promote and maintain good health.
>
> (Nutbeam, 1998: 357)

At the very beginning of this book, and in various other chapters, I have referenced the 'literacy crisis' narrative that has dominated discourses about adult literacy in Australia. In Chapter 1, I outlined how the culmination of this crisis followed publication of the results of the 2006 national adult literacy survey, the ALL (Adult Literacy and Life Skills, see Australian Bureau of Statistics, 2008a). I also explained that the ALL survey data incorporated Australia's first national health literacy survey (Australian Bureau of Statistics, 2008b), and in the years that followed it became quite common for academic health studies and health policy documents to draw on the national survey results to state that 60 per cent of Australian adults lacked the health literacy skills to cope with everyday life (e.g. Australian Commission on Safety and Quality in Health Care, 2014; Barber et al., 2009; Nutbeam, 2009; Peerson and Saunders, 2009). It has also been apparent that adults lacking in health literacy skills are predominantly disadvantaged, particularly from low socio-economic backgrounds. A key message from the ALL survey was that health literacy rates were lower for these groups of adults, based on indicators such as educational attainment and participation, parental education, labour force status and income (Australian Bureau of Statistics, 2008b), and these links have often been highlighted in the research literature (e.g. Adams et al., 2013; McCaffery et al., 2016; Muscat et al., 2020). In this book, I have referred to these disadvantaged adults as working class.

Diabetes, social support and the social practice model of health literacy

In this chapter, health literacy, and particularly diabetes literacy, a disease-specific subset of health literacy, is examined in relation to the everyday lives of a group of twenty-six adults who had been diagnosed with diabetes and were attending a diabetes centre for day patients in an Australian city location. Three of the patients were diagnosed with type 1 diabetes, the rest (23) were type 2. These adults attended the diabetes centre as outpatients with individual appointments to meet with various clinical staff, including doctors, diabetes educators, dietitians and podiatrists. The chapter focuses on how the patients managed the knowledge and practices of everyday living with diabetes (see Black et al., 2016).

Type 2 diabetes is a largely preventable lifestyle disease that affects approximately 5 per cent of the adult population, particularly older adults and those of lower socio-economic status (Abouzeid et al., 2013; Australian

Institute of Health and Welfare, 2014). The disease has been associated with sedentary lifestyles and increased obesity in society (Atlantis, Lange and Wittert, 2009; Hu, 2003; Reeves et al., 2013; Venables and Jeukendrup, 2009). It is usually progressive and is associated with a range of comorbidities including high blood pressure, high cholesterol, heart disease, stroke, depression, vision loss and kidney-related disorders (Australian Institute of Health and Welfare, 2013; Iglay et al., 2016). The self-management of diabetes often involves lifestyle modifications including food choices, physical activity, exercise and weight control. Glycaemia management may involve oral medications or injectable therapies and ongoing blood sugar monitoring (Coyle, Francis and Chapman, 2013). The disease impacts many aspects of patients' lives, including a time and emotional 'burden' on family members (Carolan, Holman and Ferrari, 2014; Stuckey et al., 2016).

The research approach to this study differed from many other health literacy studies insofar as it was a qualitative study which aimed to document the subjective perspectives of diabetes patients on how they managed the disease, and particularly in relation to social support provided by others. In recent decades, there has been an increasing research focus in health studies on exploring social contexts, drawing particularly on the role of social relationships and networks of support that affect health outcomes (e.g. Bookwala, Marshall and Manning, 2014; Cohen, 2004; Holt-Lunstad and Uchino, 2015; Martire and Franks, 2014; Umberson and Montez, 2010). Spouses and partners have been found to play an important role (Meyler, Stimpson and Peek, 2007). Specifically in relation to diabetes and other chronic diseases, family members have played a significant role in the shift from clinician-centred care to self-managed support (Piette, 2010). Self-managed health care has focused primarily on individual-centred definitions, though there has been growing recognition of the role of the wider social context including partners, relatives, friends and neighbours (Vassilev et al., 2011). Chronic illness management can thus be viewed beyond the individual as a 'collective process' involving social networks of support as 'an active extension' of the person with a long-term condition (Vassilev et al., 2014).

While health literacy studies have remained dominated by a focus on the cognitive skills and abilities of individuals, an increasing number of qualitative studies have focused on the broader social context of people's lives, examining the role of health literacy in their everyday lives. Referring to health literacy as a 'social practice', these studies, often involving semi-structured interviews and other ethnographic research methods, have challenged the individualistic bias in health literacy studies (Pinheiro, 2021; Pitt et al., 2019; Samerski, 2019). They have demonstrated the complex and multifaceted aspects of health in people's lives, and in relation to chronically ill people, they have indicated the important role played by others, including family members, peers and educators (Bernhard et al., 2017; Carolan et al., 2014; Foss et al., 2016; Hinder and Greenhalgh, 2012). These studies have suggested the need to move beyond a narrow focus on the person with the illness and the extent of their autonomy as individuals to a broader approach that explores the individual's home, work and community environment.

The conceptualization of health literacy adopted in this study was based on the social practice model promoted by Papen (2009, 2012). The aim was to explore how people used and valued health literacy practices in their everyday lives, in this case involving close observations of clinical consultations in a diabetes centre and semi-structured interviews with patients and centre staff. Papen (2009, 2012) demonstrated how individuals, often lacking skills in a normative, cognitive sense, nevertheless managed to effectively navigate their health care needs using social networks for assistance, including health care professionals and other community organization representatives. Papen (2009) concluded that health literacy was often 'distributed', by which she meant that it was not simply a property or an attribute of an individual, rather that it was 'shared knowledge and expertise' that resided in the patient's social network (see Black et al., 2016: 251). Other researchers from a similar research orientation have indicated the important role of 'health literacy mediators' in assisting people with chronic health conditions (Edwards et al., 2015). How these people accessed knowledge and information and managed their health was often a complex social practice involving a range of professional health workers, peers (those also experiencing the health condition) and social affiliations including family and friends (Lloyd, Bonner and Dawson-Rose, 2014).

The research study participants

A total of twenty-six diabetes patients were observed during clinical consultations at the diabetes centre and then later interviewed in the centre using a semi-structured format. There were sixteen female and ten male patients, and the ages ranged from forty-two to eighty-five years with a mean age of sixty-five years. Twenty-one of the twenty-six patients were born overseas where English was not the main language spoken, though fourteen patients said they spoke mainly English at home. Five patients used interpreters in their consultations. Countries of birth for the patients included Australia, Bangladesh, Chile, Columbia, Egypt, Fiji, Greece, Iran, Italy, Lebanon, Macedonia, Malta, Nepal, New Zealand, Russia, Spain, Thailand, Turkey, and Ukraine. The staff members at the centre who were interviewed for the study included doctors (6), diabetes educators (4), podiatrists (2) and one dietitian. All names of patients and staff in this chapter are pseudonyms (see Black et al., 2016 for details of the research).

The patients were predominantly from migrant and working-class backgrounds, which accorded largely with research studies on the prevalence of type 2 diabetes in Australia (e.g. Abouzeid et al., 2013). The life circumstances of a number of the patients were difficult and complex as they struggled in their everyday lives in socially disadvantaged residential areas, in some cases living alone on a welfare pension in high-rise public housing. Russian-born Larisa, aged seventy-six, was one of these. She lived alone in a public housing apartment in the inner city and experienced high levels of stress. She stated, for example, 'Every my neighbour is drug addict … I live 17 years housing commission.' She also spoke of the high number of people in her neighbourhood, often quite young, who had died in various circumstances in recent years. Doctors interviewed in the study indicated that depression and mental health issues were often associated with the lives of diabetes patients, particularly those who lived in poor socio-economic circumstances.

As background to understanding how patients managed their daily lives with type 2 diabetes, it needs to be recognized not only that their living circumstances were often difficult and stressful, but that the nature of diabetes and the extent to which it affected their daily lives varied for each patient. At one end of the spectrum, for example, were patients like Melanie, a 72-year-old Greek woman who was attending the diabetes centre for the first time to seek dietary advice following a routine blood test that revealed that she may have diabetes. At the time, she was relatively unaffected by the disease in her daily life and needed only to slightly modify her diet. At the other end of the spectrum, some of the patients had been diagnosed with diabetes decades earlier, were on daily insulin injections and experienced a wide range of comorbidities, such as 76-year-old Larisa, mentioned above, who was first diagnosed with the disease forty years ago. She required daily insulin injections, and her diabetes control was described by the diabetes educator as 'suboptimal'. In addition, she suffered from a range of other medical conditions including ischaemic heart disease (the heart is starved of oxygen due to a reduced blood supply), atrial fibrillation (irregular heart rhythm) and peripheral neuropathy (weakness, numbness and pain, usually in the hands and feet). She had also suffered a stroke (a cerebral vascular accident – CVA) and had had a total knee replacement and numerous fractures. Another patient, Ashna, also had serious comorbidities. She was fifty-two years of age, Fijian born, and lived alone in a public housing apartment. Her health conditions included severe vision loss, kidney disease, hypertension, ischaemic heart disease and arthropathy (joint disease) affecting mobility in her hands, arms and legs. How an individual patient 'self-managed' diabetes was clearly influenced by the severity of the disease and the extent of comorbidities. In the case of Ashna, her consultation with a diabetes educator indicated that she was so overwhelmed by her medical condition she had problems remembering when to take her insulin and calculating the dosage. Joint disease in her arms and hands also affected her diet insofar as she was physically unable to cook much beyond the preparation of two-minute noodles which seemed to feature prominently in her diet. This food choice was also linked with material poverty in her case (living on welfare payments and in public housing) which limited her ability to purchase healthier food.

Beyond these background contexts of poor material life circumstances and the severity of their medical conditions, an individual patient's cognitive skills in relation to language and literacy could be seen to play a role in influencing how well they independently or self-managed their health needs. Most of the patients were born overseas, and English was not their first language. Five patients had requested interpreters in their clinical consultations at the diabetes centre, and others indicated English language and literacy difficulties in the consultations. In a normative sense, and according to standardized measures of the health literacy of individuals (e.g. ABS, 2008b), most of these patients would have been assessed to be lacking in health literacy. In the following section, I outline examples of how some patients independently managed diabetes in their everyday lives and the role that language and literacy may have played.

Autonomous, self-managing patients

Some of the patients had little difficulty in 'self-managing' diabetes. Australian-born Andrew, forty-two, was one of these. He was the youngest patient interviewed and he was one of the three patients who had been diagnosed with type 1 diabetes. This diagnosis was seven years ago, and he was now required to self-inject insulin three times each day and closely monitor his blood sugar levels. The complicating factor for Andrew was that working as a courier, he spent 'twelve hours a day delivering stuff, driving'. It meant that maintaining a proper diet was difficult as his daytime food intake was 'on the run'. Nevertheless, he took responsibility for maintaining his own health and attended the diabetes centre periodically to check his blood sugar levels with a diabetes educator. At home, he did not seek any assistance from his spouse, claiming: 'What else can you do? I'm not a baby (laughs), and she's busy looking after my son as well' (his teenage son had also been diagnosed with type 1 diabetes years earlier). While he was educated in Australia and claimed he had no problems reading information about diabetes, he said that he did not bother to read the pamphlets on diabetes provided to him at the centre because he was always busy at work and at home: 'too much on the go'.

Dianne, fifty-nine, was another very independent diabetes patient. She was a secondary school teacher and well versed with managing type 2 diabetes having previously assisted her mother with the disease. Dianne had only recently been diagnosed with type 2 diabetes. She was on oral medication and her primary concern was to reduce her weight. She attended the diabetes centre regularly to consult with the dietitian and to keep her focus on weight loss. She was knowledgeable about the disease and could readily access and understand all the relevant written information, though as she stated in relation to her diet: 'knowing and doing are two different things'.

A third patient who appeared to manage the disease independently at home was Hala, fifty-three, born in Lebanon. She lived in a public housing apartment with her husband, who used a wheelchair following an accident, and her son, a hairdresser. Hala had only recently been diagnosed with type 2 diabetes, which developed following a kidney transplant. She attended the diabetes centre mainly to learn how to monitor and control her blood sugar levels. In matters relating to her diabetes, she said she managed without any assistance from her family: 'no, no, look for myself for that'. Moreover, she did more than look after herself: 'I do everything at home. I look after two men'. In the consultation with a diabetes educator, Hala was taught how to use a blood sugar monitor, and despite some initial trial-and-error attempts to prick her finger, she was unfazed. After all, she had previously learnt to manage her kidney disease: 'I do dialysis by myself … hemodialysis, six years' (Black et al., 2016: 254). Hala maintained a positive attitude, despite her medical condition, and while she described her spoken and written English as 'not really good, but all right', she felt that after 'many years in hospital' she could manage her disease independently. Her strong motivation and positive attitude appeared to compensate for any difficulties she may have had with English language and literacy skills. Most of her knowledge about diabetes was obtained through her strong desire to learn more in the face-to-face consultations with health staff at the centre: 'I have to find, I have to listen. I have to see the doctor every week, everything.'

There were other patients interviewed who indicated they were independent in their management of the disease. Australian-born William, sixty-six, for example, was a retired police detective who was diagnosed with diabetes following an operation for pancreatic cancer. His consultation with a diabetes educator indicated that he had ready access to information and a good understanding of the lifestyle changes required of him, including diet and exercise, though implementing the latter was difficult due to his weakened legs. Saliq, fifty-nine, born in Bangladesh and diagnosed with type 2 diabetes seventeen years ago, also indicated he could independently manage diabetes. He stated that he had a master's degree (in statistics), and in a consultation with the dietitian, he demonstrated good English language skills (his first language was Bengali) and a good understanding of dietary issues involving diabetes. His main problem was not lack of access to or knowledge about diabetes, rather, accommodating this knowledge with his everyday religious cultural practices. For example, he attended prayers each night and often ate a rice-based meal after 10 p.m., which contravened dietary advice. He also said that during the fasting period his doctor became angry: 'you know, because glucose is very high'.

Social support: The role of family

From observations of clinical consultations and interviews with both clinical staff and patients, social support was found to be a key factor in explaining how many of the patients managed diabetes in their everyday lives, particularly support provided by family. One of the clearest examples of the importance of family support was the case of Cesar, a 64-year-old man born and educated in Spain. He had lived in Australia for many years in a Spanish-speaking household with his wife and adult daughter. He had been diagnosed with type 2 diabetes the previous year following damage to his foot at work as a building labourer. He subsequently had two toes amputated and he visited the doctor and podiatrist at the diabetes centre for ongoing treatment for foot ulcers. He also had diabetes-related problems with one eye. Cesar always attended clinical consultations with both his wife and his daughter, and due to his English language and literacy difficulties, he relied almost entirely on them to understand and manage his diabetes care needs. He stated, '[T]hey understand what doctor tell me, everything' (Black et al., 2016: 253). Cesar seemed to believe that all he needed to do was to reduce his sugar intake: 'I don't think we need special thing (diet). The only thing, cut off sugar.' In fact, he required a special diet and ongoing foot care that his adult (Australian-born) daughter was responsible for understanding in the clinical consultations, and his wife was responsible for implementing in the home. Cesar appeared to have abrogated individual responsibility for his diabetes management in favour of his daughter and his wife.

Another prominent example of family support was Sybil, a 78-year-old Australian-born former nursing sister who had been diagnosed with type 2 diabetes more than a decade ago. She attended the diabetes centre because she had recently been admitted to a hospital emergency department for hypoglycemia. In addition to diabetes, she had Parkinson's disease, had suffered a stroke, and was experiencing short-term memory problems. Sybil was accompanied at all times by her husband, David, and she relied extensively on him during clinical consultations where he played an active mediating role, representing to a large extent her voice. David made constant references in the consultation with an educator to 'we', reinforcing that, in relation to Sybil, living with diabetes was a team effort. Sybil, though a former professional nurse, was incapable of independently managing diabetes in her daily life.

Another apparent spousal 'team effort' to managing type 2 diabetes involved the case of Peter, an Australian-born 62-year-old who had been attending the diabetes centre for eleven years. His wife took an active role in his everyday management of the disease, particularly in matters of diet and medications. For example, in the consultation with a diabetes educator, she was an advocate and a voice for Peter, resisting the idea that he would soon need insulin injections, telling the diabetes educator: 'let's wait until we see the doctor next month to decide about that' (Black et al., 2016: 253).

The role of spouses in the management of type 2 diabetes was not always straightforward within a family and could have some unintended consequences. In the case of Greek-born Costa, sixty-nine, for example, in addition to type 2 diabetes, he had been diagnosed with cancer and was receiving chemotherapy. He had also recently been in hospital with pneumonia. His wife, Athena, attended all medical consultations and treatments with him, making notes and maintaining his health records. Costa relied heavily on Athena in consultations, referring to her as his 'memory'. For her part though, Athena had given up work to look after Costa, and her caring duties were causing her considerable stress. In one consultation with an educator, she felt overwhelmed with the information she was offered on diabetes and claimed, '[N]o, it's too confusing, I will contact you (if necessary).' She explained, 'I am full time nurse, psychologist, you name it' (Black et al., 2016: 253).

In the case of Natascha, a 61-year-old Russian-born woman who had been living with type 2 diabetes for more than twenty years, the role of her husband influenced her everyday living, but not in a positive way. Her husband also had type 2 diabetes, along with heart problems. While Natascha was careful with her diet and was very concerned about her blood sugar levels and ensuring her correct insulin medication, the same could not be said for her husband whose refusal to cooperate to improve his health was a constant emotional burden for her. She commented:

> My husband is not healthy, he eats meat three times per day, he smokes. I am tired of fighting. I try to cook healthy, he does not help me with diet and food ... He does not want to take tablets. He always fights with me. I understand it's no good, but I have no power to fight with him.
>
> (Black et al., 2016: 253)

The role of adult sons and daughters within the family was also significant for several of the patients, particularly those who were first-generation migrants and whose first language was not English. Adult sons and/or daughters often transported their parents to clinical appointments and sat with them during the consultations. In cases where spoken English proficiency was a problem, they often provided interpreter services for their parents. The earlier case of Spanish-speaking Cesar was an example of this. Even if adult sons/daughters were not always available during these consultations due to their own busy working and home lives, they were often there in the background, ready to provide assistance if it was needed. In the interview with Iranian-born Batool, eighty-five, who was diagnosed with type 2 diabetes more than thirty years ago, she said she lived alone and looked after herself. She requested the presence of an interpreter during the consultation with the diabetes educator. Later in the interview, however, she mentioned that her daughter was a nurse, and her daughter-in-law was a doctor, and both lived in the same city area and provided assistance whenever she needed it.

In some cases, it was the extended family that played an important role in assisting patients to manage diabetes. In the case of Ria, fifty-five, born in New Zealand, her nieces provided that assistance. Ria was experiencing very poor health. She explained that while she had been diagnosed with type 2 diabetes a number of years earlier, she had been busy working and did not take the disease seriously until she 'just about couldn't walk or breathe'. She was subsequently hospitalized and required a heart operation. She also suffered from kidney disease, was on daily haemodialysis, 'and now they are going to do the fistula'. In her daily living, Ria relied almost entirely on her niece for her diabetes care needs: 'she does everything for me. Like, she pays for my bills, pays for my doctor's fee, everything'. She also had ready access and support from her niece's other two sisters and one of their children (a grand-niece, who was seventeen). They arranged between them to take her to all her medical appointments and watch over her. It was an interesting reciprocal family relationship because many years previously Ria had cared for the three nieces when they were babies 'while their parents were out partying' (Black et al., 2016: 254). In Ria's case, it was important to note that she relied on her network of support due to the severity of her medical conditions, not her lack of education or language/literacy abilities. She explained that previously when she was experiencing a range of medical conditions (heart problems, kidney disease requiring daily haemodialysis, diabetes), she was not in the right emotional state to confront them: 'No, I can read. Before I just wasn't listening. I just wasn't focused.'

In cases where family support was not readily available, patients mentioned receiving assistance from a range of other sources. Neighbours featured prominently, and in the case of Ashna, fifty-two, her neighbour was her primary form of assistance in her everyday management of diabetes. As indicated earlier, Ashna had severe comorbidities and lived alone in a public housing apartment. Her neighbour on the same apartment floor was an 81-year-old man from South Africa who sometimes accompanied her on the bus journey to consultations at the diabetes centre: 'If I feel dizzy, I ask him. He come with me ... to the hospital as well.' He also read correspondence for her and had assisted her with insulin injections. In some respects, the assistance was reciprocal, as Ashna explained: 'One day he fall down in the bathroom. He broke his leg, fall down. I been there. I just call the ambulance' (Black et al., 2016: 254). In the case of Greek-born Melanie, seventy-two, who had only recently been diagnosed with type 2 diabetes, there was no one in her immediate family who understood how to manage diabetes. She was living with her adult son and was separated from her husband. In her case, she turned to her Greek neighbour for advice about blood sugar levels:

> I don't have the machine at home, but a neighbour of mine, he does have diabetes and he's got the machine and sometimes I go and measure my blood sugars there. And he says to me that I've only got 5, 5.9. He says 5 is normal.

Clinical perspectives on health literacy and patients' support networks

The clinical staff at the diabetes centre, including doctors, diabetes educators, dietitians and podiatrists, had a range of views about how patients with diabetes managed their everyday lives and the role in particular of health literacy and social support from others. In cases where patients were unable to manage independently in the consultations due in part to their lack of English language proficiency, the official policy at the centre was that health interpreters should be used. The dietitian, Maroun, was strongly in agreement with this policy: 'Languages is an issue. If they don't come with an interpreter, I don't see them, full stop.' There were additional measures available to clinical staff to assist patients who were not proficient in English. The educators, for example, had written information in community languages to assist patients, such as information pamphlets on hypoglycaemia (low blood sugar levels that could lead to seizures and loss of consciousness). Several of the clinical staff referred to the use of visual materials to negate possible language and literacy difficulties. The dietitian, Maroun, for example, stated in relation to his consultations with patients:

> They go out with a written plan. It's all visual, particularly for those who can't read. They take home a visual thing that they put on their fridge and look at it. All colour coded for each meal of the day. It's very visual. I've been using these for years.

English language and literacy issues were generally not a focus for the clinical staff in terms of how patients managed their lives with diabetes. The two podiatrists, for example, tended to play down such issues. Jennifer, who had worked at the centre for more than two decades, said that, unlike the dietitian, they did not ask patients to record anything in writing as most of their consultations were based on demonstrating treatment practices. The other podiatrist, Jasmine, stated that while they did have pamphlets on basic foot care, she was not a big promoter of them: 'because I know people will take them home and chuck them out'. One of the educators at the diabetes centre, Agila, formerly a qualified nurse before undertaking post-graduate qualifications in diabetes education, stated quite specifically that she did not believe language and literacy played a prominent role in patients self-managing diabetes: 'because there are so many resources you can do … they can always find someone who can do it for them. There's no barrier really'.

Most of the professional staff were in agreement about the importance of the social support networks of patients. One of the doctors, Barbara, stated, 'I'm amazed to see who comes in with the patient. I've had people say they get the letter from the hospital about their appointment, and they take it next door. It's great, amazing' (Black et al., 2016: 254–5). Another doctor, Katrina, explained that managing diabetes was different to the management of many other diseases because it required 'everyday' management that was strongly influenced by the social circumstances of patients:

> Well, I always tell people, I always ask people who do you live with, who are your supports? Oh yes, that's how diabetes differs from our endocrine clinic because diabetes is really about what the patient is experiencing in life and everyday basis compared to thyroid or something else where those things aren't so important. But every day for a diabetic, every stress, every action that they take really impacts on their diabetes. That's where a diabetes clinic does differ. We should be allowing patients to talk to us a lot more about what's happening, not concentrating so much on sugar levels as such, but putting a lot more emphasis on their social circumstances, and I think a lot of us do that, I hope.

These 'social circumstances' included, for example, explaining food and diet not only to the patient in the clinical consultation but to the person in the family responsible for shopping and preparing food in the home environment.

One of the few negative aspects to family members assisting in the consultations was that at times the patient, often male, tended to abrogate responsibility for their care to other family members. This has already been explained in relation to Spanish-speaking Cesar who relied entirely on his daughter and wife in the consultations. One of the diabetes educators, Mary, explained that in the consultations, some male patients became disengaged, 'while his wife leans forward' (Black et al., 2016: 255). In other words, the husband abrogated his responsibility in favour of his wife, and thus Mary was occasionally required to ask the wife to leave the consultation because 'I want him to get the message it's his problem not hers' (Black et al., 2016: 255).

The issue of family members providing interpreting services for their parents in lieu of a professional health interpreter in the clinical consultations was vexed. On the one hand, family members were often the ones implementing the caring and they had deep insights into their parents' circumstances and could explain things in a way that their parents would understand. On the other hand, it was not always clear that the family members were accurately conveying the health messages, 'and some cultures do have a feeling that they don't want to bother their elderly parents with too much detail' (Angela, doctor). One of the doctors, Beatriz, suggested that family members and interpreters together in the consultation was often most useful: 'then you get an official version, and you get corroboration' (Black et al., 2016: 255).

The 'distributed' concept of health literacy

This study has implications for how health literacy is conceptualized and how it is applied in real-life contexts. Traditionally, as indicated at the beginning of this chapter with reference to a WHO definition, health literacy has been defined and operationalized as the skills and attributes of individuals in relation to how they manage their health (e.g. Nutbeam, 1998). This mirrors the conceptualization of literacy generally in the community as adopted by governments and dominant groups in Australian society. As explained in detail in Chapter 1, it serves primarily to identify those individuals and groups in society who lack the skills to cope with 'the complex demands of everyday life'. It is a deficit orientation that has continued to dominate discussions of the role of literacy at all levels of society. Health literacy appears little different, framed primarily in terms of the extent to which individuals are autonomous or not in managing their health needs.

An alternative concept of health literacy based on a social practice model has had relatively little impact to date in the research community, though the number of social practice health literacy studies is increasing (e.g. Pinheiro, 2021; Pitt et al., 2019; Samerski, 2019). The aim of these studies, adopting an ethnographic perspective, is to examine how people use and value health literacy practices in their everyday lives. Papen's (2009, 2012) research cited earlier remains one of the key social practice studies of health literacy, indicating how social networks of support can enable people to effectively manage their individual health needs. Papen (2009) concluded that health literacy is often 'distributed' based on the shared knowledge and expertise of others in social networks, as distinct from being a property or attribute of an individual.

The study outlined in this chapter followed Papen's 'distributed' concept of health literacy. While there were individual diabetes patients who could independently manage their health needs, many patients were unable to do so and drew on social networks for support. Family members comprised the main support network, and in many of the cases outlined in this chapter, patients appeared to navigate their everyday management of diabetes with family support. The cases of Cesar and Sybil were clear examples of this, and other patients (Ashna, Batool, Ria) utilized a range of family and community support networks. Family dynamics, however, could be complex, and in some cases family members could be seen to be inhibiters not enablers of health literacy, as indicated in the case of Natascha, whose husband was uncooperative at home. In the case of Costa, his diabetes health needs were met through the interventions of his wife, but this in turn caused her to become highly stressed.

By examining health/diabetes literacy as a social practice, this study also indicated that even for those patients who seemingly possessed the individual cognitive health literacy skills to act autonomously in managing diabetes, social contexts played a role. There was not necessarily a direct linear relationship between the possession of cognitive health literacy skills and improved health outcomes. For example, Andrew, the courier, claimed that he had no difficulty reading information on diabetes provided by the diabetes clinic, but he chose not to do so because he said he was too busy working. Dianne, the teacher, had little trouble comprehending information on diet, but as she indicated, 'knowing and doing are two different things'. Lebanese-born Hala felt that while she could read and write 'ok', her preferred source of knowledge about diabetes care came from her face-to-face consultations with clinical staff at the diabetes centre. Bangladesh-born Saliq appeared to possess the language and literacy skills to independently manage type 2 diabetes but putting that knowledge into practice was compromised at times by the demands of his religious practices. Ria indicated that while she could read information about diabetes, in the past she was not in the right emotional state to learn more about and confront diabetes. And one of the podiatrists, Jasmine, indicated that while she could provide pamphlets on foot care to patients, it was often a waste of time because people 'chuck them out' when they get home. These few examples were an indication that social context matters.

This study indicated the potential value of shifting beyond the usual individual deficit understandings of health literacy by examining in detail how diabetes patients managed their everyday living with the disease. While in a normative sense, many of these patients could be viewed as lacking health literacy based on their English language and literacy proficiencies, it would be inaccurate to suggest that this necessarily influenced how they managed the disease in their everyday lives. As this chapter has demonstrated, social networks of support played a key role. One of the doctors at the diabetes clinic, Angela, encapsulated the argument well, at least in relation to one category of patients, elderly males living alone. She claimed that such patients, regardless of their normative language and literacy skills, probably fared less well in relation to their everyday management of the disease compared to their male counterparts who had less proficiency in language and literacy skills but who had access to a family support network at home:

> ... an elderly man, an English-speaking man by his self probably faring worse than a non-English speaking man who's got a wife or daughter to help who's at home with them making sure their feet are ok, checking their blood sugar levels, that they're not drinking too much, that sort of thing. So, an elderly person home alone regardless of whether they speak English or not, that's often the problematic situation.

This perspective, however, is at odds with the dominant and burgeoning health literacy 'industry' of academics, policymakers and health practitioners who perceive health literacy primarily in terms of individual deficits.

10

Countering Deficit

A critique of deficit and shame

In light of the research data and discussion presented in the chapters of this book, my aim in this final chapter is to critique contemporary dominant perspectives on adult literacy in Australian society with reference to the recent TV series on adult literacy, *Lost for Words*. I will then explore in more detail the power of dominant groups to name and define literacy and the implications this has for working-class adults.

At the beginning of Chapter 1, I mentioned two recent events that have given prominence to the field of adult literacy in Australia: firstly, the release of a federal parliamentary inquiry into adult literacy and its importance (House of Representatives, 2022), and secondly, the release of the three-part TV series called *Lost for Words* on the SBS channel (SBS, 2021a). The former is significant for those involved in or professionally related to the field of adult literacy, and aspects of its findings have been cited in previous chapters, but the latter arguably has greater significance for this book due to its national promotion and appeal to a wide audience. So popular has the TV series been as a ratings success that students have been sought for a follow-up Series 2 due to be broadcast nationally at the time of writing. The peak professional association, the Australian Council for Adult Literacy (ACAL), has provided active support for the TV series and has welcomed the national spotlight being shone on the field of adult literacy. The appeal of the TV series has even extended internationally through podcast and social media links with a Canadian literacy organization, Literacy Quebec (2022). To date, a considerable number of Australian TV viewers have been exposed to and influenced by the representation of adult literacy students in this TV series, and in view of this book's focus on the role of literacy in the everyday lives of groups of Australian adults, it is important that the TV series be critically examined.

Lost for Words is described in its official website as follows:

> Lost for Words follows eight brave Australians on a life-changing opportunity to transform their lives by taking part in an intensive nine-week adult literacy programme ... It is an empowering and uplifting observational documentary that confronts Australia's staggeringly low adult literacy rate.
>
> (SBS, 2021a)

Calling the series an 'observational documentary' adds legitimacy to the real-life authenticity of the series, though it should be noted that the series does not document an existing adult literacy programme, rather, one specially developed for and funded by the TV programme and featuring students specially selected through interviews. The programme is set firmly within the literacy crisis narrative. The promotional website for the series states that '[m]ore than 43% of Australian adults don't have the necessary literacy skills needed for everyday life. That's about seven million Australian adults' (SBS, 2021b). The series highlights the 'shame and stigma' experienced by the literacy programme participants, and their perceived skill deficiencies are continually emphasized with examples of them being unable to read to their children, follow recipes, pass a driving test, navigate train timetables or order from a menu. Low-literate people are described in the series as having to 'hide their little secret' and to be fearful of others dismissing them. The participants themselves are described as 'brave beyond measure and they are you' indicating the high prevalence of literacy problems in the community and that many viewers are likely to personally identify with the low literate status of the participants.

The chapters of this book have examined aspects of adult literacy policy and practice over many decades, beginning from the 1970s, and a considerable number of adults have expressed their perspectives on the role of literacy in their lives. This leads me to be critical of the TV series *Lost for Words* for two main reasons: firstly, the inappropriate use of the statistical data that underpin the essential rationale for the series – the high prevalence of literacy 'problems' experienced by adults in the general community; and secondly, the students selected for the TV series do not generally represent either adult literacy students or adults in the community who may be considered to be low literate.

To be clear, the TV series does reflect, indeed it strengthens, dominant society's perspectives on adults with low literacy levels. The way literacy is described and the difficulties that the adult students in the series experience with literacy fit well with the 'literacy crisis' narrative outlined at the beginning of the book and discussed in several other chapters. But as I indicated in

Chapter 1, there are problems in statistically representing the extent of low literacy in adult populations. The TV series is underpinned by the statement that Australia has a 'staggeringly low adult literacy rate', and the statistics indicating that 43 per cent, or about seven million adults, 'don't have the necessary literacy skills needed for everyday life,' are repeated many times in the three-part TV series. Without these statistics, the series would have much-reduced impact. Part of the rationale for the TV series is the disquiet or shock value to viewers of being told that millions of Australian adults live with a 'little secret', low literacy, so many in fact, that 'they are you'. To legitimize the statistics used in the TV promotional material (SBS, 2021a, 2021b), they are referenced to the most recent national survey of adult skills, the Programme for the International Assessment of Adult Competencies (PIAAC; see ABS, 2013). The PIAAC survey report (ABS, 2013), however, makes no mention of adults not having a level of literacy skills needed for everyday life, and in order to make such statements, it appears the SBS has appropriated data from the previous national survey of adult literacy, the Adult Literacy and Life Skills (ALL; see ABS, 2008a). It was the ALL survey, as explained in Chapter 1, that referenced the OECD (Statistics Canada and OECD, 2005), and applied Level Three of the survey's five levels of literacy proficiency as the criterion level or 'cut-off' point that determined the 'minimum required for individuals to meet the complex demands of everyday life'. While governments and many other national agencies have drawn extensively on the ALL data derived from Level Three from the time of their release (ABS, 2008a), including as justification for the National Foundation Skills Strategy for Adults (SCOTESE, 2012), use of this criterion level is no longer appropriate, if indeed it ever was. The Level Three criterion was arbitrary, and its use as a means of determining those who can or cannot function in society has been discredited (Atkinson, 2015; Black and Yasukawa, 2014a; St. Clair, 2012), even by a senior analyst at the OECD (Thorn, 2013 cited in Smythe, 2015: 10). Use of the Level Three criterion created a dichotomy and served a purpose little different to surveys in the 1970s which claimed to determine those adults who were functionally literate or illiterate (e.g. Goyen, 1977; Northcutt, 1975). The report of the PIAAC findings in Australia has stated that the PIAAC and ALL data 'are not comparable' (ABS, 2013), and the OECD (2013: 61) has made clear that the PIAAC proficiency levels are not normative and should not be understood as 'standards' or 'benchmarks'. For these reasons, there is little justification for the SBS TV series to draw on PIAAC data to make statements that 43 per cent of Australian adults or 7 million people do not have the necessary literacy skills needed for everyday life.

It is understandable that organizations, in making their case for a focus on literacy skills, should draw on data that demonstrate the severity of the literacy crisis, and the SBS TV series is just one of the most recent examples. Another is the recent parliamentary inquiry into adult literacy and its importance (House of Representatives, 2022: 1) which states in its first two sentences:

> One in five adult Australians have low literacy and/or numeracy. This means that around three million adults do not have the skills to meet the demands of work and life.

Interestingly, it is now stated that 3 million adults and not 7 million are so lacking in literacy or numeracy skills that they cannot meet the demands of everyday life, but the same issue remains – a criterion level, now PIAAC level two, is used without justification and contrary to the OECD's published statements about proficiency level standards or benchmarks.

My second main criticism of the *Lost for Words* TV series is that the students selected for the series do not generally represent either adult literacy students or adults in the community who may be considered low literate. At the outset, however, I should acknowledge that over the decades, I have met and worked with similar types of adult literacy students to those featured in the TV series, and feelings of shame and stigma about lacking literacy ring true for some of them. But the point I make is that they are a minority, and the TV series producers have been selective in choosing participants with dispositions of shame and embarrassment towards literacy. Adult literacy students do not necessarily experience these dispositions or struggle with literacy in their everyday lives in the way depicted in the TV series, and the chapters of this book are testament to an alternative perspective.

The descriptions of adult literacy students in the TV series experiencing personal shame and stigma at having low literacy skills appear very similar to those found in studies of adult literacy up to half a century ago (British Association of Settlements, 1974; Council of Adult Education, 1974; Mezirow, Darkenwald and Knox, 1975). It has been an enduring theme over the decades, and in the recent parliamentary report on adult literacy (House of Representatives, 2022), there were submissions, mainly from volunteer tutor organizations, that emphasized these popular representations of adults who lack literacy skills (some submissions are outlined in Chapter 1 of this book). The chapters of this book, however, have rarely featured similar descriptions from the many groups of adults who have voiced their perspectives on the role of literacy in their lives. There were some prisoners (of the 'personal orientation type' according to Levine, 1986), who did appear to experience low literacy as a personal failing and who internalized shame, but others did not and were relatively untroubled in their everyday lives, often because they had social networks of support. So too with many other groups of adults. Individual feelings of shame and stigma about low literacy were not expressed by any of the unemployed adults (Chapter 3), or the local council workers (Chapter 4), or the production workers in two manufacturing companies (Chapter 5). Even within the adult literacy student groups (Chapter 6), there were few comments that indicated a disposition of shame. Quite the contrary in the case of one student who made the explicit claim: 'I never shame because I don't know this language' (a student born in Afghanistan). A contributing factor to this lack of expressed shame and stigma was that many of the students I interviewed were born overseas where English was not their main language (i.e. ESL/EAL). While they may have lacked English language and literacy proficiency, they were often multilingual and proficient in many other written scripts. This should hardly be a surprise as recent census data indicate that over 20 per cent of Australians speak a language other than English at home (ABS, 2021). From my experience, most of the students who attend adult literacy programmes in major urban areas in Australia fit this demographic profile. The case of Mei Ping in Chapter 6 was an extreme example. She was born in Indonesia to a Chinese family, and in her life trajectory to date, she had learnt seven languages and three different written scripts. English literacy was simply her latest, which she studied because she wanted to help her grandchildren in Sydney. There was no shame or stigma for her in not having proficiency in English literacy.

Overseas-born ESL/EAL adults featured in several chapters of this book, as unemployed people, as production workers, as adult literacy and VET students, and as adults experiencing diabetes. As the workplace trainer at one of the manufacturing companies (Hearing Solutions) in Chapter 5 commented fittingly, 'it's just that English is not their first language'. In the study of manufacturing companies in Chapter 5, it was found that while in a normative sense many workers were assessed to lack English language and literacy skills, according to the perspectives of local managers, supervisors, workplace trainers and the workers themselves, this was not a matter of concern in terms of workplace performance. Furthermore, these workers expressed no shame at being assessed to lack these English language and literacy skills. These were highly proficient workers managing the language and literacy practices required in their workplaces, and they were also proficient in a range of languages and literacies other than English. Their assessed low (English) literacy skills however could be seen to render them deficient as workers in the eyes of dominant groups, as reflected in policy discourses on language and literacy (Hunter, 2012; Hunter and Cooke, 2014). The CEO of the manufacturing company (Insulation Products) typified this viewpoint, describing his migrant ESL/EAL workers as 'foreign ... your less educated people' and the only ones left for him to employ. But these dominant perspectives on overseas-born migrants as deficient Others were effectively countered in the chapters of this book through ethnographic perspectives that demonstrated how they managed language and literacy practices in their everyday lives.

Lack of self-worth and feelings of shame about lack of literacy are dispositions associated mainly with adults born in Australia or in English-speaking communities who for various reasons have not acquired literacy skills in their early years and have not been well served by their schooling experiences. These dispositions have been described in one UK study as the 'hidden injuries' of disadvantaged working-class lives (Cieslik and Simpson, 2015), and in a Canadian study as 'wounded learners' (Lange et al., 2015). The volunteer tutor programme that reported on students' deficits and shame in the recent parliamentary report on adult literacy focused primarily on Australian-born students, those who had 'fallen through the cracks in the school system' (House of Representatives, 2022: 128–9). The students specially selected for the TV series *Lost for Words* appeared to be predominantly Australian born (place of birth was not stated in the series). Each of the students felt personally afflicted by low literacy and their shame was expressed on screen with plentiful tears of emotion. In this respect, the TV series accurately reflected how some adults can be damaged emotionally by low literacy. Describing these students as 'brave' in their efforts to overcome fears about their 'little secret' appeared to accord with a characterization of adult literacy students referred to in Chapter 6 as 'heroic victims' (Belzer and Pickard, 2015), in which adult learners drew on the redemptive power of literacy to heal emotional injuries. However, according to Belzer and Pickard (2015: 6), 'heroic victim' stories 'are less relevant for research purposes than they are for public relations and marketing', which may help to account for their absence in my book chapters and their prominence as marketing appeal in *Lost for Words*. The students in the TV series appeared to have been specially selected for their emotional appeal for TV audiences. One selected participant had even travelled from interstate in order to participate in the series. While the students' emotions were, of course, genuine and heartfelt, the series in effect commodified these emotions for purchase in the entertainment media. It was a case of commercializing deficit and shame.

The TV series *Lost for Words* and the recent parliamentary inquiry into adult literacy present contemporary (and long held) dominant perspectives on adult literacy in Australia. Statistics from recent national adult literacy (and numeracy) surveys have been used (I would argue misused) to bolster claims of a literacy crisis, and adults who fall within the lowest levels of literacy on these surveys are represented essentially as non-functioning members of society who lack the skills for everyday life and experience a high degree of personal shame.

Alternative perspectives based on the voices of working-class adults

The chapters of this book provide a counter to both the literacy crisis discourse and its related representations of low-literate adults as illustrated in *Lost for Words*. I refer to these adults as working class, and my aim throughout has been to examine the role of literacy in their lives from their own perspectives, their own 'voices'. Adopting an ethnographic perspective commensurate with a 'social practice' approach to literacy, and through a dialogical process of semi-structured interviews, my aim has been to provide 'thick' descriptions of the lives of people who are usually silenced or marginalized (Angus et al., 2013). Each group of adults has provided insights into the role of literacy in the contexts of their everyday lives that are rarely found in mainstream studies of literacy. Invariably, these sociocultural insights have provided contrasts, indeed contradictions, not only with the neoliberal perspectives of the dominant groups who largely speak for literacy in contemporary society but with society generally due to the power of the dominant discourse on literacy. It may be useful to provide a brief summary of the chapters to highlight these contradictions:

- I began with prisoners (Chapter 2), commonly known to be largely functionally illiterate, and whose criminality is often linked with their lack of literacy. All the prisoners I interviewed had been assessed by the prison system as lacking in literacy, and the prisoners themselves self-reported that they experienced difficulties with literacy. These prisoners explained that they managed the literacy practices of their everyday prison lives largely by drawing on a support network of fellow prisoners. There were complexities of course due to variations in individual prisoner skills, attitudes and dispositions, but they managed their lives – they functioned in prison largely through the support of others. So too in their lives beyond prison, at home and at work where social support was provided mainly by spouses and fellow workers. While not the focus of the study, any causal links between their literacy abilities and criminal behaviour appeared tenuous relative to the impact of their poor socio-economic life circumstances.

- In the case of long-term unemployed people (Chapter 3), they were sent to (in some cases coerced into) a literacy programme for jobseekers because low literacy was seen to cause unemployment. Some students could see advantages, particularly those born overseas who believed their spoken English proficiency was limiting their job opportunities, but others failed to see any link between their literacy abilities and obtaining a job. Literacy had not prevented them being employed in the past, and they were unemployed at the time largely because there was a recession. There was less a skills gap, more a jobs gap. The literacy=jobs axiom served the interests of several stakeholders, including employment agencies, VET providers and governments but not many of those identified as low-literate 'jobseekers' and sent to the literacy programme. Effectively, they were being blamed for being unemployed because they lacked literacy skills, shifting the focus away from the macro-economic structural factors that could be seen to be the primary cause of the recession and unemployment.
- The outdoor workers in a local council featured in Chapter 4 were engaged in traditional manual work constructing concrete footpaths. Their enterprising manager and supervisor were resolved to restructure the work and culture of these outdoor workers into 'competitive teams' required as part of the 'new work order'. The dominant human capital argument was that more advanced literacy skills were essential for work in restructured 'team' workplaces. The problem, however, was that despite the managerial rhetoric of workers needing to be more literate in this new workplace culture, there was no evidence that literacy skills had any major role to play in this type of manual work. Moreover, the workers were already working very effectively in their job roles in teams (and traditional 'gangs'), and they privately resisted managerial efforts to change them. It was concluded that literacy was used as a code by managers and supervisors to indicate that the workers did not meet managerial expectations of the social identities required of new knowledge workers.
- In Chapter 5, two manufacturing companies were selected to examine the workplace literacy and numeracy crisis in production work. Both companies

were at varying stages of introducing lean production training in which, according to national industry skills organizations, more advanced literacy and numeracy skills were seen to be integral. In the routine work of both companies, the mainly overseas-born production workers were found to be highly effective in their work roles and problems with literacy and numeracy skills were considered a non-issue by workers, workplace trainers and line managers. If any literacy/numeracy problems did arise, particularly in the high-performance company, Hearing Solutions, the work 'teams' provided all the necessary support for individual workers. In the lean production training, literacy and numeracy issues played only a minor role in one company, and no role in the other. At Hearing Solutions, the training was provided as part of regular work routines on the production floor. It was focused largely on visual representations (graphs etc.), and the work teams provided all the support that workers needed. The research study effectively invalidated the workplace literacy skills crisis as it related to routine production work and lean production training in these two manufacturing companies.

- The adult literacy students interviewed in Chapter 6 provided a different picture to the common perception that they were non-functioning ('hobbled') adults in the community experiencing personal shame. Most did not speak English as their first language and were multilingual, the norm in most literacy programmes in urban TAFE colleges in Australia. There was little evidence of personal shame about lack of (English) literacy skills. Students sought to improve their English literacy as a means to improve their own self-concepts, and more generally, their social and economic well-being. Many were already 'functioning' as active and engaged members of family, community and work networks, but in the process of learning literacy as part of a student group, they were practising new roles in expanded English-speaking social networks. Students were introduced to different groups and social networks (bridging and linking ties) previously unknown or inaccessible to them. Improved social relations (social capital) at home, in the community and at work were a major programme outcome for the students, in addition to improving their technical literacy skills.

- Chapter 7 featured young people who were disengaged from the school system and were participants in a 'flexible' TAFE programme designed to enable them to obtain the equivalent of a school leaving certificate (Year 10).

The dominant perspective on these types of students was that they were 'at risk' troublemakers in need of fixing, and they were particularly at risk of becoming NEET (not in education, employment or training). The students in this study were successful in gaining the qualification due to the 'flexible' course structure (the absence of school-type regulations), but more importantly, to social relationships (social capital). They developed strong friendship networks with fellow students, and they related well with teachers, despite their previous fractured relationships in the school system. The new relationships with TAFE teachers involved friendship, trust and reciprocal respect that often extended beyond the school site. These relations were in stark contrast to the 'relational power' they experienced at school where they were alienated by dominant middle-class norms of social control.

- In the field of post-school vocational education and training (Chapter 8), the dominant human capital discourse views many vocational students to be in need of improved literacy (and language and numeracy, i.e. LLN) in order to obtain qualifications for work. A range of vocational education students in TAFE were interviewed and for most students (particularly in hairdressing and aged care courses) LLN was not found to restrict them from successfully completing their studies. Most students could manage their studies independently, while others received informal assistance from peers and work colleagues, particularly with theoretical aspects of their courses. In the case of aged care students, some of them had to overcome a lack of academic self-esteem resulting from their own poor schooling experiences. In courses where LLN support was provided, some students indicated dissatisfaction with deficit models that focused primarily on assisting students with LLN problems.
- Chapter 9 featured older patients with diabetes and examined how they managed the disease in their everyday lives and in clinical consultations with professional health workers. The chapter focused on the concept of health literacy, which traditionally has highlighted poor health outcomes resulting from individuals lacking cognitive (i.e. 'autonomous') literacy skills. The qualitative study demonstrated that individual patients were supported in large part by social networks, mainly from family and friends, to manage the disease in their everyday lives. Health literacy was thus viewed as a 'distributed' concept, involving 'shared knowledge and expertise', rather than a set of cognitive skills that many individuals lacked.

The power to name and define literacy

For each of these groups of adults there were contradictions between the predominantly deficit perspectives expressed by dominant groups and the sociocultural perspectives of members of the adult groups in terms of the role of literacy in their everyday lives. Street (2001: 6–7) has long argued from his literacy studies in various parts of the world, that he hears 'dominant voices characterising local people as "illiterate" while on the ground ethnographic and literacy-sensitive observation indicates a rich variety of practices'. Jackson (2005b: 769) refers to these seemingly contradictory perspectives as the significant mismatch or 'gap' between the 'standardisations and normalisations' of policy and the 'messy, lived practices of those who are the targets of policy'. To understand these gaps and contradictions we need to consider the exercise of power by dominant groups. Street (2011) refers to the significance of 'the power to name and define' literacy by dominant groups, which includes the power to determine what counts as inequality in society. Thus, inequality from this perspective 'is not simply a given that we, as moral and committed reformers need to respond to, but a construct that needs careful analysis and justification' (Street, 2011: 580). This power to define literacy extends across the whole spectrum of the adult literacy field, including the power

> to determine policy, to fund and develop literacy programmes in international contexts, to prescribe ways of teaching, development of educational materials, texts books, assessment etc.
>
> (Street, 2011: 581)

Most commonly, as this book has highlighted throughout, literacy is understood by dominant groups as a 'single uniform thing' (Street, 2011: 580), a set of skills acquired and developed initially in early schooling and seen to lead to a range of benefits in society, including better jobs, prosperity, health and socio-economic well-being more generally. This 'autonomous' model of literacy (Street, 1984) forms the basis of the literacy crisis promoted by dominant groups on the grounds that individuals lacking literacy will necessarily have poorer employment and health outcomes and generally reduced levels of socio-economic well-being. This taken-for-granted, common-sense understanding of literacy and the powerful interests promoting it are rarely questioned in the general community.

Street (2011) argues that ethnographic perspectives on literacy, as represented by social practice approaches, provide an alternative understanding of literacy as practices that are 'multiple and culturally varied' that can help to avoid the 'one dimensional and culturally narrow' autonomous model of literacy. He also argues that the ethnographic perspective 'can sensitise us to the ways in which the power to name and define is a crucial component of inequality' (2011: 580). I would contend that the chapters of this book and this concluding chapter serve to illustrate both of Street's points of argument.

The OECD and neoliberal capitalism

Key international organizations have demonstrated the power to name and define literacy and, in so doing, provide an explanation for continuing poverty and inequality in societies. Street (2011) named UNESCO with its Global Monitoring Reports (UNESCO, 2006) as one such key organization, particularly influencing the Global South with its promotion of general, universal accounts of literacy consistent with autonomous models. In the context of my studies of literacy in the Global North, I refer to the role of the OECD as the key international organization responsible for naming and defining literacy in a way that dominates literacy policy and understandings not only in Australia but in countries such as the UK, the United States and Canada. The OECD performs this role largely through the considerable power of its international surveys designed to measure adult proficiencies in information-processing skills – literacy, numeracy and problem-solving (Black and Yasukawa, 2016). These OECD surveys, implemented and published by the ABS (1997, 2008a, 2013), have dominated adult literacy policy and practice in Australia for the past two decades. To a very large extent, what counts as literacy for adults and how it is measured in Australia are determined by these surveys. The findings of the first survey undertaken in 1996 (ABS, 1997) had relatively little impact in Australia (Mendelovits, 2011), but the second one, the ALL (ABS, 2008a), as explained in Chapter 1 and earlier in this chapter, had a major impact on adult literacy policy and practice. This was due primarily to the use of the Level Three criterion or cut-off point on the five-point scale of literacy proficiencies which determined the 'minimum required for individuals to meet the complex demands of everyday life in the emerging knowledge-based economy'. The ABS adopted the criterion level from an OECD publication (Statistics Canada and the OECD, 2005), and the fact that neither the ABS nor the OECD has found it necessary to provide justification for this criterion level is a measure of the power of the OECD to name and define literacy. Leading Australian statisticians in Australia have commented on the use of the Level Three criterion only that 'the message is simplified' (Caldwell and Webster, 2013: 107). And yet this Level Three criterion has been responsible for providing the statistical rationale for the National Foundation Skills Strategy for Adults (SCOTESE, 2012) and for providing the key level of skills promoted by the nation's peak intergovernmental forum, the Council of Australian Governments (COAG; see SCOTESE, 2012; Productivity Commission, 2020). In Canada also, the Level Three criterion has had a major impact on policy and practice in adult literacy (Atkinson, 2015; Elfert and Walker, 2020; Smythe, 2015). I would contend that it was largely the absence of a criterion level of literacy skills for functioning in society that resulted in the other two OECD-derived national surveys (ABS, 1997, 2013) failing to gain much national interest in the news media in Australia following the release of the survey reports (Yasukawa, 2019; Yasukawa and Black, 2016).

The OECD's interest in adult literacy coincided with the rise in the importance of human capital theory. In policy terms in Australia, the Australian Language and Literacy policy (ALLP; see DEET, 1991), with its focus on promoting jobseeker and workplace literacy programmes, represented this shift to human capital orientations. Around the same time, the OECD was beginning to promote the economic costs of low literacy (OECD, 1992) in the lead up to its first major international adult literacy survey (OECD and Statistics Canada, 1995). Since the early 1990s, the OECD has been a significant international policy actor in the field of education (Sellar and Lingard, 2013), but educational development has not been its primary goal; rather, it is secondary to economic growth (Valiente, 2014). Literacy in the human capital model plays a key part as an economic resource to be invested in and profited by. As explained in Chapter 3, literacy is viewed as a resource 'just like farmland or goldmines' (DEET, 1992a: 1) to be developed for a country's growth and prosperity. To a large extent the OECD's surveys, with their focus on labour-market competencies, encouraged an international 'vocational turn' in adult literacy (Druine and Wildemeersch, 2000), and in Australian adult literacy policy this vocationalism has been reflected in the shift from more traditional understandings of literacy to the more economically encompassing term 'foundation skills' (SCOTESE, 2012), that includes not only literacy but employability. As indicated in Chapter 1, similar shifts have occurred in Canada with 'essential skills' (Hayes, 2013; Jackson, 2005a) and in the UK with 'functional skills' (Burgess and Hamilton, 2011).

The OECD's international literacy surveys exert power through numbers, through the survey data (Hamilton, Maddox and Addey, 2015). Literacy has thus become quantified, and the prime example in Australian policy and practice of the power of numbers is the significance of the Level Three criterion. The surveys are based on an assumed (autonomous) model of literacy, internationally recognized, accepted and seemingly offering 'certainty and closure on issues of what literacy is and who it is for' (Hamilton, Maddox and Addey, 2015: xiv). This global literacy represents 'the single story, the only way literacy is understood and acted upon' (Addey, 2018: 327). It is a privileged model of literacy that fails to account for how local literacies are used in people's everyday lives and indeed is seen to devalue them (Hamilton, 2001; Hamilton and Barton, 2000). The powerful and dominating influence of the OECD's surveys and concepts of literacy has translated into many national adult literacy policies, curriculum documents and assessment practices (Hamilton, 2001, 2016, 2017; Hamilton, Maddox and Addey, 2015; Pinsent-Johnson, 2015). In Australia, the influence of the OECD has already been examined in relation to the National Foundation Skills Strategy and government skills targets, and it has extended to literacy assessment regimes following the mapping of the OECD's ALL proficiency ratings with the country's main literacy and numeracy assessment tool, the Australian Core Skills Framework (Circelli et al., 2013).

The surveys and the model of literacy on which they are based are part of the OECD's ideological agenda to promote neoliberal capitalism (Rubenson, 2009, 2015; Teodora, 2020). They are designed to form global citizens for a competitive global economy, and the surveys measure 'a new capitalism literacy, an ideal literacy of what all people should have to be able to engage in a neo-liberal society' (Addey, 2018: 328). As explained in Chapter 1, the surveys have been referred to as 'technologies of neoliberal governance' (Atkinson, 2012: 81) due to their promotion of market values in which individuals are expected to take personal responsibility for their own well-being. Individuals are thus viewed primarily as units of human capital for which they themselves are wholly responsible. These neoliberal tenets of individualization and responsibilization were discussed briefly in Chapter 1 as the dominant blame-the-victim approach inherent in the current National Foundation Skills Strategy (Argent, Brown and Kelly, 2022). As Atkinson (2019: 151) points out, the neoliberal imperative for individuals to treat education as a form of investment in themselves 'weighs particularly heavily on those who have had the least access to education and who face the most barriers to having their credential recognised'. This describes most of the individuals who feature in the chapters of this book: prisoners, unemployed people, outdoor workers in local councils, manufacturing workers, adult literacy and vocational students, and many adults experiencing chronic health problems. These adults, referred to in this book as working class, are all defined by dominant society as deficient in literacy skills based on normative constructions of literacy, the 'single story' of literacy. This does not mean that they are unable to manage the literacy demands of their everyday lives, as the chapters of this book clearly demonstrate, rather, that based on the power of dominant groups to define what counts as literacy, chief among them being the OECD, these groups of adults are deemed by virtue of their normatively assessed literacy deficiencies to be less worthy people.

The violence of literacy

The dominant discourse on literacy promoted strongly by the OECD's international literacy surveys over the past several decades can be seen to oppress the values and practices of working-class adults. It has imposed inequality on them (Street, 2011: 581); it performs a violence against them. In making this statement, I draw on critical educators who have presented class-based analyses of adult literacy education. Atkinson (2009) refers in part to Allman (1999) to explain that literacy, as represented in OECD literacy surveys, 'becomes a mask which disguises the essence of capitalist relations'; it ignores how capitalism systematically devalues the labour of particular groups of people as it relentlessly seeks increased profits. Atkinson (2009) states that in order to understand and resist this dominant literacy discourse, 'we must name what "epistemic violence" it enacts, by whom and in whose interests'. Hopefully this book has contributed to this naming. Other researchers in recent times have referred to the violence of literacy. Duckworth and colleagues in their UK studies (Ade-Ojo and Duckworth, 2019; Duckworth, 2013; Duckworth and Ade-Ojo, 2016; Duckworth and Cochrane, 2012; Duckworth and Smith, 2018; Duckworth and Tett, 2019) draw extensively on Bourdieu's reproduction theory (Bourdieu and Passeron, 1990) to invoke the concept of symbolic violence as it relates to working-class students in adult literacy and further education courses. In these studies, students describe violence and trauma in their lives at home, at work and in their further education studies as dominant society imposes its values and meanings and invariably constructs these students as deficient. Adult literacy programmes based on critical and emancipatory principles are positioned to offer resistance to this symbolic violence.

In each of the chapters of this book, I have demonstrated how conceptualizations of literacy promoted by dominant groups have presented working-class adults as deficient and unworthy, representing a violence against working-class people. The standardized autonomous form of literacy, that promoted by the OECD, is an ideological tool that represents dominant society's values and norms, and it is used against working-class people; it oppresses them. In capitalist society, as Stuckey (1991: 93) notes, literacy is 'reproductive of the material relationships of people'; it serves to maintain the inequalities of the existing social order. This is not a new argument. Graff (1979, 1987, 2017), for example, has long argued the literacy myth that while historically promoted as the means to upward social mobility and economic development, literacy, from at least the mid-nineteenth century in Western urban societies, has been used in the interests of capital to regulate and discipline working-class people (Black and Yasukawa, 2014b).

The chapters of this book provide multiple examples of the violence of literacy against working-class adults. In the case of long-term unemployed adults (Chapter 3), it was primarily poorer, lower-skilled adults who were targeted for literacy assessments, and those assessed as lacking literacy skills were directed, under threat of losing their welfare benefits, to jobseeker literacy programmes. They were made to accept responsibility for being unemployed because they lacked literacy skills, and yet as the chapter demonstrated, literacy may have played little or no role in their previous employment. In the case of outdoor workers in a local council in Chapter 4, workers were being told by management that they lacked literacy skills, and their jobs could be under threat. And yet, there was no evidence that literacy played a role in the everyday work of most of these workers. Literacy was being used to change their workplace identities with the view to extract more of their surplus labour. In the case of manufacturing workers undertaking training in lean production in Chapter 5, the dominant discourse stated clearly that literacy skills were an integral component of this work, and yet at one company, Hearing Solutions, any literacy (and/or language) difficulties experienced by the largely overseas-born workforce were overcome, indeed they became a non-issue, due mainly to the way workplace training was introduced and the support provided within the work teams. The case of the other manufacturing company, Insulation Products, needs to be recounted in more detail because it provides a prime example of symbolic violence perpetuated against production workers based on their assessed literacy deficiencies. At the time of the research, the company was in the process of introducing lean production, but the training focus was exclusively on the changes required by the workers, not management personnel or workplace systems. One of the first actions of the external training consultant responsible for introducing lean production to the company was to assess the whole workforce for their literacy skills using the standardized assessment tool, the Australian Core Skills Framework (ACFS). Unsurprisingly, many production workers fell below the benchmark level of the ACFS and were thus deemed in a normative sense to be deficient and a literacy programme was introduced at the company to assist these workers. And yet, in terms of job performance, the same external trainer analysed the work role of each production worker (she called it a 'process map') and concluded that, beyond some minor issues relating to pronunciation, there were no examples of deficiencies in workplace performance; the production workforce was operating very efficiently. Lack of literacy (or language or numeracy), as measured by the standardized ACFS, played no major role in the workplace efficiency of the production workforce. The one area of the company's operations that did cause problems, however, was the communication work of the sales teams which comprised personnel with more professional backgrounds and educational qualifications. They were identified by managers and workers as responsible for costly mistakes caused by insufficient or incorrect technical knowledge of the company's products, or they made mistakes when placing information on the job cards. But because the personnel in the sales teams all recorded literacy assessment scores above the benchmark level, they were ineligible for training provided by the external trainer and exempt from remedial attention. The focus on literacy levels thus targeted only the production workers for remedial training, despite their efficient workplace performance.

In the two manufacturing companies outlined above, teamwork on the production floor was integral, highlighting a central feature of contemporary workplace organization. As a team leader at Hearing Solutions commented, 'there is no I. I always remind them every day in the meeting there's no I; it's we, we as a team'. So too with the local council workers in Chapter 3 who worked in 'gangs' or newly created 'competitive teams'. Working together in teams can be seen as emblematic of the broader role of social networks in people's everyday lives, which, as the chapters of this book illustrate, are not confined only to workplaces. Prisoners, at least those who acknowledged difficulties with literacy, relied extensively on social networks of mainly fellow prisoners to help them manage the literacy practices of their everyday prison lives. In their lives outside prison, they also relied on social networks of support, often involving spouses at home, and colleagues at work. For the students in post-compulsory education – adult literacy students, marginalized young people and vocational education students in TAFE, relationships with others in social networks, particularly relationships with fellow students and teachers, were key to successful learning outcomes in their studies and to improving aspects of their socio-economic well-being.

For most of the diabetes patients in Chapter 9, understanding and managing their health needs would have been highly problematic if not for their access to social networks of support, particularly from family members. This was highlighted by the diabetes doctor cited at the conclusion of the chapter, who stated that elderly patients, lacking normative language and/or literacy skills but with access to strong social support from family, probably fared better in terms of managing their diabetes than elderly people living alone regardless of their language/literacy skills. Support provided by social networks is a defining feature of this book, and literacy in these examples can be seen to be 'distributed' based on the knowledge and expertise of others in social networks (Papen, 2009).

Dominant constructions of literacy take no account of local contexts, including social networks. The focus primarily is on independent individuals expected in neoliberal times to take personal responsibility for their own skills (human capital) and well-being. There is a tension, indeed contradiction, between this autonomous literacy skills approach which promotes neoliberal capitalism and identifies those individuals who fail to meet its standards as deficient, and a social practice approach to literacy, demonstrated in the chapters of this book, that details how people actually manage literacy practices in their everyday lives, invariably drawing on social networks for support. In the former, dominant power relations are effectively hidden by a seemingly common-sense, hegemonic literacy discourse. In the latter, the power and politics of literacy become evident. This skills versus practices tension has featured in every chapter of this book. It is a long-standing tension first highlighted in the pioneering work of social practice researchers such as Graff (1979), Heath (1983) and Street (1984). My hope is that this book contributes to debates and alternative voices on the role of literacy in society, highlighting how groups of working-class adults manage their everyday lives while subject to a dominant discourse on literacy that oppresses them and subjects them to symbolic violence.

References

Abouzeid, M., Philpot, B., Janus, E.D., Coates, M. and Dunbar, J. (2013). 'Type 2 diabetes prevalence varies by socio-economic status within and between migrant groups: Analysis and implications for Australia'. *BMC Public Health*, 13 (1): 252.

ACIL Allen Consulting. (2015). *SEE Programme Evaluation*. Melbourne: ACIL Allen Consulting.

Adams, R., Piantadosi, C., Ettridge, K., Miller, C., Wilson, C., Tucker, G. and Hill, C. (2013). 'Functional health literacy mediates the relationship between socio-economic status, perceptions and lifestyle behaviours related to cancer risk in an Australian population'. *Patient Education and Counselling*, 91 (2): 206–12.

Addey, C. (2018). 'Assembling literacy as global: The danger of a single story'. In M. Milano, S. Webb, J. Holford, R. Waller and P. Jarvis (eds), *The Palgrave International Handbook of Adult and Lifelong Education and Learning*, 315–35. London: Palgrave.

Addey, C. (2021). 'Passports to the Global South, UN flags, favourite experts: Understanding the interplay between UNESCO and OECD within the SDG4 context'. *Globalisation, Societies and Education*, 19 (5): 593–604.

Ade-Ojo, G. and Duckworth, V. (2019). 'Forms of institutionalised symbolic violence and resistance in the journey of a cohort of adult literacy learners'. *International Journal of Educational Research*, 98: 336–44.

Adult Learning Australia. (2021). 'Australia's adult literacy crisis'. *Quest, Adult Learning Australia*, (1): 1–5.

Allman, P. (1999). *Revolutionary Social Transformation: Democratic Hopes, Political Possibilities and Critical Education*. Westport, CT: Bergin & Garvey.

Ananiadou, K., Jenkins, A. and Wolf, A. (2004). 'Basic skills and workplace literacy: What do we actually know about the benefits?' *Studies in Continuing Education*, 26 (2): 289–308.

Angus, L., Golding, B., Foley, A. and Lavender, P. (2013). 'Promoting "learner voice" in VET: Developing democratic, transformative possibilities or further entrenching the status quo?' *Journal of Vocational Education and Training*, 65 (4): 560–74.

Apple, M. (1987). 'Foreword'. In C. Lankshear and M. Lawler, *Literacy, Schooling and Revolution*, vii–xii. London: Falmer Press.

Apple, M. (1999). 'Freire, neo-liberalism and education'. *Discourse: Studies in the Cultural Politics of Education*, 20 (1): 5–20.

Appleby, Y. and Barton, D. (2009). 'Adults' lives and learning in different contexts: A view over time'. In S. Reder and J. Bynner (eds), *Tracking Adult Literacy and Numeracy Skills: Findings from Longitudinal Research*, 349–64. New York: Routledge.

Argent, G., Brown, S. and Kelly, P. (2022). 'The responsibilisation of learners in the Australian Foundation Skills apparatus: Making up motivated, choice-making customers'. *Discourse: Studies in the Cultural Politics of Education*, 43 (1): 48–60.

Atkins, L. (2013). 'From marginal learning to marginal employment? The real impact of "learning" employability skills'. *Power and Education*, 5 (1): 28–37.

Atkinson, T. (2009). 'Commodifying literacy, justifying inequality: Timely relations in the international adult literacy survey (IALS)'. Paper presented at the 39th Annual SCUTREA Conference, 7–9 July, University of Cambridge.

Atkinson, T. (2012). 'Beyond disempowering counts: Mapping a fruitful future for adult literacies'. In L. Tett, M. Hamilton and J. Crowther (eds), *More Powerful Literacies*, 75–87. Leicester: National Institute of Adult Continuing Education.

Atkinson, T. (2015). 'Counting "what you want them to want": Psychometrics and social policy in Ontario'. In M. Hamilton, B. Maddox and C. Addey (eds), *Literacy as Numbers: Researching the Politics and Practices of International Literacy Assessment*, 207–22. Cambridge: Cambridge University Press.

Atkinson, T. (2019). 'Calculating normative literacy, constituting human capital'. In D. Brock (eds), *Governing the Social in Neoliberal Times*, 138–58. Vancouver: UBC Press.

Atlantis, E., Lange, K. and Wittert, G.A. (2009). 'Chronic disease trends due to excess body weight in Australia'. *Obesity Reviews*, 10 (5): 543–53.

Auerbach, E. (1994). 'Walking the competence tightrope'. Paper presented at the National Conference of the Australian Council for Adult Literacy, Perth.

Aulich, C. (1999). 'From convergence to divergence: Reforming Australian local government'. *Australian Journal of Public Administration*, 58 (3): 12–23.

Australian Bureau of Statistics. (1997). *Aspects of Literacy: Assessed Skill Levels*. Canberra: ABS.

Australian Bureau of Statistics. (2004). *Measuring Social Capital: An Australian Framework and Indicators*. Canberra: ABS.

Australian Bureau of Statistics. (2008a). *Adult Literacy and Life Skills Survey, Summary Results, Australia, 2006*. Canberra: ABS.

Australian Bureau of Statistics. (2008b). *Health Literacy, Australia, 2006*. Canberra: ABS.

Australian Bureau of Statistics. (2013). *Programme for the International Assessment of Adult Competencies, Australia, 2011–2012*. Canberra: ABS.

Australian Bureau of Statistics. (2019). *National Health Survey: Health Literacy*. Canberra: ABS.

Australian Bureau of Statistics. (2021). *Cultural Diversity Census, 2021*. Canberra: ABS.

Australian Commission on Safety and Quality in Health Care [ACSQHC]. (2014). *National Statement on Health Literacy: Taking Action to Improve Safety and Quality*. Sydney: ACSQHC.

Australian Committee on Technical and Further Education [Kangan Report]. (1974). *TAFE in Australia: Report on Needs in Technical and Further Education*. Canberra: Australian Government Publishing Service.

Australian Council for Adult Literacy. (2021). 'Submission 66 to Inquiry into adult literacy and its importance'. Available online: Sub 66 – ACAL – 10 Mar 2021 (1).pdf (accessed 22 May 2022).

Australian Council of Social Service [ACOSS]. (1994). *Down, but Not Out: Helping People Most Deeply Disadvantaged in the Labour Market*. Sydney: ACOSS.

Australian Council of Trade Unions [ACTU] and Trade Development Council [TDC]. (1987). *Australia Reconstructed: ACTU/TDC Mission to Western Europe*. Canberra: Australian Government Publishing Service.

Australian Government. (2022). 'National Foundation Skills Framework 2022 to 2032'. Available online: https://www.skillsreform.gov.au/images/documents/National-Foundation-Skills-Framework-2022-to-2032.pdf (accessed 22 May 2022).

Australian Industry Group. (2010). *Employer Views on Workplace Literacy and Numeracy Skills, Their Impact on Business and the Most Effective Measures for Improving Skills*. North Sydney: AIG.

Australian Industry Group. (2012). *When Words Fail: National Workforce Literacy Project. Final Project Report*. North Sydney: AIG.

Australian Industry Group. (2015). *Investing in Workplace Literacy Pays: Building Employer Commitment to Workplace Language, Literacy and Numeracy Programs*. North Sydney: AIG.

Australian Industry Group. (2016). *Tackling Foundation Skills in the Workforce*. North Sydney: AIG.

Australian Industry Group and University of Technology Sydney. (2012). *A More Competitive Manufacturing Industry: Management and Workforce Skills and Talent*. North Sydney: AIG.

Australian Institute of Health and Welfare. (2013). *Diabetes and Disability: Impairments, Activity Limitations, Participation Restrictions and Comorbidities*. Canberra: AIHW.

Australian Institute of Health and Welfare. (2014). *Cardiovascular Disease, Diabetes and Chronic Kidney Disease – Australian Facts: Prevalence and Incidence*. Canberra: AIHW.

Australian Institute of Health and Welfare. (2019). *The Health of Australia's Prisoners, 2018*. Canberra: AIHW.

Avis, J. (2010). 'Workplace learning, knowledge, practice and transformation'. *Journal for Critical Education Policy Studies*, 8 (2): 165–93.

Avis, J. (2017). 'Beyond cynicism, comfort radicalism and emancipatory practice: FE teachers'. In M. Daley, K. Orr and J. Petrie (eds), *The Principal: Power and Professionalism in FE*, 195–202. London: UCL Institute of Education Press.

Avis, J. (2021). 'Beyond neo-liberalism a new settlement – Three crises and postsecondary education'. *Journal for Critical Education Policy Studies*, 19 (1): 158–83.

Bak, T. and O'Maley, P. (2015). 'Towards professional responsibility for language and literacy: Exploring vocational teachers' emerging language and literacy understandings and identities'. *Literacy and Numeracy Studies*, 23 (1): 50–72.

Baker, A. (2013). *Not Looking for Work: The Rise of Non-Jobseekers on Unemployment Benefits.* Policy Monograph 136. Sydney: The Centre for Independent Studies.

Baker, D. (1998). 'Numeracy as social practice'. *Literacy and Numeracy Studies*, 8 (1): 37–50.

Balatti, J. and Black, S. (2011). 'Constructing learners as members of networks'. In R. Catts, I. Falk and R. Wallace (eds), *Vocational Learning: Innovative Theory and Practice*, 63–76. Dordrecht: Springer.

Balatti, J., Black, S. and Falk, I. (2006). *Reframing Adult Literacy and Numeracy Course Outcomes: A Social Capital Perspective.* Adelaide: National Centre for Vocational Education Research.

Balatti, J., Black, S. and Falk, I. (2007). 'Teaching for social capital outcomes: The case of adult literacy and numeracy courses in VET'. *Australian Journal of Adult Learning*, 47 (2): 245–63.

Balatti, J., Black, S. and Falk, I. (2009). *A New Social Capital Paradigm for Adult Literacy: Partnerships, Policy and Pedagogy.* Adelaide: National Centre for Vocational Education Research.

Balatti, J. and Falk, I. (2002). 'Socioeconomic contributions of adult learning to community: A social capital perspective'. *Adult Education Quarterly*, 52 (4): 281–98.

Bandura, A. (1995). *Self-Efficacy in Changing Societies.* Cambridge: Cambridge University Press.

Barber, M., Staples, M., Osborne, R., Clerehan, R., Elder, C. and Buchbinder, R. (2009). 'Up to a quarter of the Australian population may have suboptimal health literacy depending upon the measurement tool: Results from a population-based survey'. *Health Promotion International*, 24 (3): 252–61.

Barker, J. (2012). 'Social capital, homeless young people and the family'. *Journal of Youth Studies*, 15 (6): 730–43.

Barton, D. (2007). *Literacy: An Introduction to the Ecology of Written Language* (2nd ed.). Oxford: Blackwell Publishing.

Barton, D. (2009). 'Researching adult learners' lives to understand engagement and progression in learning'. *Literacy and Numeracy Studies*, 16 (2)/17 (1): 51–61.

Barton, D. (2012). 'Ethnographic approaches to literacy research'. In C. Chapelle (ed), *The Encyclopedia of Applied Linguistics.* Chichester: Wiley Blackwell.

Barton, D. and Hamilton, M. (2012). *Local Literacies: Reading and Writing in One Community* (2nd ed.). London: Routledge.

Barton, D., Hamilton, M. and Ivanič, R. (eds) (2000). *Situated Literacies: Reading and Writing in Context.* London: Routledge.

Barton, D., Appleby, Y., Hodge, R., Ivanič, R. and Tusting, K. (2007). *Literacy, Lives and Learning.* London: Routledge.

Bassani, C. (2007). 'Five dimensions of social capital theory as they pertain to youth studies'. *Journal of Youth Studies*, 10 (1): 17–34.

Basu, K., Maddox, B. and Robinson-Pant, A. (eds) (2009). *Interdisciplinary Approaches to Literacy and Development.* London: Routledge.

Bates, S. (2004). 'A model for pedagogical change: The course in applied vocational study skills'. *Fine Print*, 27 (1): 3–7.

Baynham, M. (1988). 'Literate, biliterate or multiliterate? Some issues for literacy research'. In J. McCaffery and B. Street (eds), *Literacy Research in the UK: Adult and School Perspectives*, 51–63. Lancaster: RaPAL.

Baynham, M. (1993). 'Code switching and mode switching: Community interpreters and mediators of literacy'. In B. Street (ed), *Cross Cultural Approaches to Literacy*, 294–314. Cambridge: Cambridge University Press.

Baynham, M. (1995). *Literacy Practices: Investigating Literacy in Social Contexts*. New York: Longman.

Baynham, M. and Lobanga Masing, H. (2000). 'Mediators and mediation in multilingual literacy events'. In M. Martin-Jones and K. Jones (eds), *Multilingual Literacies: Reading and Writing Different Worlds*, 189–207. Amsterdam: John Benjamins.

Baynham, M. and Prinsloo, M. (eds) (2009). *The Future of Literacy Studies*. London: Palgrave Macmillan.

Bean, R. (1994). 'Integrating communication and skills training'. *Open Letter: Australian Journal for Adult Literacy Research and Practice*, 5 (1): 17–30.

Beckett, D. (1999). 'Past the guru and up the garden path: The new organic management learning'. In D. Boud and J. Garrick (eds), *Understanding Learning at Work*, 83–97. London: Routledge.

Bee, B. (1993). 'Critical literacy and the politics of gender'. In C. Lankshear and P. McLaren (eds), *Critical Literacy: Politics, Praxis and the Postmodern*, 105–31. New York: State University of New York Press.

Belfiore, M., Defoe, T., Folinsbee, S., Hunter, J. and Jackson, N. (2004). *Reading Work: Literacies in the New Workplace*. Mahwah, NJ: Lawrence Erlbaum Associates.

Belzer, A. and Pickard, A. (2015). 'From heroic victims to competent comrades: Views of adult literacy learners in the research literature'. *Adult Education Quarterly*, 65 (3): 250–66.

Bernhard, G., Ose, D., Baudendistel, I., Seidling, H., Stutzle, M., Szecsenyi, J., Wensing, M. and Mahler, C. (2017). 'Understanding challenges, strategies, and the role of support networks in medication self-management among patients with type 2 diabetes'. *Diabetes Education*, 43 (2): 190–205.

Birrell, R., Healy, E. and Kinnaird, R. (2007). 'Cooks galore and hairdressers aplenty'. *People and Place*, 15 (1): 30–44.

Black, S. (1989a). *Low Literate Prisoners: Their Needs and Factors Affecting Their Participation in Prison Literacy Programmes*. Unpublished MA (Hons) thesis. Sydney University.

Black, S. (1989b). 'Prison education: For what purpose?' *Interlink, Newsletter of the Australian Association of Adult Education New South Wales Branch*, (1): 3–4.

Black, S. (1995a). *Literacy and the Unemployed*. Research report no. 1. Sydney: University of Technology Sydney.

Black, S. (1995b). 'Literacy as hegemony'. *Open Letter: Australian Journal for Adult Literacy Research and Practice*, 6 (1): 17–28.

Black, S. (1996). *Literacy/Numeracy Support and Team Teaching in VET: TAFE Teachers Reflect on Their Practice*. Blacktown: Foundation Studies Training Division.

Black, S. (2001). *Literacy as Critical Social Practice: A Challenge to Dominant Discourses on Literacy and (Un)Employment*. Unpublished PhD thesis. University of Technology Sydney.

Black, S. (2004). 'Whose economic wellbeing?: A challenge to dominant discourses on the relationship between literacy/numeracy skills and (un)employment'. *Literacy and Numeracy Studies*, 13 (1): 7–17.

Black, S. (2007). 'Non-English speaking background students in TAFE: Exploring the factors behind their module completion rates'. Paper presented at the 10th Annual Conference of the Australian Vocational Education and Training Research Association (AVETRA), 11–13 April, Victoria University, Melbourne.

Black, S. (2008a). 'The certificate III in aged care work in TAFE: Perspectives on unemployed, mature-aged women training to become assistants in nursing'. In J. Guenther, I. Falk and A. Arnott, *The Role of Vocational Education and Training in Welfare to Work; Support Document*, 42–54. Adelaide: National Centre for Vocational Education Research.

Black, S. (2008b). *Non-English Speaking Background Students in TAFE: Exploring the Factors behind Their Module Completion Rates in Selected TAFE NSW Courses*. Sydney: TAFE NSW Multicultural Education Unit.

Black, S. (2009). 'Editorial'. *Literacy and Numeracy Studies*, 16 (2)/17 (1): 1–4.

Black, S. (2010). 'Working the interstices: Adult basic education teachers respond to the audit culture'. *Literacy and Numeracy Studies*, 18 (2): 6–25.

Black, S. (2018). 'From "empowerment" to "compliance": Neoliberalism and adult literacy provision in Australia'. *Journal for Critical Education Policy Studies*, 16 (1): 104–44.

Black, S. (2020). 'Class experiences: A lifelong educational journey to political consciousness'. *Journal for Critical Education Policy Studies*, 18 (2): 30–69.

Black, S., Balatti, J. and Falk, I. (2006). 'Social capital outcomes: The new focus for adult literacy and numeracy courses'. *Australian Journal of Adult Learning*, 46 (3): 317–36.

Black, S., Balatti, J. and Falk, I. (2010). 'Reconnecting young people with learning: A social capital approach in VET'. *International Journal of Training Research*, 8 (2): 103–15.

Black, S. and Bee, B. (2018a). 'Adult literacy provision and social class: Australian contexts'. *Studies in the Education of Adults*, 50 (1): 92–110.

Black, S. and Bee, B. (2018b). 'Adult literacy and liberal-progressive pedagogy: Australian contexts'. *Research in Post-Compulsory Education*, 23 (2): 181–201.

Black, S., Lucchinelli, M. and Flynn, M. (2006). *Community Volunteering: Towards a Cross-Sectoral Model of Integrated Literacy Provision*. Canberra: Department of Education, Science and Training.

Black, S., Maitland, C., Hilbers, J. and Orinuela, K. (2016). 'Diabetes literacy and informal social networks: A qualitative study of patients at a diabetes centre'. *Journal of Clinical Nursing*, 26 (1&2): 248–57.

Black, S., McGregor, J. and Lucchinelli, M. (2006). *Marketing Adult Basic Education: Business Principles for Equity Outcomes*. Sydney: Northern Sydney Institute.

Black, S. and Sim, S. (1989). 'Adult literacy, political opportunism and basic skills testing in schools'. *Education Australia*, (6): 20–1.

Black, S. and Sim, S. (1990). *The Learning Experience: Perspectives of Former Students from Two Adult Literacy Programmes*. Sydney: Adult Literacy Information Centre.

Black, S. and Thorp, K. (1997). 'Everyday literacy practices and multilingual students: Implications for ABE pedagogy'. *Prospect: A Journal of Australian TESOL*, 12 (1): 63–75.

Black, S. and Yasukawa, K. (2011a). 'A tale of two councils: Alternative discourses on the "literacy crisis" in Australian workplaces'. *International Journal of Training Research*, 9 (3): 218–33.

Black, S. and Yasukawa, K. (2011b). *Working Together: Integrated Language, Literacy and Numeracy Support in Vocational Education and Training*. Sydney: University of Technology Sydney.

Black, S. and Yasukawa, K. (2012). 'Shared delivery: Integrating ELT in Australian vocational education'. *ELT Journal*, 66 (3): 347–55.

Black, S. and Yasukawa, K. (2013a). 'Beyond deficit models for integrating language, literacy and numeracy in Australian VET'. *Journal of Further and Higher Education*, 37 (4): 574–90.

Black, S. and Yasukawa, K. (2013b). 'Disturbing the pedagogical status quo: LLN and vocational teachers working together'. *Pedagogies: An International Journal*, 8 (1): 44–59.

Black, S. and Yasukawa, K. (2014a). 'Level 3: Another single measure of adult literacy and numeracy'. *Australian Educational Researcher*, 41 (2): 125–38.

Black, S. and Yasukawa, K. (2014b). 'The literacy myth continues: Adapting Graff's thesis to contemporary policy discourses on adult "foundation skills" in Australia'. *Critical Studies in Education*, 55 (2): 213–28.

Black, S. and Yasukawa, K. (2016). 'Research that counts: OECD statistics and "policy entrepreneurs" impacting on Australian adult literacy and numeracy policy'. *Research in Post-Compulsory Education*, 21 (3): 165–80.

Black, S., Yasukawa, K. and Brown, T. (2013). *Investigating the Crisis: Production Workers' Literacy and Numeracy Practices*. Adelaide: National Centre for Vocational Education Research.

Black, S., Yasukawa, K. and Brown, T. (2014). 'Changing conceptualisations of literacy and numeracy in lean production training: Two case studies of manufacturing companies'. *Studies in the Education of Adults*, 46 (1): 58–73.

Black, S., Yasukawa, K. and Brown, T. (2015). 'The literacy and numeracy "crisis" in Australian workplaces: Discursive rhetoric vs. production floor realities'. *Journal of Education and Work*, 28 (6): 607–30.

Block, D. (2014). *Social Class in Applied Linguistics*. London: Routledge.

Bloome, D. (2012). 'Classroom ethnography'. In M. Grenfell, D. Bloome, C. Hardy, K. Pohl, J. Rowsell and B. Street (eds), *Language, Ethnography and Education: Bridging New Literacy Studies and Bourdieu*, 7–26. London: Routledge.

Bloome, D. and Green, J. (2015). 'The social and linguistic turns in studying language and literacy'. In K. Pahl and J. Rowsell (eds), *The Routledge Handbook of Literacy Studies*, 19–34. London: Routledge.

Boeck, T. (2009). 'Social capital and young people'. In J. Wood and J. Hine (eds), *Work with Young People: Theory and Policy for Practice*, 88–103. London: Sage.

Bookwala, J., Marshall, K. and Manning, S. (2014). 'Who needs a friend? Marital status transitions and physical health outcomes in later life'. *Health Psychology*, 33 (6): 505–15.

Bottrell, D. (2008). 'Dealing with disadvantage: Resilience and the social capital of young people's networks'. *Youth and Society*, 40 (4): 476–501.

Bourdieu, P. and Passeron, J. (1990) *Reproduction in Education, Society and Culture* (2nd ed.). London: Sage.

Bradshaw, D. (2001). 'Life is respect: Extending and implementing early learnings'. *Fine Print*, 24 (1): 10–12.

Brennan, B., Clark, R. and Dymock, D. (1989). *Outcomes of Adult Literacy Programs*. Armidale, NSW: University of New England.

Brennan, M. and Brennan, R. (1984). *Literacy and Learning: The Human Factor*. Wagga Wagga: Charles Sturt University – Riverina.

Brennan-Kemmis, R. and Ahern, S. (2010). 'Workforce development for the hair and beauty industry'. Paper presented at VET Research: Leading and responding in turbulent times, 13th Annual AVETRA Conference, 8–9 April, Surfers Paradise, Queensland.

Brewer, K., McLean, P., Perkins, K., Tout, D. and Wyse, L. (2008). *Australian Core Skills Framework*. Canberra: Commonwealth of Australia.

Brine, J. (2006a). 'The everyday classificatory practices of selective schooling: A fifty-year retrospective'. *International Studies in Sociology of Education*, 16 (1): 37–55.

Brine, J. (2006b). 'Lifelong learning and the knowledge economy: Those that know and those that do not – the discourse of the European Union'. *British Educational Research Journal*, 32 (5): 649–65.

British Association of Settlements. (1974). *A Right to Read: Action for a Literate Britain*. London: BAS.

Brown, B. and Baker, S. (2012). *Responsible Citizens: Individuals, Health and Policy under Neoliberalism*. London: Anthem, London.

Brown, S. (2019). 'ESOL, emancipation and "comfort radicalism": Perceptions of ESOL practitioners in the Scottish further education sector'. In F. Mishan (ed), *ESOL*

Provision in the UK and Ireland: Challenges and Opportunities, 183–209. Oxford: Peter Lang.

Brown, T., Yasukawa, K. and Black, S. (2014). 'Seeing and hearing: Examining production workers' literacy and numeracy practices in a context of crisis'. *Studies in Continuing Education*, 36 (2): 188–200.

Buggy, J. (1991). *Working Smarter*. Canberra: Australian Government Publishing Service.

Burgess, A. and Hamilton, M. (2011). *Back to the Future? Functional Literacy and the New Skills Agenda*. Discussion paper. Lancaster: Lancaster University.

Caldwell, B. and Webster, A. (2013). 'Adult literacy surveys in Australia'. *Australian Economic Review*, 46 (1): 103–9.

Campbell, B. (2010). *Reading the Fine Print – a History of the Victorian Adult Literacy and Basic Education Council (VALBEC) 1978-2008*. Springvale South: Victorian Adult Literacy and Basic Education Council.

Canning, R. (2007). 'Reconceptualising core skills'. *Journal of Education and Work*, 20 (1): 17–26.

Carolan, M., Holman, J. and Ferrari, M. (2014). 'Experiences of diabetes self-management: A focus group study among Australians with type 2 diabetes'. *Journal of Clinical Nursing*, 24 (7–8): 1011–23.

Carroll, B. (2010). *Vintage Keating: His Wit and Wisdom*. Dural, NSW: Rosenberg Publishing.

Casey, H., Olga, C., Eldred, J., Grief, S., Hodge, R., Ivanič, R., Jupp, T., Lopez, D. and McNeil, B. (2006). *You Wouldn't Expect a Maths Teacher to Teach Plastering: Embedding Literacy and Language in Post 16 Vocational Programmes – the Impact on Learning and Achievement*. London: National Research and Development Centre for Adult Literacy and Numeracy.

Castleton, G. (2002). 'Workplace literacy as a contested site of educational activity'. *Journal of Adolescent and Adult Literacy*, 45 (7): 556–66.

Charnley, A.H., and Jones, H.A. (1980). *The Concept of Success in Adult Literacy*. London: Adult Literacy and Basic Skills Unit.

Chesters, J., Ryan, C. and Sinning, M. (2013). *The Returns to Literacy Skills in Australia*. Adelaide: National Vocational Education and Training Research.

Chodkiewicz, A., Widin, J. and Yasukawa, K. (2010). 'Making connections to re-engage young people in learning: Dimensions of practice'. *Literacy and Numeracy Studies*, 18 (1): 35–51.

Cieslik, M. and Simpson, D. (2015). 'Basic skills, literacy practices and the "hidden injuries of class"'. *Sociological Research Online*, 20 (1).

Circelli, M., Gillis, S., Dulhunty, M., Wu, M. and Calvitto, L. (2013). *Does 1 = 1? Mapping Measures of Adult Literacy and Numeracy*. Adelaide: National Centre for Vocational Education Research.

Clark, C., Geer, T. and Underhill, B. (1996). *The Changing of Australian Manufacturing*. Canberra: Industry Commission.

Clemans, A. and Seddon, T. (2000). 'Technical and further education: Social justice solution and social justice problem'. *Australian Educational Researcher*, 27 (3): 117–30.

Clemente, C., Higgins, M. and Sughrua, W. (2011). '"I don't find any privacy around here": Ethnographic encounters with local practices of literacy in the state prison of Oaxaca'. *Language and Education*, 25 (6): 491–513.

Coates, S., Fitzpatrick, L., McKenna, R. and Makin, A. (1996). *National Reporting System*, Canberra: ANTA and Department of Employment, Education and Training.

Cohen, L.C. (2010). 'When it pays to be friendly: Employment relationships and emotional labour in hairdressing'. *The Sociological Review*, 58 (2): 197–218.

Cohen, S. (2004). 'Social relationships and health'. *American Psychologist*, 59 (8): 676–84.

Colley, H. (2006). 'Learning to labour with feeling: Class, gender and emotion in childcare education and training'. *Contemporary Issues in Early Childhood*, 7 (1): 15–29.

Collinson, D. (1994). 'Strategies of resistance: Power, knowledge and subjectivity in the workplace'. In J. Jermier, D. Knights and W. Nord (eds), *Resistance and Power in Organizations*, 25–68. London: Routledge.

Committee on Employment Opportunities. (1993). *Restoring Full Employment: Background Papers*. Canberra: Australian Government Publishing Service.

Community Justice Coalition. (2016). *Prisoner Education NSW 2016*. Available online: https://www.communityjusticecoalition.org/images/05092016.pdf (accessed 22 May 2022).

Community Justice Coalition. (2018). *Effects of the Privatisation of Prisoner Education in NSW Correctional Centres*. Available online: http://www.communityjusticecoalition.org/images/pdf_files/Education/EffectsPrivEdn071218.pdf (accessed 22 May 2022).

Connell, R. (2013). 'Why do market "reforms" increase inequality?' *Discourse: Studies in the Cultural Politics of Education*, 34 (2): 279–85.

Cook-Gumperz, J. (ed) (2006). *The Social Construction of Literacy* (2nd ed.). Cambridge: Cambridge University Press.

Cope, B. and Kalantzis, M. (1997). *Productive Diversity: A New, Australian Model for Work and Management*. Annandale, NSW: Pluto Press.

Council of Adult Education. (1974). *The Way Out: A Pilot Project in Adult Literacy*. Melbourne: Council of Adult Education.

Courtenay, M. and Mawer, G. (1995). *Integrating English Language, Literacy and Numeracy into Vocational Education and Training: A Framework*. Sydney: TAFE NSW.

Coyle, M., Francis, K. and Chapman, Y. (2013). 'Self-management activities in diabetes care: A systematic review'. *Health Review*, 37 (4): 513–22.

Cruickshank, K. (2006). *Teenagers, Literacy and School: Researching in Multilingual Contexts*. New York: Routledge.

Crump, S., Connell, B. and Seddon, T. (1997). *Learning Needs, Disadvantage and Student Diversity in Vocational Education in TAFE*. Brisbane: Australian National Training Authority.

Czerniawski, G. (2015). 'A race to the bottom – prison education and the English and Welsh policy context'. *Journal of Education Policy*, 31 (2): 198–212.

Darkenwald, G. and Valentine, T. (1985). 'Outcomes of participation in adult basic skills education'. *Lifelong Learning*, 8 (5): 17–22.

Darrah, C. (1996). *Learning and Work: An Exploration in Industrial Ethnography*. New York: Garland Publishing.

Davison, C., Taylor, E. and Hatcher, L. (1994). *Pedagogy and Politics: Developing Ethno-Inclusive Practices in the ALBE Profession*. Canberra: Department of Employment, Education and Training.

Dawkins, J. and Holding, C. (1987). *Skills for Australia*. Canberra: Australian Government Publishing Service.

Department for Education and Employment [DfEE]. (1999). *Skills for Life: The National Strategy for Improving Adult Literacy and Numeracy Skills*. London: DfEE.

Department of Education, Science and Training. (2005). *Review Report of the Language, Literacy and Numeracy Programme*. Canberra: DEST.

Department of Education, Skills and Employment. (2020). Ministerial statement – 20 November 2020. Available online: https://www.dese.gov.au/skills-reform/resources/ministerial-statement-20-november-2020 (accessed 22 May 2022).

Department of Education, Skills and Employment. (2021). 'Submission 86 to inquiry into adult literacy and its importance'. Available online: https://www.aph.gov.au/parliamentary_business/committees/house/employment_education_and_training/adultliteracy/submissions (accessed 22 May 2022).

Department of Employment, Education and Training [DEET]. (1991). *Australia's Language: The Australian Language and Literacy Policy*. Canberra: DEET.

Department of Employment, Education and Training [DEET]. (1992a), *Getting the Word Out*. Canberra: DEET.

Department of Employment, Education and Training [DEET]. (1992b). *Department of Employment, Education and Training Review*. Canberra: Australian Government Publishing Service.

Department of Employment, Education and Training [DEET]. (1996). *Evaluation of the Language and Literacy Elements of the Special Intervention Program: 1994–1995. Interim Report Case Study Component*. Canberra: DEET.

Derrick, J. (2012). *Embedding Literacy and Essential Skills in Workplace Learning: Breaking the Solitudes*. Quebec: The Centre for Literacy.

Dodd, G. (1980). *The Gapadol Test and Illiteracy in Prisons*. Research Notes. Sydney: NSW DCS.

Dollery, B. and Marshall, N. (1997). *Australian Local Government: Reform and Renewal*. Melbourne: Macmillan Education Australia.

Druine, N. and Wildemeersch, D. (2000). 'The vocational turn in adult literacy education and the impact of the international adult literacy survey'. *International Review of Education*, 46 (5): 391–405.

Duckworth, V. (2013). *Learning Trajectories, Violence and Empowerment amongst Adult Basic Skills Learners*. London: Routledge.

Duckworth, V. and Ade-Ojo, G. (2016). 'Journey through transformation: A case study of two literacy learners'. *Journal of Transformative Education*, 14 (4): 285–304.

Duckworth, V. and Cochrane, M. (2012). 'Spoilt for choice, spoilt by choice: Long-term consequences of limitations imposed by social background'. *Education + Training*, 54 (7): 579–91.

Duckworth, V. and Smith, R. (2018). 'Breaking the triple lock: Further education and transformative teaching and learning'. *Education + Training*, 60 (6): 529–43.

Duckworth, V. and Tett, L. (2019). 'Transformative and emancipatory literacy to empower'. *International Journal of Lifelong Learning*, 38 (4): 366–78.

Dumbrell, T., de Montfort, R. and Finnegan, W. (2004). 'Equity in VET: An overview of the data for designated equity groups'. In K. Bowman (ed), *Equity in Vocational Education and Training: Research Readings, 19–40*. Adelaide: National Centre for Vocational Education Research.

Dymock, D. (1982). *Adult Literacy Provision in Australia: Trends and Needs*. Armidale: Australian Council for Adult Literacy.

Eberle, A. and Robinson, S. (1980). *The Adult Illiterate Speaks Out: Personal Perspectives on Learning to Read and Write*. Washington DC: US Department of Education.

Edwards, M., Wood, F., Davies, M. and Edwards, A. (2015). 'Distributed health literacy: Longitudinal qualitative analysis of the roles of health literacy mediators and social networks of people living with a long-term health condition'. *Health Expectations: An International Journal of Public Participation in Health Care and Health Policy*, 18 (5): 1180–93.

Edwards, R. and Miller, K. (2011). 'Literacies in the learning careers of students'. In R. Catts., I. Falk and R. Wallace (eds), *Vocational Learning: Innovative Theory and Practice*, 191–201. Dordrecht: Springer.

Eldred, J., Robinson-Pant, A., Nabi, R., Chopra, P., Nussey, C. and Bown, L. (2014). 'Women's right to learning and literacy: Women learning literacy and empowerment'. *Compare: A Journal of Comparative and International Education*, 44 (4): 655–75.

Elfert, M. and Walker, J. (2020). 'The rise and fall of adult literacy: Policy lessons from Canada'. *European Journal for Research on the Education and Learning of Adults*, 11 (1): 109–25.

Falk, I. (2001). 'Sleight of hand: Job myths, literacy and social capital'. In J. Lo Bianco and R. Wickert (eds), *Australian Policy Activism in Language and Literacy*, 203–20. Melbourne: Language Australia.

Falk, I., Golding, B. and Balatti, J. (2000). *Building Communities: ACE, Lifelong Learning and Social Capital*. Melbourne: Adult, Community and Further Education Board.

Farrall, S. and Maruna, S. (2004). 'Desistance-focused criminal justice policy research: Introduction to a special issue on desistance from crime and public policy'. *The Howard Journal of Criminal Justice*, 43 (4): 358–67.

Farrell, L., Newman, T. and Corbel, C. (2021). 'Literacy and the workplace revolution: A social view of literate work practices in Industry 4.0'. *Discourse: Studies in the Cultural Politics of Education*, 42 (6): 898–912.

Field, J. (2003). 'Civic engagement and lifelong learning: Survey findings on social capital and attitudes towards learning'. *Studies in the Education of Adults*, 35 (2): 142–56.

Fingeret, A. (1983). 'Social networks: A new perspective on independence and illiterate adults'. *Adult Education Quarterly*, 33 (3): 133–46.

Foley, G. (1994). 'Adult education and capitalist reorganisation'. *Studies in the Education of Adults*, 26 (2): 121–43.

Foley, G. (1999). *Learning in Social Action: A Contribution to Understanding Informal Education*. London: Zed Books.

Foley, P. (2007). *The Socio-Economic Status of Vocational Education and Training Students in Australia*. Adelaide: National Centre for Vocational Education Research.

Fooks, D. (1994). 'The life and times of Cinderella'. In P. Kearns and W. Hall (eds), *Kangan: 20 Years On: A Commemoration: TAFE 1974–1994*, 29–43. Adelaide: National Centre for Vocational Education Research.

Foss, C., Knutsen, I., Kennedy, A. et al. (2016). 'Connectivity, contest and the ties of self-management support for type 2 diabetes: A meta-synthesis of qualitative literature'. *Health and Social Care in the Community*, 24 (6): 672–86.

Fraser, N. and Honneth, A. (2003). *Redistribution or Recognition?: A Political-Philosophical Exchange*. London New York: Verso.

Freire, P. (1972). *Pedagogy of the Oppressed*. Harmondsworth: Penguin.

Fuller, A. and Unwin, L. (2004). 'Expansive learning environments: Integrating organizational and personal development'. In A. Fuller, A. Munro and H. Rainbird (eds), *Workplace Learning in Context*, 126–44. London: Routledge.

Galloway, S. (2019). 'Social practices or functional skills? Rehabilitation or rights? An Analysis of Scottish prison learning contracts'. *Encyclopaideia – Journal of Phenomenology and Education*, 23 (53): 67–80.

Galloway, S. (2021). 'Unseen roots and unfolding flowers? Prison learning, equality and the education of socially excluded groups'. *British Educational Research Journal*, 47 (5): 1416–33.

Gebre, A.H., Rogers, A., Street, B. and Openjuru, G. (2009). *Everyday Literacies in Africa: Ethnographic Studies of Literacy and Numeracy Practices in Ethiopia*. Kampala: Fountain Publishers.

Gee, J. (1990). *Social Linguistics and Literacies: Ideology in Discourses*. London: Falmer.

Gee, J. (2000). 'The new literacy studies: From "socially situated" to the work of the social'. In D. Barton, M. Hamilton and R. Ivanič (eds), *Situated Literacies: Reading and Writing in Context*, 180–96. London: Routledge.

Gee, J. (2015). 'The new literacy studies'. In K. Pahl and J. Rowsell (eds), *The Routledge Handbook of Literacy Studies*, 35–48. London: Routledge.

Gee, J. and Lankshear, C. (1995). 'The new work order: Critical language awareness and "fast capitalist" texts'. *Discourse: Studies in the Cultural Politics of Education*, 16 (1): 5–19.

Gee, J., Hull, G. and Lankshear, C. (1996). *The New Work Order: Behind the Language of the New Capitalism*. St Leonards: Allen & Unwin.

Gibb, T. (2015). 'Literacy and language education: The quantification of learning'. *New Directions for Adult and Continuing Education*, 146: 53–63.

Gorski, P. (2018). *Reaching and Teaching Students in Poverty: Strategies for Erasing the Opportunity Gap* (2nd ed.). New York: Teachers College Press.

Gowen, S. (1992). *The Politics of Workplace Literacy: A Case Study*. New York: Teachers College Press.

Gowen, S. (1994). 'The "literacy myth" at work: The role of print literacy in school-work transitions'. In R. Lakes (ed), *Critical Education for Work: Multidisciplinary Approaches*, 35–49. Norwood NJ: Ablex Publishing.

Gowen, S. (1996). 'How the reorganisation of work destroys everyday knowledge'. In J. Hautecoeur (ed), *Alpha 96: Basic Education at Work*, 11–32. Toronto: Culture Concepts.

Goyen, J. (1977). *Adult Illiteracy in Sydney*. Canberra: Australian Association of Adult Education.

Graff, H. (1979). *The Literacy Myth: Literacy and Social Structure in the Nineteenth-century City*. New York: Academic Press.

Graff, H. (1987). *The Labyrinths of Literacy: Reflections on Literacy Past and Present*. London: The Falmer Press.

Graff, H. (2017). *Literacy, Myths, Legacies and Lessons: New Studies on Literacy*. New York: Routledge.

Graham, H. and McNeill, F. (2017). 'Desistance: Envisioning futures'. In P. Carlen and L.A. Franca (eds), *Alternative Criminologies*, 433–52. London: Routledge.

Grant, A. (1985). 'Learning from the life stories of adult literacy students'. *Literacy Link: Readings in Adult Basic Education*, 19–33. Melbourne: Australian Council for Adult Literacy.

Grant, A. (1987). *Opportunity to Do Brilliantly: TAFE and the Challenge of Adult Literacy Provision in Australia*. Canberra: Australian Government Publishing Service.

Grant, A. and Hayles, L. (1981). *Literacy for Adults: An Evaluation Study of the Council of Adult Education's Literacy Program*. Melbourne: Council of Adult Education.

Green, B., Hodgens, J. and Luke, A. (1994) *Debating Literacy in Australia: A Documentary History, 1945–1994*. Sydney: Australian Literacy Federation.

Grotlüschen, A., Desjardins, R. and Liu, H. (2020). 'Literacy and numeracy: Global and comparative perspectives'. *International Review of Education*, 66 (2–3): 127–37.

Guadalupe, C. (2015). 'How feasible is it to develop a culturally sensitive large scale standardised assessment of literacy skills?' In M. Hamilton, B. Maddox and C. Addey (eds), *Literacy as Numbers: Researching the Politics and Practice of International Literacy Assessment*, 111–28. Cambridge: Cambridge University Press.

Guenther, J., Falk, I. and Arnott, A. (2008). *The Role of Vocational Education and Training in Welfare to Work*. Adelaide: National Centre for Vocational Education Research.

Hamilton, M. (1999). 'Ethnography for classrooms: Constructing a reflective curriculum for literacy'. *Curriculum Studies*, 7 (3): 429–44.

Hamilton, M. (2001). 'Privileged literacies: Policy, institutional process and the life of the IALS'. *Language and Education*, 15 (2–3): 178–96.

Hamilton, M. (2016). 'Imagining literacy: A sociomaterial approach'. In K. Yasukawa and S. Black (eds), *Beyond Economic Interests: Critical Perspectives on Adult Literacy and Numeracy in a Globalised World*, 3–17. Rotterdam: Sense.

Hamilton, M. (2017). 'How international large-scale skills assessments engage with national actors: Mobilising networks through policy, media and public knowledge'. *Critical Studies in Education*, 58 (3): 280–94.

Hamilton, M. and Barton, D. (2000). 'The international adult literacy survey: What does it really mean?' *International Review of Education*, 46 (5): 377–89.

Hamilton, M., Barton, D. and Ivanič, R. (eds) (1994). *Worlds of Literacy*. Clevedon: Multilingual Matters.

Hamilton, M. and Hillier, Y. (2006). *The Changing Face of Adult Literacy, Language and Numeracy 1970–2000: A Critical History*. London: Trentham Books.

Hamilton, M., Maddox, B. and Addey, C. (eds) (2015). *Literacy as Numbers: Researching the Politics and Practice of International Literacy Assessment*. Cambridge: Cambridge University Press.

Hamilton, M. and Pitt, K. (2011). 'Challenging representations: Constructing the adult literacy learner over 30 years of policy and practice in the United Kingdom'. *Reading Research Quarterly*, 46 (4): 350–73.

Hamilton, M. and Stasinopoulos, M. (1987). *Literacy, Numeracy and Adults. Evidence from the National Child Development Study*. London: Adult Literacy and Basic Skills Unit.

Hammond, J., Wickert, R., Burns, A., Joyce, H. and Miller, A. (1992). *The Pedagogical Relations between Adult ESL and Adult Literacy*. Canberra: Department of Employment, Education and Training.

Hancock, K. and Zubrick, S. (2015). *Children and Young People at Risk of Disengagement from School*. Perth: University of Western Australia.

Hart, M. (1992). *Working and Educating for Life: Feminist and International Perspectives on Adult Education*. London: Rutledge.

Hart-Landsberg, S. and Reder, S. (1995). 'Teamwork and literacy: Teaching and learning at Hardy Industries'. *Reading Research Quarterly*, 30 (4): 1016–52.

Hartley, R. (1989). *The Social Costs of Inadequate Literacy. A Report for International Literacy Year*. Canberra: Australian Institute of Family Studies.

Harvey, D. (1990). *The Condition of Postmodernity. An Inquiry into the Origins of Cultural Change*. Oxford: Blackwell.

Hayes, B. (2013). *IALS and Essential Skills in Canadian Literacy Policy and Practice: A Descriptive Overview*. Montreal: The Centre for Literacy.

Healy, J. and Moskos, M. (2005). *How Do Aged Care Workers Compare with Other Australian Workers?* Adelaide: National Institute of Labour Studies.

Heath, S.B. (1980). 'The functions and uses of literacy'. *Journal of Communication*, 30 (1): 123–33.

Heath, S.B. (1983). *Ways with Words: Language, Life and Work in Communities and Classrooms*. London: Cambridge University Press.

Higgins, T. (2017). *Literacy and Numeracy Demands and Usage in the Workplace*. PhD thesis. Cardiff University.

Hill, D. and Kumar, R. (eds) (2009). *Global Neoliberalism and Education and Its Consequences*. London: Routledge.

Hill, D., Greaves, N. and Maisuria, A. (2009). 'Education, inequality, and neoliberal capitalism: A classical Marxist analysis'. In D. Hill and R. Kumar (eds), *Global Neoliberalism and Education and Its Consequences*, 102–26. London: Routledge.

Hilmer, F. (1993). *National Competition Policy (the Hilmer Report)*. Canberra: Australian Government Publishing Service.

Hinder, S. and Greenhalgh, T. (2012) '"This does my head in": Ethnographic study of self – management by people with diabetes'. *BMC Health Services Research*, 12: 83.

Hoddinott, S. (2000). 'The worker basic skills "crisis": Some industrial relations implications'. In H. Rainbird (ed), *Training in the Workplace*, 169–88. London: Palgrave.

Hodge, R., Barton, D. and Pearce, I. (2008). *Progression: Moving on in Life and Learning*. London: National Research and Development Centre for Adult Literacy and Numeracy.

Hodgens, J. (1994). 'How adult literacy became a public issue in Australia'. *Open Letter, Australian Journal for Adult Literacy Research and Practice*, 4 (2): 13–24.

Holland, J., Reynolds, T. and Weller, S. (2007). 'Transitions, networks and communities: The significance of social capital in the lives of children and young people'. *Journal of Youth Studies*, 10 (1): 97–116.

Holmes, J. and Storrie, T. (1985). *Consett: A Case Study of Education and Unemployment*. London: Further Education Unit.

Holt-Lunstad, J. and Uchino, N. (2015). 'Social support and health'. In K. Glanz, B.K. Rimer and K. Viswanath (eds), *Health Behavior: Theory, Research, and Practice*, 183–214. San Francisco: Jossey Bass.

House of Representatives Standing Committee on Employment, Education and Training. (1991). *Words at Work*. Canberra: Australian Government Publishing Service.

House of Representatives Standing Committee on Employment, Education and Training. (2022). *Don't Take It as Read: Inquiry into Adult Literacy and Its Importance.* Canberra: Parliament of the Commonwealth of Australia.

Hoyles, M. (1977). 'Cultural deprivation and compensatory education'. In M. Hoyles (ed), *The Politics of Literacy*, 172–81. London: Writers and Readers Publishing Cooperative.

Hu, F. (2003). 'Sedentary lifestyle and risk of obesity and type 2 diabetes'. *Lipids*, 38 (2): 103–8.

Hull, G. (1993). 'Hearing other voices: A critical assessment of popular views on literacy and work'. *Harvard Educational Review*, 63 (1): 20–49.

Hull, G., Jury, M. and Zacher, J. (2007). 'Possible selves: Literacy, identity, and development in work, school, and community'. In A. Belzer (ed), *Towards Defining and Improving Quality in Adult Basic Education*, 299–318. Mahwah, NJ: Lawrence Erlbaum Associates.

Hunter, C. and Harman, D. (1979). *Adult Illiteracy in the United States: A Report to the Ford Foundation.* New York: McGraw-Hill.

Hunter, J. (2012). 'Language and literacy on the ground: Disconnects between government policy and employer perspectives'. *Discourse: Studies in the Cultural Politics of Education*, 33 (2): 299–31.

Hunter, J. and Cooke, D. (2014). 'Education for power: English language in the workplace'. *Power and Education*, 6 (3): 253–67.

Iglay, K., Hannachi, H., Howie, P. et al. (2016). 'Prevalence and co-prevalence of comorbidities among patients with type 2 diabetes mellitus'. *Current Medical Research and Opinion*, 32 (7): 1243–52.

Industry Skills Councils. (2011). *No More Excuses: An Industry Response to the Language, Literacy and Numeracy Challenge.* Canberra: Australian Government.

Ivanič, R., Appleby, Y., Hodge, R., Tusting, K. and Barton, D. (2006). *Linking Learning and Everyday Life: A Social Perspective on Adult Language, Literacy and Numeracy Classes.* London: NRDC.

Ivanič, R., Edwards, R., Barton, D., Martin-Jones, M., Fowler, Z., Hughes, B., Mannion, G., Miller, K., Satchwell, C. and Smith, J. (2009). *Improving Learning in College: Rethinking Literacies across the Curriculum.* London: Routledge.

Jackson, D. and Daly, J. (2004). 'Current challenges and issues facing nursing in Australia'. *Nursing Science Quarterly*, 17 (4): 352–5.

Jackson, N. (2005a). 'Essential skills: Essential confusion?' *Literacies*, (6): 38–43.

Jackson, N. (2005b). 'Adult literacy policy: Mind the gap'. In N. Bascia, A. Cumming, A. Datnow, K. Leithwood and D. Livingstone (eds), *International Handbook of Educational Policy*, 763–78. Dordrecht: Springer.

Jackson, N. and Slade, B. (2008). '"Hell on my face": The production of workplace illiteracy'. In M. DeVault (ed), *People at Work: Life, Power, and Social Inclusion in the New Economy*, 25–39. New York: New York University.

Jamrozik, K. (2010). 'Health literacy, victim blaming and the mission of public health'. *Australian and New Zealand Journal of Public Health*, 34 (3): 227.

John, D. (2004). *Identifying the Key Factors Affecting the Chance of Passing Vocational Education and Training Subjects*. Adelaide: National Centre for Vocational Education Research.

Jones, H. and Charnley, A. (1978). *Adult Literacy: A Study of Its Impact*. Leicester: National Institute of Adult Education.

Jones, K. (2016). *Education in Britain: 1944 to the Present* (2nd ed.). Cambridge: Polity Press.

Jones, M. (1989). *Managing Local Government: Leadership for the 21st Century*. Melbourne: Hargreen Publishers.

Joyce, H. (1992). *Workplace Texts in the Language Classroom*. Sydney: NSW AMES.

Joyce, S. (2019). *Strengthening Skills Expert Review of Australia's Vocational Education and Training System*. Canberra: Commonwealth of Australia, Department of the Prime Minister and Cabinet.

Kalman, J. and Reyes, I. (2016). 'On literacy, reading, and learning to read in Mexico'. *Prospects*, 46 (3–4): 407–21.

Kalman, J. and Street, B. (eds) (2013). *Literacy and Numeracy in Latin America: Local Perspectives and Beyond*. New York: Routledge.

Kamler, B. (1999). 'Literacy narratives of crisis and blame'. *Literacy and Numeracy Studies*, 9 (1): 65–73.

Karpin, D. (1995). *Enterprising Nation: Renewing Australia's Managers to Meet the Challenge of the Asia-Pacific Century*. Canberra: Australian Government Printing Service.

Keddie, A. (2016). 'Children of the market: Performativity, neoliberal responsibilisation and the construction of student identities'. *Oxford Review of Education*, 42 (1): 108–22.

Keddie, N. (1973). *Tinker, Tailor: The Myth of Cultural Deprivation*. Harmondsworth: Penguin Education.

Kell, C., Guy, S., Hastwell, K. and Harvey, S. (2009). *Upskilling Partnership Programme: In-House Literacy, Language and Numeracy Initiatives in New Zealand Workplaces*. Wellington: Department of Labour.

Kell, M. (2005). 'Learning by experience: Reconstructing the literacy engagement of nine men who self-report literacy difficulties'. PhD thesis. University of Western Sydney.

Kell, P. (2006). *TAFE Futures: An Inquiry into the Future of Technical and Further Education in Australia*. South Melbourne: Australian Education Union.

Kelly, S. (1989). 'Literacy screens for TAFE students'. *Good Practice in Australian Adult Literacy and Basic Education*, (5): 9.

Kilpatrick, S., Field, J. and Falk, I. (2003). 'Social capital: An analytical tool for exploring lifelong learning and community development'. *British Educational Research Journal*, 29 (3): 417–33.

King, D. (2016). 'It's frustrating! Managing emotional dissonance in aged care work'. *Australian Journal of Social Issues*, 47 (1): 51–70.

Klope, E. and Hedlin, M. (2023). 'Always happy: An ideal is reproduced and challenged in hairdressing vocational education and training'. *Journal of Education and Work*, Published online 05 Feb 2023.

Kozol, J. (1980). *Prisoners of Silence: Breaking the Bonds of Adult Illiteracy in the United States*. New York: Continuum Corporation.

Kral, I. (2012). *Talk, Text and Technology: Literacy and Social Practice in a Remote Indigenous Community*. Bristol: Multilingual Matters.

Lamb, S., Long, M. and Malley, J. (1998). *Access and Equity in Vocational Education and Training: Results from Longitudinal Surveys of Australian Youth*. ACER Research Monograph No. 55. Melbourne: Australian Council for Educational Research.

Lange, E., Chovanec, D., Cardinal, T., Kajner, T. and Smith Acuña, N. (2015). 'Wounded learners failed by schooling: Symbolic violence and re-engaging low income adults'. *Canadian Journal for the Study of Adult Education*, 27 (3): 893–104.

Lankshear, C. and Lawler, M. (1987). *Literacy, Schooling and Revolution*. London: The Falmer Press.

Latham, T. (2010). 'Embedding literacy'. In N. Hughes and I. Schwab (eds), *Teaching Adult Literacy: Principles and Practice*, 344–64. Maidenhead: Open University Press.

Lave, J. (2011). *Apprenticeship in Critical Ethnographic Practice*. Chicago: University of Chicago Press.

Lave, J. (2019). *Learning and Everyday Life: Access, Participation, and Changing Practice*. Cambridge: Cambridge University Press.

Lave, J. and Wenger, E. (1991). *Situated Learning: Legitimate Peripheral Participation*. Cambridge: Cambridge University Press.

Lea, M. and Street, B. (1998). 'Student writing in higher education: An academic literacies approach'. *Studies in Higher Education*, 23 (2): 157–72.

Lea, M. and Street, B. (2006). 'The "academic literacies" model: Theory and applications'. *Theory into Practice*, 45 (4): 368–77.

Leach, L., Zepke, N., Haworth, P. and Isaacs, P. (2010). *'One Size Does Not Fit All'. How Five Tertiary Organizations Embed Literacy, Language and Numeracy. Case Study Findings*. Wellington: New Zealand Ministry of Education.

Leathwood, C. and Archer, L. (2004). 'Social class and educational inequalities: The local and the global'. *Pedagogy, Culture and Society*, 12 (1): 5–13.

Lee, A. and Wickert, R. (1995). 'Reading the discourses of adult basic education'. In G. Foley (ed), *Understanding Adult Education and Training*, 134–46. Sydney: Allen & Unwin.

Levett, A. and Lankshear, C. (1994). 'Literacies, workplaces, and the demands of new times'. In M. Brown (eds), *Literacies and the Workplace: A Collection of Original Essays*, 27–54. Geelong: Deakin University.

Levine, K. (1980). *Becoming Literate*. Nottingham: Nottingham University.

Levine, K. (1982). 'Functional literacy: Fond illusions and false economies'. *Harvard Educational Review*, 52 (3): 249–66.

Levine, K. (1986). *The Social Context of Literacy*. London: Routledge & Kegan Paul.

Levy, S., Briede, M. and Frost-Camilleri, L. (2021). 'Literacy and numeracy support in vocational education: Perceptions from engineering apprentices in Victoria'. *Issues in Educational Research*, 31 (3): 891–913.

Lillis, T. (2019). '"Academic literacies": Sustaining a critical space on writing in academia'. *Journal of Learning Development in Higher Education*, 15, November.

Lillis, T. and Tuck, J. (2016). 'Academic Literacies: A critical lens on writing and reading in the academy'. In K. Hyland and P. Shaw (eds), *The Routledge Handbook of English for Academic Purposes*, 30–43. London: Routledge.

Literacy Quebec. (2022). 'What's literacy got to do with it? A podcast'. 8 January. Available at: https://anchor.fm/literacy-quebec/episodes/Episode-51----Lost-For-Words-Part-2-with-Literacy-Experts-Joanne-Medlin--Adam-Nobilia-e1chgl6 (accessed 22 May 2022).

Livingstone, D. and Sawchuk, P. (2005). 'Hidden knowledge: Working – class capacity in the "knowledge-based economy"'. *Studies in the Education of Adults*, 37 (2): 110–22.

Lloyd, A., Bonner, A. and Dawson-Rose, C. (2014). 'The health information practices of people living with chronic health conditions'. *Journal of Librarianship and Information Science*, 46 (3): 207–16.

Lo Bianco, J. (1987). *National Policy on Languages*. Canberra: Commonwealth Department of Education.

Lo Bianco, J. (1993). 'Shaping policy for professional development'. *Open Letter*, 3 (2): 4–15.

Lo Bianco, J. and Wickert, R. (eds) (2001). *Australian Policy Activism in Language and Literacy*. Melbourne: Language Australia.

Luke, A. (1992). 'Literacy and work in "New Times"'. *Open Letter*, 3 (1): 3–15.

Mace, J. (1979). *Working with Words: Literacy beyond School*. London: Writers and Readers Publishing Cooperative.

Malicky, G. and Norman, C. (1996). 'Perceptions of adult learners about themselves and their lives'. *Adult Basic Education*, 6 (1): 3–20.

Mannion, G., Miller, K., Gibb, I. and Goodman, R. (2009). 'Reading, writing, resonating: Striking chords across the contexts of students' everyday and college lives'. *Pedagogy, Culture and Society*, 17 (3): 323–39.

Manufacturing Skills Australia. (2012). *Environmental Scan 2012*. North Sydney: MSA.

Marshall, N., Witherby, A. and Dollery, B. (1999). 'Management, markets and democracy: Australian local government reform in the 1990s'. *Local Government Studies*, 25 (3): 34–57.

Martin-Jones, M. and Jones, K. (eds) (2000). *Multilingual Literacies: Reading and Writing Different Worlds*. Amsterdam: John Benjamins.

Martire, L. and Franks, M. (2014). 'The role of social networks in adult health: Introduction to the special issue'. *Health Psychology*, 33 (6): 501–4.

Mawer, G. (1999). *Language and Literacy in Workplace Education: Learning at Work*. London: Routledge.

McCaffery, K.J., Morony, S., Muscat, D.M., Smith, S.K., Shepherd, H.L., Dhillon, H.M., Hayen, A., Luxford, K., Meshreky, W., Comings, J. and Nutbeam, D. (2016). 'Evaluation of an Australian health literacy program for socially disadvantaged adults attending adult basic education classes: Study protocol for a cluster randomised controlled trial'. *BMC Public Health*, 27 (16): 454.

McCulloch, G. (1998). *Failing the Ordinary Child?: The Theory and Practice of Working-Class Secondary Education*. Buckinghamshire: Open University Press.

McCulloch, G. (2011). *Educational Reconstruction: The 1944 Education Act and the Twenty-First Century*. London: Routledge.

McGinty, S., Bursey, S. and Babacan, H. (2018). 'I just want an education! Young people's perspectives'. In S. McGinty, K. Wilson, J. Thomas and B. Lewthwaite (eds), *Gauging the Value of Education for Disenfranchised Youth: Flexible Learning Options*, 63–81. Leiden: Brill.

McGinty, S., Wilson, K., Thomas, J. and Lewthwaite, B. (eds) (2018). *Gauging the Value of Education for Disenfranchised Youth: Flexible Learning Options*. Leiden: Brill.

McGregor, F. (2020). *Learning to Desist: Exploring the Relationship between Engagement in Prison Education and Desistance from Crime*. PhD thesis. University of Technology Sydney.

McGregor, G., Mills, M., te Riele, K. and Hayes, D. (2015). 'Excluded from school: Getting a second chance at a "meaningful" education'. *International Journal of Inclusive Education*, 19 (6): 608–25.

McKenna, R. and Fitzpatrick, L. (2005). *Integrated Approaches to Teaching Adult Literacy in Australia: A Snapshot of Practice in Community Services*. Adelaide: National Centre for Vocational Education Research.

McLean, P., Perkins, K., Tout, D., Brewer, K. and Wyse, L. (2012) *Australian Core Skills Framework (ACSF)*. Canberra: Commonwealth of Australia.

McLean, P., Oldfield, J. and Stevens, A. (2017). *Australian Core Skills Framework, Pre-level 1*. Canberra: Commonwealth of Australia.

Meadows, P. and Metcalf, H. (2008). 'Does literacy and numeracy training for adults increase employment and employability? Evidence from the Skills for Life Programme in England'. *Industrial Relations Journal*, 39 (5): 254–369.

Mendelovits, J. (2011). 'A slow burn: The impact of IALS in Australia'. Paper presented at the *IALS (International Adult Literacy Survey): Its Meaning and Impact for Policy and Practice*, Banff. October 23–5.

Meyler, D., Stimpson, J.P. and Peek, M.K. (2007). 'Health concordance within couples: A systematic review'. *Social Science and Medicine*, 64 (11): 2297–310.

Mezirow, J., Darkenwald, G. and Knox, A. (1975). *Last Gamble on Education: Dynamics of Adult Basic Education*. Washington DC: Adult Education Association of the United States.

Miller, P. and Chiswick, B. (1997). 'Literacy, numeracy and the labour market'. In ABS, *Aspects of Literacy: Assessed Skill Levels Australia 1996*, 73–9. Canberra: ABS.

Mills, A. (2017). 'Privatisation of Criminal Justice'. In A. Deckert and R. Sarre (eds), *The Palgrave Handbook of Australian and New Zealand Criminology, Crime and Justice*, 467–81. London: Palgrave Macmillan.

Mills, M. and McGregor, G. (2010). *Re-engaging Students in Education: Success Factors in Alternative Education*. Brisbane: Youth Affairs Network Queensland (YANQ).

Miralles, J. (2004). *Factors Impacting on Vocational Education and Training Participation and Completion in Selected Ethnic Communities*. Adelaide: National Centre for Vocational Education Research.

Mjaya, A. (2022). *Literacies, Power and Identities in Figured Worlds in Malawi*. London: Bloomsbury Academic.

Monden, Y. (1994). *Toyota Production System*. London: Chapman & Hall.

Morken, F., Jones, LØ. and Helland, W.A. (2021). 'Disorders of language and literacy in the prison population: A scoping review'. *Education Sciences*, 11 (2): 77.

Munns, G. and McFadden, M. (2000). 'First chance, second chance or last chance? Resistance and response to education'. *British Journal of Sociology of Education*, 21 (1): 59–76.

Muñoz, V. (2009). 'The right to education of persons in detention: Summary of report presented to the UN Human Rights Committee in June 2009'. *Journal of Prisoners on Prisons*, 18 (1&2): 164–74.

Murray, S. and Mitchell, J. (2016). 'Teaching practices that re-engage early school leavers in further education: An Australian study'. *Journal of Further and Higher Education*, 40 (3): 372–91.

Muscat, D., Morony, S., Nutbeam, D. et al. (2020). 'Learners" experience and perceived impact of a health literacy program in adult basic education: A qualitative study"'. *Public Health Research and Practice*, 30 (2).

National Board of Employment, Education and Training. (1992). *Disadvantaged Jobseekers: Casual, Part-time, and Temporary Work*. Commissioned Report No. 18. Canberra: Australian Government Publishing Service.

National Food Industry Training Council Ltd. (1995). *Team Work: Effective Communication in the Restructured Workplace*. Carlton North: National Food Industry Council.

National VET Equity Advisory Council (NVEAC). (2010). *Overcoming Disadvantage through VET: Beginning the Conversation*. Melbourne: NVEAC.

Neef, D., Siesfeld, G. and Cefola, J. (eds) (1998). *The Economic Impact of Knowledge*. Boston: Heinemann.

Newcombe, J. (1994). *Literacy at Work: The Workplace Basic Education Project Model of Delivery*. Geelong: Deakin University.

Nicholas, J. (2011). *Lean Production for Competitive Advantage: A Comprehensive Guide to Lean Methodologies and Manufacturing Practices*. New York: Productivity Press.

Noad, B. and Hancock, G. (1984). 'Programming for prisoners in New South Wales'. In B. Noad (ed), *Developmental Programmes for Prisoners*, 13–36. Seminar Proceedings No 5. Canberra: Australian Institute of Criminology.

Northcutt, N. (1975). *Adult Functional Competency: A Report to the Office of Education Dissemination Review*. Austin: University of Texas.

NSW Department of Corrective Services. (1984). *Annual Report*. Sydney: DCS.

NSW Government. (1978). *Report of the Royal Commission into New South Wales Prisons*. Sydney: NSW Government.

NSW Government Workplace Literacy Taskforce. (1990). *Workplace Language, Literacy and Maths: Discussion Paper*. Sydney: NSW Government Workplace literacy Taskforce.

Nutbeam, D. (1998). 'Health promotion glossary'. *Health Promotion International*, 13 (4): 349–64.

Nutbeam, D. (2009). 'Building health Literacy in Australia'. *Medical Journal of Australia*, 191 (10): 525–6.

Nutbeam, D., Levin-Zamir, D. and Rowlands, G. (2018). 'Health literacy and health promotion in context'. *Global Health Promotion*, 25 (4): 3–5.

O'Connor, P. (1993). 'Workplace literacy in Australia: Competing agenda'. In P. Freebody and A. Welch (eds), *Knowledge, Culture and Power: International Perspectives on Literacy as Policy and Practice*, 187–208. London: Falmer Press.

O'Grady, A. and Atkin, C. (2006). 'Choosing to learn or chosen to learn: The experience of Skills for Life learners'. *Research in Post-Compulsory Education*, 11 (3): 277–87.

Olivella, J., Cuatrecasas and Gavilan, N. (2008). 'Work organisation practices for lean production'. *Journal of Manufacturing Technology Management*, 19 (7): 798–811.

O'Maley, P. (2014). 'Book review of Talk, Text and Technology: Literacy and Social Practice in a Remote Indigenous Community by Inge Kral'. *Fine Print*, 37 (3): 37–8.

Organization for Economic Co-operation and Development (OECD). (1992). *Adult Illiteracy and Economic Performance*. Paris: OECD.

Organization for Economic Co-operation and Development (OECD) and Statistics Canada. (1995). *Literacy, Economy and Society: Results of the First International Adult Literacy Survey*. Paris and Ottawa: OECD & Statistics Canada.

Organization for Economic Co-operation and Development (OECD) and Human Resources Development Canada. (1997). *Literacy Skills for the Knowledge Society: Further Results of the International Adult Literacy Survey*. Paris and Ottawa: OECD & Human Resources Development Canada.

Organization for Economic Co-operation and Development (OECD) and Statistics Canada. (2000). *Literacy in the Information Age: Final Report of the International Adult Literacy Survey*. Paris and Ottawa: OECD & Statistics Canada.

Organization for Economic Co-operation and Development (OECD). (2001). *The Well-Being of Nations: The Role of Human and Social Capital*. Paris: OECD.

Organization for Economic Co-operation and Development (OECD). (2013), *OECD Skills Outlook 2013: First Results from the Survey of Adult Skills*. Paris: OECD Publishing.

Organization for Economic Co-operation and Development (OECD). (2017). *Building Skills for All in Australia: Policy Insights from the Survey of Adult Skills*. Paris: OECD.

Orr, K. (2018). 'Further education colleges in the United Kingdom: Providing education for other people's children'. In R. Latiner Raby and E.J. Valeau (eds), *Handbook of Comparative Studies on Community Colleges and Global Counterparts*, 253–69. Cham, Netherlands: Springer.

Osborne, D. and Gaebler, T. (1993). *Reinventing Government: How the Entrepreneurial Spirit is Transforming the Public Sector*. New York: Addison-Wesley.

Osborne, R., Batterham, R., Elsworth, G., Hawkins, M. and Buchbinder, R. (2013). 'The grounded psychometric development and initial validation of the Health Literacy Questionnaire (HLQ)'. *BMC Public Health*, 13 (1): 658.

Osmond, P. (2021). *Developing Social Equity in Australian Adult Education: Lessons from the Past*. London: Routledge.

Papen, U. (2005). *Adult Literacy as Social Practice: More Than Skills*. London: Routledge.

Papen, U. (2009). 'Literacy, learning and health: A social practices view of health'. *Literacy and Numeracy Studies*, 16 (17): 19–34.

Papen, U. (2010). 'Literacy mediators, scribes or brokers?: The central role of others in accomplishing reading and writing'. *Langage et Societe*, 133 (3): 63–82.

Papen, U. (2012). 'Informal, incidental and ad hoc: The information-seeking and learning strategies of health care patients'. *Language and Education*, 26 (2): 105–19.

Peerson, A. and Saunders, M. (2009). 'Health literacy revisited: What do we mean and why does it matter?' *Health Promotion International*, 24 (3): 285–96.

Pennycook, A. (2015). 'Review essay: Class is out: Erasing social class in applied linguistics'. *Applied Linguistics*, 36 (2): 270–7.

Perkins, K. (2009). *Adult Literacy and Numeracy: Future Research and Strategy*. Adelaide: National Centre for Vocational Education Research.

Perry, K. and Homan, A. (2015). '"What I feel in my heart": Literacy practices of and for the self among adults with limited or no schooling'. *Journal of Literacy Research*, 46 (4): 422–54.

Peters, M. (2017). 'From state responsibility for education and welfare to self-responsibilisation in the market'. *Discourse: Studies in the Cultural Politics of Education*, 38 (1): 138–45.

Piette, J. (2010). 'Editorial: Moving beyond the notion of "self" care'. *Chronic Illness*, 6 (1): 3–6.

Pinheiro, P. (2021). 'Conceptualizations of health literacy: Past developments, current trends, and possible ways forward toward social practice'. *Health Literacy Research and Practice*, 5 (2): e91–e95.

Pinsent-Johnson, C. (2015). 'From an international adult literacy assessment to the classroom: How test development methods are transposed into curriculum'. In M.

Hamilton, B. Maddox and C. Addey (eds), *Literacy as Numbers: Researching the Politics and Practices of International Literacy Assessment*, 187–206. Cambridge: Cambridge University Press.

Pitt, R., Davis, T., Manganello, J., et al. (2019). 'Health literacy in a social context: A meta-narrative review'. In O. Okan, U. Bauer, D. Levin-Zamir, P. Pinheiro and K. Sørensen (eds), *International Handbook of Health Literacy. Research, Practice and Policy across the Lifespan*, 665–88. Bristol: Policy Press.

Power, S., Edwards, T., Whitty, G. and Wigfall, V. (2003) *Education and the Middle Class*. Buckingham: Open University Press.

Price, K., Alde, P., Provis, C., Harris, R. and Stack, S. (2004). 'What hinders and what helps? Searching for solutions to mature aged unemployment and the residential aged care workforce crisis'. *Australasian Journal on Ageing*, 23 (4): 177–83.

Prince, D. (1992). *Literacy in the Workplace: A Self-Study Guide for Teachers*. Sydney: NSW AMES.

Prinsloo, M. and Breier, M. (eds) (1996). *The Social Uses of Literacy: Theory and Practice in Contemporary South Africa*. Amsterdam: John Benjamins.

Productivity Commission. (2010). *Staff Working Paper: Links between Literacy and Numeracy Skills and Labour Market Outcomes*. Canberra: Productivity Commission.

Productivity Commission. (2020). *National Agreement for Skills and Workforce Development Review, Interim Report*. Canberra: Productivity Commission.

Putnam, D. (2000). *Bowling Alone: The Collapse and Revival of American Community*. New York: Simon & Schuster.

Quigley, A. (2021). '"Naming the elephant": Literacy classism, human rights and the need for a new conversation'. *Adult Literacy Education*, 3 (3): 41–6.

Raffo, C. and Reeves, M. (2000). 'Youth transitions and social exclusion: Developments in social capital theory'. *Journal of Youth Studies*, 3 (2): 147–66.

Rahmani, Z., Crosier, T. and Pollack, S. (2002). *Evaluating the Impact of the Literacy and Numeracy Training Programme for Job Seekers*. Canberra: Department of Education, Science and Training.

Randazzo, S. (1989). 'Literacy support in a trade course', *Good Practice in Australian Adult Literacy and Basic Education*, (6): 5.

Reay, D. (2006). 'The zombie stalking English schools: Social class and educational inequality'. *British Journal of Educational Studies*, 54 (3): 288–307.

Reay, D. (2017). *Miseducation: Inequality, Education and the Working Classes*. Bristol: Policy Press.

Reeves, M.M., Healy, G.N., Owen, N., Shaw, J.E., Zimmet, Z. and Dunstan, D.W. (2013). 'Joint associations of poor diet quality and prolonged television time with abnormal glucose metabolism in Australian men and women'. *Preventive Medicine*, 57 (5): 471–6.

Richardson, S. and Martin, B. (2004). *The Care of Older Australians: A Picture of the Residential Aged Care Workforce*. Adelaide: National Institute of Labour Studies, Flinders University.

Roberts, A. and Wignall, L. (2010). *Briefing on Foundation Skills for the National VET Equity Advisory Council*. Melbourne: NVEAC.

Roberts, C., Baynham, M., Shrubshall, P., Brittan, J., Cooper, B., Gidley, N., Windsor, V., Eldred, J., Castillino, C. and Walsh, M. (2005). *Embedded Teaching and Learning of Adult Literacy, Numeracy and ESOL: Seven Case Studies*. London: National Research and Development Centre for Adult Literacy and Numeracy.

Robinson-Pant, A. (ed) (2004). *Women, Literacy and Development: Alternative Perspectives*. London: Routledge.

Robinson-Pant, A. (2015). 'Women, literacy, and development: An overview'. In B. Street and S. May (eds), *Literacies and Language Education. Encyclopaedia of Language and Education*. Cham: Springer.

Robinson-Pant, A. (2016). *Promoting Health and Literacy for Women's Empowerment*. Hamburg: UNESCO.

Robinson-Pant, A. (2018). 'Academic literacies: Ethnographic perspectives'. In H. Callan (ed), *The International Encyclopedia of Anthropology*. Oxford: Wiley Blackwell.

Rogers, A. and Gizaw, A.M. (2022). 'Wider benefits of adult literacy teaching: A preliminary exploration of the impact of teaching literacy to adults on some facilitators'. *International Review of Education*, 68 (1): 55–79.

Rogers, A. and Street, B. (2012). *Adult Literacy and Development: Stories from the Field*. Leicester: National Institute of Adult Continuing Education.

Rose, M. (2004). *The Mind at Work: Valuing the Intelligence of the American worker*. London: Penguin.

Ross, S. and Gray, J. (2005). 'Transitions and re-engagement through second chance education'. *The Australian Educational Researcher*, 32 (3): 103–40.

Rubenson, K. (1989). 'The economics of adult basic education'. In M. Taylor and J. Draper (ed), *Adult Literacy Perspectives*, 387–98. Toronto: Culture Concepts.

Rubenson, K. (2009). 'Lifelong learning: Between humanism and global capitalism'. In P. Jarvis (ed), *The Routledge International Handbook of Lifelong Learning*, 411–22. London: Routledge.

Rubenson, K. (2015). 'Framing the adult learning and education policy discourse: The role of the Organization for Economic Co-operation and Development'. In M. Milana and T. Nesbit (eds), *Global Perspectives on Adult Education and Learning Policy*, 179–93. New York: Palgrave.

Rushbrook, P. (2010). 'Bringing Cinderella to the ball: Constructing a federal system of technical and further education in Australia, 1971–1975'. *Journal of Educational Administration and History*, 42 (1): 33–54.

Ryan, C. and Sinning, M. (2012). *Training Requirements of Foreign-Born Workers in Different Countries*. Adelaide: National Centre for Vocational Education Research.

Ryan, M., Gwinner, K., Mallan, K. and Livock, C. (2016). 'Juggling priorities: Balancing economic and social drivers to address the language, literacy and numeracy needs of students in the VET sector'. *International Journal of Training Research*, 14 (2): 145–60.

Samerski, S. (2019). 'Health literacy as a social practice: Social and empirical dimensions of knowledge on health and healthcare'. *Social Science and Medicine*, 226: 1–8.

Sanderson, M. (2007). 'Education and the labour market'. In N. Crafts, I. Gazeley and A. Newell (eds), *Work and Pay in Twentieth Century Britain*, 264–99. Oxford: Oxford University Press.

Sanguinetti, J. (2007). 'Meanings, traditions and contemporary policy discourse in adult literacy'. *Literacy Link*, 27 (1): 6–8.

Sawchuk, P. (2003). *Adult Learning and Technology in Working-Class Life*. Cambridge: Cambridge University Press.

Sawyer, W. (2006). 'Just add "progressivism" and stir: How we cook up literacy crises in Australia'. In B. Doecke, M. Howie and W. Sawyer (eds), *Only Connect: English Teaching, Schooling and Community*. Kent Town, SA: Wakefield Press and English Teachers Association.

SBS. (2021a). *Lost for Words: Documentary*. Available online: https://www.sbs.com.au/ondemand/program/lost-for-words (accessed 22 May 2022).

SBS. (2021b). 'Heartwarming "Lost for Words" documentary looks at learning to read as an adult'. Available online: https://www.sbs.com.au/guide/article/2021/08/18/heartwarming-lost-words-documentary-looks-learning-read-adult (accessed 22 May 2022).

Schultz, K. (1997). 'Discourses of workplace education: A challenge to the new orthodoxy'. In G. Hull (ed), *Changing Work, Changing Worker: Critical Perspectives on Language, Literacy and Skills*, 43–83. New York: State University of New York.

Scott, B. (1990). *TAFE Restructuring: Building a Dynamic Vocational Education and Training Enterprise for the 1990s*. Sydney: New South Wales Education Portfolio, Management Review.

Sefton, R., Waterhouse, P. and Deakin, R. (1994). *Breathing Life into Training: A Model of Integrated Training*. Melbourne: National Automotive Industry Training Board.

Sellar, S. and Lingard, B. (2013). 'The OECD and global governance in education'. *Journal of Education Policy*, 28 (5): 710–25.

Shildrick, T. and MacDonald, R. (2008). 'Understanding youth exclusion: critical moments, social networks and social capital'. *Youth and Policy*, 99: 43–54.

Shomos, A. (2010). *Links between Literacy and Numeracy Skills and Labour Market Outcomes*. Canberra: Productivity Commission.

Shomos, A. and Forbes, M. (2014). *Literacy and Numeracy and Labour Market Outcomes in Australia*. Canberra: Productivity Commission.

Simmons, R. and Smyth, J. (eds) (2018). *Education and Working-Class Youth: Reshaping the Politics of Inclusion*. London: Palgrave Macmillan.

Skills Australia. (2010). *Australian Workforce Futures: A National Workforce Development Strategy*. Canberra: Commonwealth of Australia.

Smyth, J. and McInerney, P. (2013). 'Making "space": Young people put at a disadvantage re-engaging with learning'. *British Journal of Sociology of Education*, 34 (1): 39–55.

Smythe, S. (2015). 'Ten years of adult literacy policy and practice in Canada: Literacy policy tensions and workarounds'. *Language and Literacy*, 17 (2): 4–20.

Spielhofer, T., Marson-Smith, H. and Evans, K. (2009). *Non-Formal Learning: Good Practice in Reengaging Young People Who Are NEET*. Slough: National Foundation for Educational Research.

St. Clair, R. (2012). 'The limits of levels: Understanding the international adult literacy surveys (IALS)'. *International Review of Education*, 58 (6): 759–76.

Standing Council for Tertiary Education Skills and Employment (SCOTESE). (2012). *National Foundation Skills Strategy for Adults*. Canberra: Australian Government.

Statistics Canada and Organization for Economic Co-operation and Development (OECD). (2005). *Learning a Living: First Results from the Adult Literacy and Life Skills Survey*. Paris and Ottawa: OECD & Statistics Canada.

Street, B. (1984). *Literacy in Theory and Practice*. Cambridge: Cambridge University Press.

Street, B. (1990). 'Putting literacies on the political agenda'. *Open Letter*, 1 (1): 5–16.

Street, B. (ed) (1993). *Cross Cultural Approaches to Literacy*. Cambridge: Cambridge University Press.

Street, B. (1995). *Social Literacies: Critical Approaches to Literacy Development, Ethnography and Education*. Harlow, Essex: Longman.

Street, B. (ed) (2001). *Literacy and Development: Ethnographic Perspectives*. London: Routledge.

Street, B. (2003). 'What's new in new literacy studies? Critical approaches to literacy in theory and practice'. *Current Issues in Comparative Education*, 5 (2): 77–91.

Street, B. (2011). 'Literacy inequalities in theory and practice: The power to name and define'. *International Journal of Educational Development*, 31 (6): 580–6.

Street, B. (2012a). 'New literacy studies'. In M. Grenfell, D. Bloome, C. Hardy, K. Pohl, J. Rowsell and B. Street (eds), *Language, Ethnography and Education: Bridging New Literacy Studies and Bourdieu*, 27–48. London: Routledge.

Street, B. (2012b). 'LETTER: Learning for empowerment through training in ethnographic-style research'. In M. Grenfell, D. Bloome, C. Hardy, K. Pohl, J. Rowsell and B. Street (eds), *Language, Ethnography and Education: Bridging New Literacy Studies and Bourdieu*, 73–88. London: Routledge.

Street, J. and Street, B. (1991). 'The schooling of literacy'. In D. Barton and R. Ivanič (eds), *Writing in the Community*, 143–66. London: Sage.

Stromquist, N.P. (1997). *Literacy for Citizenship: Gender and Grassroots Dynamics in Brazil*. Albany, NY: State University of New York.

Stuckey, H., Mullan-Jensen, C., Kalra, S. et al. (2016). 'Living with an adult who has diabetes: Qualitative insights from the second Diabetes Attitudes, Wishes and Needs (DAWN2) study'. *Diabetes Research and Clinical Practice*, 116: 270–8.

Stuckey, J.E. (1991). *The Violence of Literacy*. Portsmouth, NH: Boynton/Cook Heinemann.

Tannock, S. (1997). 'Positioning the worker: Discursive practices in a workplace literacy program'. *Discourse and Society*, 8 (1): 85–116.
Teodora, A. (2020). *Contesting the Global Development of Sustainable and Inclusive Education*. New York: Routledge.
te Riele, K. (2006). 'Youth "at risk": Further marginalising the marginalised'. *Journal of Educational Policy*, 21 (2): 129–45.
te Riele, K. (2007). 'Educational alternatives for marginalised youth'. *The Australian Educational Researcher*, 34 (3): 53–68.
te Riele, K. (2018). 'Reflecting on belonging, space, and marginalised young people'. In C. Halse (ed), *Interrogating Belonging for Young People in Schools*, 247–59. London: Palgrave Macmillan.
te Riele, K. (2019). 'A framework for quality flexible learning programs'. In B. Shelley, K. te Riele, N. Brown and T. Crellin (eds), *Harnessing the Transformative Power of Education*, 119–37. Leiden, Netherlands: Brill.
Tett, L. and Maclachlan, K. (2007). 'Adult literacy and numeracy, social capital, learner identities and self-confidence'. *Studies in the Education of Adults*, 39 (2): 150–67.
Thompson, R. (2009). 'Social class and participation in Further Education: Evidence from the Youth Cohort Study of England and Wales'. *British Journal of Sociology of Education*, 30 (1): 29–42.
Trudell, B. (2019). 'Reading in the classroom and society: An examination of "reading culture" in African contexts'. *International Review of Education*, 65 (3): 427–42.
Umberson, D. and Montez, J.K. (2010). 'Social relationships and health: A flashpoint for health policy'. *Journal of Health and Social Behaviour*, 51 (1 suppl): S54–S66.
United Nations Educational, Scientific and Cultural Organization (UNESCO). (2006). *EFA Global Monitoring Report: Literacy*. Paris: UNESCO.
United Nations Educational, Scientific and Cultural Organization (UNESCO). (2012). *Youth and Skills: Putting Education to Work. EFA Global Monitoring Report*. Paris: UNESCO.
UNESCO Institute for Statistics. (2009). *The Next Generation of Literacy Statistics: Implementing the Literacy Assessment and Monitoring Programme (LAMP)*. Montreal: UNESCO Institute for Statistics.
Valencia, R. (2010). *The Evolution of Deficit Thinking: Educational Thought and Practice*. New York: Routledge.
Valiente, O. (2014). 'The OECD skills strategy and the education agenda for development'. *International Journal of Educational Development*, 39: 40–8.
Vassilev, I., Rogers, A., Kennedy, A. and Koetsenruijter, J. (2014). 'The influence of social networks on self-management support: A metasynthesis'. *BMC Public Health*, 14 (1): 719.
Vassilev, I., Rogers, A., Sanders, C., Kenneday, A., Blickem, C., Protheroe, J., Bower, P., Kirk, S., Chew-Graham, C. and Morris, R. (2011). 'Social networks, social capital and chronic illness self-management: A realist review'. *Chronic Illness*, 7 (1): 60–86.

Venables, M. and Jeukendrup, A. (2009). 'Physical inactivity and obesity: Links with insulin resistance and type 2 diabetes mellitus'. *Diabetes/Metabolism Research and Reviews*, 25 (S1): S18–S23.

Vincent, C. and Braun, A. (2013). 'Being "fun" at work: Emotional labour, class, gender and childcare'. *British Educational Research Journal*, 39 (4): 751–68.

Vinson, T. (1999). *Unequal in Life: The Distribution of Social Disadvantage in Victoria and New South Wales*. Melbourne: Jesuit Social Services.

Virgona, C. (1994). 'Language learning in the new industry context: Issues of language and power'. In M. Brown (ed), *Literacies in the Workplace: A Collection of Original Essays*, 103–51. Geelong: Deakin University.

Volkoff, V. (2004). 'Tangled threads: Issues faced by non-English speaking background people in vocational education and training'. In K. Bowman (ed), *Equity in Vocational Education and Training: Research Readings*, 120–40. Adelaide: National Centre for Vocational Education Research, Adelaide.

Vorhaus, J. (2014). 'Prisoners' right to education: A philosophical survey'. *London Review of Education*, 12 (2): 162–74.

Walker, J. (2009). 'The inclusion and construction of the worthy citizen through lifelong learning: A focus on the OECD'. *Journal of Education Policy*, 24 (3): 335–51.

Wardhough, R. (1992). *An Introduction to Sociolinguistics* (2nd ed.). Oxford: Blackwell.

Watson, L., Kearns, P., Grant, P. and Cameron, B. (2000). *Equity in the Learning Society: Rethinking Equity Strategies for Post-Compulsory Education and Training*. Adelaide: National Centre for Vocational Education Research.

Watts, B. and Fitzpatrick, S. (2018). *Welfare Conditionality*. London: Routledge.

Wenger, E. (1998). *Communities of Practice: Learning, Meaning, and Identity*. Cambridge: Cambridge University Press.

White, K. (1983). 'Conflict, principles and practice in adult literacy'. *Australian Journal of Reading*, 6 (3): 117–27.

White, K. (1986). 'Influences on adult literacy in Australia'. In A. Nelson and D. Dymock (eds), *Adult Literacy and Community Development*, 32–9. Armidale, NSW: University of New England.

Wickert, R. (1989). *No Single Measure: A Survey of Australian Adult Literacy*. Sydney: University of Technology Sydney.

Wickert, R. (1993). 'Constructing adult literacy: Mythologies and identities'. In A. Luke and P. Gilbert eds), *Literacy in Contexts: Australian Perspectives and Issues*, 29–38. St Leonards: Allen and Unwin.

Wickert, R. and Baynham, M. (1994). '"Just like farmland and goldmines": Workplace literacies in an era of long-term unemployment'. In M. Brown (ed), *Literacies and the Workplace: A Collection of Original Essays*, 153–83. Geelong: Deakin University.

Wilson, A. (2000). 'There is no escape from third-space theory: Borderland discourse and the in-between literacies of prison'. In D. Barton, M. Hamilton and R. Ivanič (eds), *Situated Literacies: Reading and Writing in Context*, 54–69. London: Routledge.

Wilson, A. (2004). 'Four days and a breakfast: Time, space and literacy/ies in the prison community'. In K. Leander and M. Sheehy (eds), *Spatializing Literacy Research and Practice*, 67–90. New York: Peter Lang.

Wilson, A. (2007). '"1 go to get away from the cockroaches": Educentricity and the politics of education in prisons'. *The Journal of Correctional Education*, 58 (2): 185–203.

Wolf, A., Aspin, L., Waite, E. and Ananiadou, K. (2010). 'The rise and fall of workplace basic skills programmes: Lessons for policy and practice'. *Oxford Review of Education*, 36 (4): 385–405.

Wolf, A. and Evans, K. (2011). *Improving Literacy at Work*. London: Routledge.

Womack, J.P., Jones, D.T. and Ross, D. (1990). *The Machine that Changed the World*. New York: Rawson Associates.

Wood, E.M. (1995). *Democracy against Capitalism: Renewing Historical Materialism*. Cambridge: Cambridge University Press.

Worthen, H. (2008). 'Using activity theory to understand how people negotiate the conditions of their work'. *Mind, Culture, Activity*, 15 (4): 322–38.

Wyn, J. (2006). 'Youth transition to work and further education in Australia'. In J. Chapman, P. Cartwright and J. McGilp (eds), *Lifelong Learning, Participation and Equity*, 217–42. Dordrecht, Netherlands: Springer.

Wyn, J. and White, R. (1997). *Rethinking Youth*. London: Routledge.

Wyse, L. and Casarotto, N. (2004) 'Literacy in the world of the aged care worker'. *Literacy and Numeracy Studies*, 13 (1): 19–30.

Yasukawa, K. (2018). 'The workplace as a site for learning critical numeracy practice'. In K. Yasukawa, A. Rogers, K. Jackson and B. Street (eds), *Numeracy as Social Practice: Global and Local Perspectives*, 225–40. London: Routledge.

Yasukawa, K. (2019). 'The role of national media in adult literacy and numeracy policy: A case study from Australia'. *Canadian Journal of Science, Mathematics and Technology Education*, 19 (1): 35–47.

Yasukawa, K. and Black, S. (2016). 'Policy making at a distance: A critical perspective on Australia's National Foundation Skills Strategy for adults'. In K. Yasukawa and S. Black (eds), *Beyond Economic Interests: Critical Perspectives on Adult Literacy and Numeracy in a Globalised World*, 19–39. Rotterdam: Sense.

Yasukawa, K., Brown, T. and Black, S. (2012). 'Workplace literacy and numeracy learning: An opportunity for trade union renewal in Australia'. *International Journal of Training Research*, 10 (2): 73–148.

Yasukawa, K., Brown, T. and Black, S. (2013). 'Production workers' literacy and numeracy practices: Using cultural-historical activity theory as an analytical tool'. *Journal of Vocational Education and Training*, 65 (3): 369–84.

Yasukawa, K., Brown, T. and Black, S. (2014). 'Disturbing practices: Training workers to be lean'. *Journal of Workplace Learning*, 26 (6/7): 392–405.

Yasukawa, K. and Osmond, P. (2019). 'Adult basic education in Australia: In need of a new song sheet?' In L. Tett and M. Hamilton (eds), *Resisting Neoliberalism in*

Education: Local, National and Transnational Perspectives*, 195–207. Bristol: Policy Press.

Yasukawa, K., Rogers, A., Jackson, K. and Street, B. (eds) (2018). *Numeracy as Social Practice: Global and Local Perspectives*. London: Routledge.

Zacharakis, J., Becker Patterson, M. and Quigley, A. (2021). 'Working class, social class, and literacy classism'. In T. Rocco, M. Smith, R. Mizzi, L. Merriweather and J. Hawley (eds), *The Handbook of Adult and Continuing Education 2020 Edition*, 420–7. Sterling, Virginia: Stylus Publishing.

Zavala, V. (2018). 'Language as social practice: Deconstructing boundaries in intercultural bilingual education'. *Trabalhos em Linguística Aplicada*, 57 (3): 1313–38.

Index

accountability 16, 58, 130
adult basic education (ABE) 56, 137
Adult Literacy and Life Skills (ALL) 11, 158, 175
adult literacy students
    community literacy programmes 4, 25, 77–8, 99
    'desperately hobbled' 100, 117
    formal classroom network 114–16
    friendship networks 106, 112–13
    'heroic victims' characterization 100, 117, 178
    letter writing strategy 114
    motivations to participate 103–4
    multilingual students 106–8, 117, 122, 177, 181
    popular media constructions 12, 100
    self-confidence 9, 15, 101, 105, 112, 134
    social isolation 113
    socio-economic well-being 9, 183
    TAFE literacy programmes 3, 49, 54, 78, 121
adult literacy teachers 8–9, 77–8, 111
apprentices/apprenticeships 69, 92, 131, 142, 151
'at risk' groups 11, 45, 120, 182
Australian-born students 48, 49, 147–8, 150, 178
Australian Bureau of Statistics (ABS)
    cultural diversity survey 177
    health surveys 15, 17, 158, 162
    literacy surveys 11, 16–17, 74–5, 158, 175, 184–5
    social capital survey 112, 122
Australian Core Skills Framework (ACSF) 85, 138, 186, 189
Australian Council for Adult Literacy (ACAL) 41, 51, 173
Australian Language and Literacy Policy (ALLP) 13, 39–41, 44, 74, 185

Australia's underclass 12, 42, 45
autonomous (model of literacy) 2–3, 7, 13, 25–6, 45, 86, 122, 137, 171, 182–4, 186, 188, 190

'benchmarks' (proficiency levels) 17, 175–6
blame-the-victim 15, 16–17, 186

Canada 7, 14, 184–5
capitalism
    crisis in 44
    nature of 56
    neoliberal 5, 15–16, 184, 186, 190
    rediscovery 58
class inequalities 5–6, 12, 16, 188
classroom norms 113–14, 129–30
coerced (into jobseeker programmes) 6, 43, 180
cognitive literacy skills 137, 157, 159–60, 162, 171, 182
common sense understanding (of literacy) 16, 46
contradictory understandings (of literacy) 78, 179, 183
critical educators 44, 187
curriculum 6, 8–9, 16, 102, 121, 138, 140, 144, 186

deficit ideology 11–12, 15, 17–18, 99, 154
diabetes patients
    abrogating individual responsibility 165, 169
    comorbidities 159, 161–2, 167
    family members as social support 159–60, 169–71
    interpreter services 160, 162, 166, 168–70
    neighbours 159, 167
    self-managing 162, 168
    social relationships 159
    visual materials 168

Index

disadvantaged adults 5, 11, 18, 42–3, 121, 136, 158, 161, 178
distributed (concept of literacy) 36, 160, 170, 182, 190
dominant discourse 2, 12, 179, 187–8, 190

emancipatory pedagogy 8–9, 187
embarrassment at low literacy 12, 34, 130, 176
employability 8, 12, 14, 45, 185
enterprising culture 59, 77, 180
ethnographic
    approaches/style 3, 65, 80, 101
    Australia 2
    global contexts 7
    research methods 140, 159, 183
    perspectives 140, 170, 178–9, 183–4
    tools/stance 102
    understandings of local practices 7
    workplace case studies 58, 76–7

foundation skills 9, 12–15, 17, 185
functionally illiterate 21–2, 179

Global North 7, 16, 184
Global South 7, 76, 184

health literacy 15, 17, 19, 157–60, 162, 168, 170–2, 182
human capital
    acquiescence of teachers 79
    discourses 112, 182
    individual level of skills 15, 186, 190
    'just like farmland and goldmines' 40, 185
    literacy and employment 41, 44, 47, 185
    literacy and national economy 40
    orientations of OECD 44, 185
    outcomes from literacy programme 131, 134
    rationale for literacy 12, 14, 74, 95, 101, 180
    support from industry 14–15
    workplace literacy 76

ideological role of literacy 22, 25, 76, 188
individualization 16, 186
industry groups 2, 9
inequality 42, 183–4, 187
international adult literacy surveys 16, 185

lack of/deficient in literacy skills 1, 3, 19, 22, 28, 31, 35, 42, 45, 51, 53, 70, 73, 78, 100, 116, 158, 174–6, 187–8, 190
Level Three 11, 17, 85–6, 138, 175, 185, 186
literacy as social practice 3, 13, 19, 26–7, 36, 65, 76, 80, 115–16, 140–1, 158–60, 170–1, 183, 190
literacy crisis 1, 15, 158, 174, 179, 183
literacy mediators 27, 36, 109, 160
literacy myth 46, 51, 188
literacy oppresses 6, 188, 190
literacy practices
    adult literacy students 101, 106, 109–10
    diabetes patients 160, 170
    everyday lives 2, 13
    jobseekers 43
    local 7
    local council workers 63–5, 70
    managing with social support 190
    manufacturing/production workers 57–8, 92, 177
    politics 25
    prisoners 24, 27–8, 30–4, 36, 179, 189
    VET students 140–1, 146
literacy skills
    additional language 103, 110, 153, 164, 190
    Arabic 108
    blame for unemployment or failing courses 54, 137, 188
    choosing to improve 14, 15, 24, 44, 54, 85, 114
    cognitive health 171
    demonstrate at work 65
    employment 107, 180–1, 188
    health literacy 15, 158
    highly valued 110
    lack of self-worth 178
    low-skilled jobs 75
    measuring levels 138, 185, 189
    moral virtue 12
    more than skills 13, 46
    name and define 7
    personal shame 176–7
    range of 102
    responding to audits 79
    spousal/family support 52, 172
    survey 10

technical literacy 92
unproductive workers 101, 177
workplace performance 177
literacy stakeholders 11, 14–15, 22, 54, 74–5, 78, 180
local councils/maintenance workers
  absence of literacy practices 63–4
  'business units' 58
  competitive teams 4, 56, 59–60, 65–7, 180, 189
  contradictions at work 65
  finding meaning in work 57–8, 61, 65
  flexible workplace practices
  knowledge workers 57, 61, 70, 97
  lack of monetary reward 66, 70
  literacy as managerial code 70
  maintenance and construction workers 55–6, 59–62
  manual labour 56, 61
  National Competition Policy 58
  new technology 57
  numeracy practices 63–4
  restructured workplaces 57
  social identities of workers 70, 180
  team leaders as linchpins 62
  use value 67
  work 'gangs' 55–6, 59–60, 180, 189
Long term unemployed/jobseeker programmes
  accommodating the literacy programme 48
  Commonwealth Employment Service (CES) 42–3, 47–51, 53–4
  critical educators 44
  Language, Literacy and Numeracy Programme (LLNP) 40
  literacy = jobs axiom 41, 44, 47, 180
  Literacy and Numeracy Training (LANT) 40
  literacy programmes 40–4, 46–7, 54, 188
  mutual obligation 43
  Newstart 39, 42–3, 50
  previous jobs 48, 51
  reciprocal obligation 43
  resisting the literacy programme 49
  shifting the blame 44–5
  Skills for Education and Employment (SEE) 40
  skills formation 40
  Special Intervention Programme (SIP) 40, 42–4, 47–8, 50–4
  welfare conditionality 43
Lost for Words 1, 12, 100, 173–4, 176, 178–9
low-literate adults 2–3, 18, 24–5, 30, 36, 100–1, 174, 179

Manufacturing companies/workers
  audiologist 91
  competitive manufacturing 75
  computer modelling 90–1
  'earning a living' 81, 87
  embedded LLN 91
  'English-only' policy 82–83, 93, 95–6
  expansive-restricted models 86, 95–6
  Hearing Solutions 73, 88–97
  'hidden knowledge' of workers 84, 91
  Insulation Products 80, 84–9, 91, 93
  job cards 82, 84, 91, 189
  lean production 75, 80–81, 84–9, 93–4, 96, 181, 188
  Literacy 40, 92
  machine cutting 81, 84
  productive diversity 93
  soft-touch hegemony 97
  unions 40, 79
  visual documentation 93–4, 181
marginalised young people
  'connection' between students and teachers 128–9
  feeling safe 129–30
  'flexible' learning programmes 123–4, 130
  integrated literacy and numeracy 121, 123
  making friends 125, 127, 129
  not in employment, education or training (NEET) 120, 182
  re-engagement programmes 121–2
  'relational power' 120, 182
  School Certificate 119–22, 134
  'second chance' education 136, 143
  social-emotional classroom environment 129

National Centre for Vocational Education Research (NCVER) 4, 73, 75, 80, 111, 119, 122, 146
National Foundation Skills Strategy for Adults 12, 14–17, 41, 74–5, 101, 185–6

neoliberal
    'apparatus'/governance 16, 186
    capitalism 5, 15–16, 185–6, 190
    dominant groups 179
    education reforms 16
    era/society consumed with efficiencies 6, 8–9, 19, 186
    ideology 24
    the individual 14–16, 186, 190
new literacy studies (NLS) 25, 58, 80, 101
new work order 4, 56–7, 61, 65, 67, 70, 74, 180

Organization for Economic Co-operation and Development (OECD)
    adult literacy, numeracy/competencies surveys 11, 16, 17, 41, 76, 184–5
    'autonomous' literacy 13, 188
    Global North 7
    human capital orientations 44, 111–12, 185
    international policy actor 185
    interplay with UNESCO 16
    Level Three criterion 175, 184–5
    neoliberal capitalism 184–6
    neoliberal education reforms 16
    not in employment, education or training (NEET) 120
    oppress working-class adults 187–8, 190
    power through numbers 185
    power to define literacy 187
    proficiency standards or benchmarks 176
    review of Australian skills 136
overseas-born 73, 81, 94–5, 177–8, 181, 188

politics of literacy 1, 8, 10, 25, 76–7, 79, 190
poverty 4, 12, 18, 37, 44–5, 136, 162, 184
power to name and define literacy 7, 183–4, 187
practice field 115–16, 129
prisoners and literacy
    crime and illiteracy 21–3, 33, 36–38, 41
    education as human right 23
    fellow prisoners 28–9, 38, 179, 189
    literacy practices 24–5, 27–8, 30–6, 53
    'personal fulfilment' 27, 30
    prisoners' everyday lives 24, 25, 33, 36–8

prison officers 29
recidivism 22–4
rehabilitation 23–4
role of spouses 28–9, 32, 33–4, 38
proficiency levels 16–17, 175
Programme for the International Assessment of Adult Competencies (PIAAC) 17, 76, 136, 175–6
pronunciation 84–5, 94, 105, 189

recession 12, 40–1, 44, 46, 52, 54, 180
'remedial English' teacher 3, 22, 24
remedial literacy 45, 137–8, 141, 189
reproduction theory 47, 187
responsibilization 16, 186
'Right to Read' campaign 99

'schooled' literacy 64, 122, 134
semi-structured interviews 25, 159–60
sense of efficacy 112, 132, 134
shame (at low literacy) 11–12, 18, 34, 99–100, 117–18, 173–4, 176–9, 181
situated literacy/learning 2, 13, 36, 69, 76, 90, 139
social capital 4, 9, 46, 104, 110–12, 117–18, 119, 122–3, 129, 131–2, 134, 181–2
social circumstances 169
social class 5–6, 8, 38, 135–6, 141
social context of literacy 22, 25, 38, 58, 76, 159, 171
social networks
    adult literacy students 110, 112, 181
    diabetes patients 159, 170–1, 182, 190
    marginalized young people 122–3, 126, 132, 189
    navigating health care 160, 170
    obtaining jobs 46
    prisoners 25, 27, 29, 31, 33, 37, 189
    spouses 52–3
    VET students 150, 155, 189
    working in teams 189
socio-economic
    benefits and community development 111
    disadvantaged, working-class families/ areas 36, 121, 125, 136, 154, 158, 161, 180
    indicators (income, occupation) 4, 103
    status, lack of power 4, 158

TAFE/VET 136
  well-being 112, 117, 183, 189–90
spoken English 24, 48, 82, 85, 92, 105, 112, 153, 166, 180
'staggeringly low adult literacy rate' 12, 174, 175
Statistics Canada 11, 44, 175, 184–5

team leaders 57, 59–60, 62–6, 81, 89–90, 93–4, 96
team meetings 57, 86, 89, 93–4
teamwork 57, 63, 68, 95, 97, 146, 189
training programmes 43, 55, 60, 67–9, 86–7
transformation (of students) 9, 134
type 2 diabetes 157–8, 161, 163–7, 171

United Kingdom (UK)
  'embedding literacy' 139
  employability programmes 8
  'functional skills' 14, 185
  Global North 7
  further education (FE) 5, 136
  literacy and numeracy crisis 74
  literacy programmes for the unemployed 54
  literacy research 9, 26, 101–2, 106, 178
  prisoner research 26, 27
  'Right to Read' campaign 99
  Skills for Life 46
  student perspectives 151
  violence of literacy 187
  workplace literacy 77, 79
United Nations Educational, Scientific and Cultural Organization (UNESCO) 7, 13–14, 16, 76, 184

violence of literacy 47, 54, 187–8, 190
Vocational Education and Training (VET) students and literacy
  aged care 117, 135, 140, 146–50, 154–5, 182
  Assistant-in-Nursing (AIN) 146
  beauty 136, 150–1, 153, 155

'beyond deficit models' 140
bonding with classmates and employers 145–6
electrical trades 136, 150–1, 154–5
'fit in' to the vocational status quo 139–40
fitness 136–8
hairdressing 135–6, 142–6, 146, 152, 154–5, 182
integrating literacy and numeracy 139
lack of confidence 147–8, 150
'learner voice' 136, 154
literacy and numeracy 'screens' 138
love and passion for hairdressing 143–4, 146, 155
non-English-speaking background (NESB) students 141–2
'other people's children' 5, 136
shared delivery 140–1, 152–5
TAFE as 'Cinderella' institution 136
team teaching 112, 138–40, 152, 154
unemployed, mature-aged women 146
vocational literacies 140
vocational socialisation 140
volunteer tutors 8, 18, 116–17, 176, 178

well-being 9, 17, 19, 103, 112, 181, 183, 186, 190
working-class
  adults 1–2, 4, 6, 8, 18, 38, 45, 47, 54, 173, 179, 187, 190
  area of Sydney 35, 103
  backgrounds/childhoods 36, 38, 120, 136, 161, 178
  control, disempower 8, 188
  East London 5
  jobs 56, 96, 136
  poorly paid 70, 100
  status/classification 4–5
  students 150, 187
  symbolic violence 187–8
working smarter 6, 56–8, 60, 66, 70
Workplace English Language and Literacy (WELL) 77–9, 85

www.ingramcontent.com/pod-product-compliance
Lightning Source LLC
Chambersburg PA
CBHW071832300426
44116CB00009B/1515